THE WORD OF GOD AND
THE WORD OF MAN

THE WORD OF GOD
AND
THE WORD OF MAN

by KARL BARTH

translated with a new Foreword by
DOUGLAS HORTON

GLOUCESTER, MASS.

PETER SMITH

1978

TO HIS MOTHER
THIS BOOK IS DEDICATED
BY THE AUTHOR

TO THE MEMBERS OF THE
COMMISSION ON EVANGELISM
AND THE DEVOTIONAL LIFE
OF THE
CONGREGATIONAL CHURCHES
IN THE UNITED STATES,
IN RECOGNITION OF
THEIR BROAD INTEREST
IN THE THOUGHT OF THE WORLD,
THIS TRANSLATION IS DEDICATED.

THE WORD OF GOD AND THE WORD OF MAN

Copyright, 1928, by Sidney A. Weston
Copyright, 1956, 1957, by Douglas Horton

Printed in the United States of America

ISBN 0-8446-1599-4

First HARPER PAPERBACK edition published 1957

Reprinted, 1978, by
Peter Smith Publisher, Inc.

This book is a translation of
Das Wort Gottes und die Theologie

CONTENTS

FOREWORD

Providence, I have come to believe, had a good deal to do with making this the book through which the thought of Karl Barth was first introduced to readers of English. Certainly it was not through any studied judgment of mine.

It was a generation ago that I ran across the German text, published under the title *Das Wort Gottes und die Theologie,* on the "New Books" shelf in the Andover-Harvard Theological Library in Cambridge, Massachusetts, near which at the time I was serving as a parish minister. At first I glanced idly through it for the chapter titles, then found myself reading some of the more arresting paragraphs, and presently succumbed so completely to the spell of its passionate intensity and penetrating faith that I lost track of the passage of time—not to be brought back to myself for two or three hours.

It seemed clear to me from that moment that the book should be translated, and it was not long after that Dr. Barth gave me his gracious permission to try my hand at it.

Only those who are old enough to remember the particular kind of desiccated humanism, almost empty

1

of other-worldly content, which prevailed in many Protestant areas in the early decades of this century, can understand the surprise, the joy, the refreshment which would have been brought by the book to the ordinary and, like myself, somewhat desultory reader of the religious literature of that time. To question evolutionary modes of thought in that day was something like questioning the Ptolemaic theory in the time of Copernicus, with the stupendous difference that Copernicus seemed at first to shut the transcendent God out of the world and Barth seemed immediately to let him in.

The experience of discovering Barth was of the bitter-sweet variety, producing an emotional dialectic which Barth himself would have prized. On the one hand it was the thin end of the wedge which was eventually to topple the impressive philosophical structure which had been built up by the idea of the progressive advance of the divine into the world. This had become a veritable faith: to many it was the substance of things hoped for, the evidence of things not seen. To have it suggested that this was unsound thinking—to see it now beginning to totter under Barth's pressure—was to be filled with misgivings, to anticipate crisis. On the other hand, there was undeniable exhilaration in rehearing and relearning that God is God, that he *will* will what he will *will*, that he is not caught in the trammels of the world he himself has created, and that man can produce him neither as the conclusion of a syllogism, the Q.E.D. of an experiment, nor the crown of a civilization. To encounter the unsettling quality of this frighteningly new and securely old thinking was to enter into a situation Barth called "existential"—a word to whose modern currency Barth himself was one of the first to contribute.

Since those early days Barth and his contemporaries have seen the whole world change. Even the theological world, whose movement has been likened by some to the burdened advance or recession of a glacier, has shown itself to be more like a rolling Mississippi, ready to cut a new channel. And who can deny Barth's part in dredging the new channel for it to flow in?

The events of the world since the first publication of this little book of addresses in English have illustrated its basic theses with too dreadful actuality. If the generation needed proof that there is a difference between Christians as the Christ-possessed and Christians as "the multitude of the baptized" [Barth's phrase], there has been a war, a globe-girdling war, whose circumstances proved that among the innumerable masses in the several nations the name Christian too often simply classified a person for purposes of census-taking, had little to do with his morals, and nothing to do with his religion. If the world needed to know the truth of Barth's fundamental thesis that though a real Christian can do no more than witness, he can witness *to his Lord,* it had to look no further than to the spectacle of the response to Nazism in Germany. Before this new political discipline with its ruthless claims upon the human soul and its demonic and swift instruments to make the claims good, everything that the pre-Barth world had considered "values" seemed to wilt. The

vaunted independent thinking of the universities was
seen to be the bruised reed and smoking flax that Barth
had said it was—easy enough for a resolute Hitler who
thought with his blood to break and to quench. The
great business combinations and labor organizations
which had seemed mountainous and invincible in their
power proved to be mere Ossa and Pelion in the hands
of a man with titanic faith in himself. In the grim
assizes of those days, all German Christendom was
judged—and when history had cleared the courtroom
after the trial, swept out the bodies of the million slain,
closed the books of the half-true but wholly bloody
philosophy that had almost won its verdict, and locked
the door on another episode in the exceeding sinfulness
of man, the only Christians who were then seen to have
had the courage to resist the evil, to die if need be—in
a word, to live their faith—were those whose spirits
had been nurtured on the kind of truth that Barth
taught. Never again can our generation listen with
equanimity to the teaching that an optimistic humanism is all that man needs to be himself.

Since the end of the war the theological world has
accepted Barth in the sense that it has given him the
leading seat on its Olympus. It may discount the existence of his influence with the same lifted eyebrow
which it has for the existence of Zeus, but that his
influence not only exists but exists dominantly is proved
by the very cordiality with which intellectual enemies
attack him. You may agree with him or you may dis-
agree, but you cannot disregard him. While various
schools of thought meet in the valleys and clash con-

cerning the rightness or wrongness of the Barthian idea, the man himself sits at his desk on the heights, reads, thinks, and continues to pour volume after volume of his works into the mind of today.

Like the world, Karl Barth himself has undergone change since he first gave the addresses recorded in this book. Through the long intellectual give-and-take he has had with his theological colleagues in every land —a process which the Germans discerningly call an *Auseinandersetzung*, combining the ideas of mutual analysis, of making clear one's position in discussion, and of setting oneself properly in relation to others—he has acquired a mellower and more effective apologetic, and a new vocabulary to go with it. Today he would hardly, I think, use the phrase *totaliter aliter*—"wholly other"—in his description of God's ways and God's world. But yet it is undoubtedly true that the foundation of his thought has not been altered. His mighty *Dogmatik* has grown out of the soil which is to be found in *The Word of God and the Word of Man*.

It is because this little book with its forthrightness and simplicity seems to give so honest an account of Barth's basic thought, even in his theological maturity, that I have ventured to believe that Providence had a hand in introducing him to readers of English by this means. I can still with truth repeat what I said in the translator's note for the first edition:

"This book contains the essence of his message.

"Parish ministers have found his utterances stimulating because, having been one of them himself, he speaks and writes from their standpoint. Theologians and historians have variously hailed, challenged, condemned, and acclaimed his books because they see in them—in thoroughly modern form but in all its ancient strength —a resurgence of the Calvinism of Calvin. People in general have heard Professor Barth gladly because he seems to understand their inner needs.

"And now to the English world, with its own people, its theologians and historians and its ministers, I give this book, hoping that the glow of its contents may not have been unduly dimmed by the ineptitudes of the translation."

DOUGLAS HORTON

Harvard Divinity School
Cambridge, Massachusetts
January, 1957

Author's Introduction

My publisher's suggestion that a new and combined edition of these addresses be issued meets a desire of my own. I am glad of the opportunity of repeating in better form certain things I have already said and of bringing together utterances made at various times and places.

As the reader takes his way between the first and last of these addresses he will find the landscape changing. This will be true not only of the style (as a Swiss country parson I shall be pardoned for employing somewhat different speech from that which I use as a professor of the Reformed Church in Göttingen), not only of the ideas (naturally I would no longer speak of "the voice of him that crieth in the wilderness," as I have done here on the first page, as "the voice of conscience"), but also of the material*. A good deal once stood in the foreground of my mind which has since had to recede into the background, and *vice versa*. And there are not lacking places where in the course of the years I have had to accept additions and excisions in my thought. I do not, however, feel

---

* The address appearing last in this translation has been removed for logical reasons from the chronological order.—D.H.

occasion today to deny my earlier work, which, for all its one-sidedness, is yet my own. Understanding readers will keep these circumstances in mind and read the whole work as — a whole.

The subjects of these addresses were almost all supplied and to some extent defined by the organizers of the gatherings before which they were delivered. If, in spite of this, the collection may still be called a whole, it is such by virtue of an inner unity.

Göttingen.   KARL BARTH.

I.

THE RIGHTEOUSNESS OF GOD

"THE voice of him that crieth in the wilderness, Prepare ye the way of the Lord, make straight in the desert a highway for our God. Every valley shall be exalted, and every mountain and hill shall be made low; and the crooked shall be made straight, and the rough places plain; and the glory of the Lord shall be revealed!" This is the voice of our conscience, telling us of the righteousness of God. And since conscience is the perfect interpreter of life, what it tells us is no question, no riddle, no problem, but a fact — the deepest, innermost, surest fact of life: God is righteous. Our only question is what attitude toward the fact we ought to take.

We shall hardly approach the fact with our critical reason. The reason sees the small and the larger but not the large. It sees the preliminary but not the final, the derived but not the original, the complex but not the simple. It sees what is human but not what is divine.

We shall hardly be taught this fact by men. One

This address was delivered in the Town Church of Aarau in January, 1916.

man may speak about it to another, to be sure. One man may perhaps provoke another to reflect upon "the righteousness of God." But no man may bring another to the peculiar, immediate, penetrating certainty which lies behind the phrase. We must first learn again to speak to each other with authority and not as the scribes. For the present we are all much too clever and unchildlike to be of real mutual help.

We must let conscience speak, for it tells of the righteousness of God in such a way that that righteousness becomes a certainty. Conscience, as everybody knows, may be reduced almost to silence or crushed into oblivion; it may be led astray to the point of folly and wrongdoing; but it remains forever the place, the only place between heaven and earth, in which God's righteousness is manifest. As with a blare of trumpets from another world it interrupts one's reflections concerning himself and his life, concerning his duties to family, calling, and country. It interrupts even the cultivation of his religious thoughts and feelings! It comes with its message, now as a bitter, pressing accusation, now as a quiet, firm assertion, now as an imperious task set for the will, now as an obstruction opposing against you an inexorable No, now as a curse and condemnation which crushes you to earth, now as a holy joy which lifts you above yourself and all that is — but always awaking and agitating in you fundamentally the same thought, pointing you in the same direction. In every chance and change of experience

it convinces you that all your living and learning
have a goal. In every coming and going of sensa-
tion, joyful or painful, it speaks of an existence
higher than joy and deeper than pain. In every rise
and fall of the sincerity, strength, and purity of the
will, it speaks of a will which remains true to itself.
And that is the righteousness of God.

What delight to discover a will which seems to be
clear and constant in itself, free from caprice and
fickleness, possessing a dominant and inflexible idea!
And now the conscience tells us that the last and
deepest essence of all things is such a will — that
God is righteous. We live by knowing this. We
forget it often, to be sure; we overlook it; we spurn
it. And yet we could not even keep on living, did
we not profoundly know that God is righteous.

For we suffer from unrighteousness. We dread
it. All that is within us revolts against it. We
know more about it, it is true, than we do about
righteousness. We have constantly before us, in
the great and small occurrences of life, in our own
conduct and in that of others, another kind of will,
a will which knows no dominant and inflexible idea
but is grounded upon caprice, vagary, and self-seeking — a will without faithfulness, logic, or correlation, disunited and distraught within itself. The
more sharply we look, the more clearly we see it. Of
such are we, of such is life, of such is the world.
The critical reason may come and prove to us that
it has always been so and always must be so. But
we have before our eyes the consequences of this

unrighteous will — disquiet, disorder, and distress in forms minute and gross, obscure and evident. We have before us the fiendishness of business competition and the world war, passion and wrongdoing, antagonism between classes and moral depravity within them, economic tyranny above and the slave spirit below. We may indeed argue about these things and prove to ourselves and others quite shrewdly that they all have their necessary reasons. We may imagine ourselves thus becoming inwardly free from them. But we do not escape the simple fact that we suffer from them. The unjust will which imbues and rules our life makes of it, with or without our sanction, a weltering inferno. How heavily it lies upon us! How unendurably! We live in the shadow. We may temporarily deceive ourselves about it. We may temporarily come to an understanding with it. Obviously it will never do so with us. For the unrighteous will is by nature the unendurable, the impossible. We live by knowing that there is really something else in the world.

But many times the fearful apprehension seizes us that unrighteousness may triumph in the end. The frightful fancy comes, that the unrighteous will which now persecutes and tortures us may be the only, the profoundest, will in life. And the impossible resolve suggests itself — make peace with it! Surrender yourself to the thought that the world is a hell, and conform! There seems nothing else to do.

But now into the midst of this sense of need and apprehension, as resistless and unbroken as the theme of a Bach fugue, comes the assurance of conscience — No, it is not true! There is above this warped and weakened will of yours and mine, above this absurd and senseless will of the world, another which is straight and pure, and which, when it once prevails, must have other, wholly other, issues than these we see today. Out of this will, when it is recognized, another life must grow. Out of this will, when it emerges, a new world will arise. Our home is where this will prevails; we have wandered away, but we can return. There is a will of God which is righteous.

As a drowning man grasps at a straw, all that is within us reaches out for the certainty which the conscience gives. If only we might stand in the shining presence of the other will, not doubtfully but with assurance! If only, instead of merely guessing at it as men who can only hope and wish, we might contemplate it quietly and take enjoyment in it! If only we might approach it, come to know it, and have it for our own! The deepest longing in us is born of the deepest need: oh that Thou wouldest rend the heavens, that thou wouldest come down! Oppressed and afflicted by his own unrighteousness and the unrighteousness of others, man — every man — lifts up from the depths of his nature the cry for righteousness, the righteousness of God. Whoever understands him at this point, understands him wholly. Whoever can reach a hand to him here, can really help him. This is the reason that such prophets as Moses, Jeremiah, and

John the Baptist are figures never to be erased
from the memory of humanity. They uncovered to
men their deepest need; they made articulate their
conscience within them; they wakened and kept
awake the longing within them for the righteousness
of God. They prepared the way of the Lord.

But now comes a remarkable turn in our relation
with the righteousness of God. The trumpet of conscience sounds; we start with apprehension; we feel
the touch of holiness upon us — but at first we do
not dream of appealing beyond ourselves for help
in our need and anxiety. Quite the opposite. "They
said one to another, Go to, let us make brick, and
burn them throughly. Let us build us a city and a
tower whose top may reach unto heaven; and let us
make a name, lest we be scattered abroad upon the
face of the whole earth!" We come to our own rescue and build the tower of Babel. In what haste we
are to soothe within us the stormy desire for the
righteousness of God! And to soothe means, un-
fortunately, to cover up, to bring to silence. It is as
if we could not long endure our own perfervid cry.
It is as if we were afraid of a too real and complete
fulfillment of our longing. The conscience speaks;
we hear; something must be done! But we do not
let conscience speak to the end. We hear the alarm
and rush out sleepily before we have found out what
is really the matter and what must first be done if
anything else is to be done.

We stand here before the really tragic, the most

fundamental, error of mankind. We long for the righteousness of God, and yet we do not let it enter our lives and our world — cannot let it enter because the entrance has long since been obstructed. We know what the one thing needful for us really is, but long ago we set it aside or put it off till later "better times" — in the meanwhile making ourselves sicker and sicker with substitutes. We go off and build the pitiable tower at the Babel of our human righteousness, human consequence, human significance. Our answer to the call of conscience is one great makeshift, extending over the whole of life, a single gigantic "as if" (als ob)! And because and as long as we are willing to think, speak, and act "as if" — *as if* our tower were important, as if something were happening, as if we were doing something in obedience to the conscience — the reality of the righteousness after which we hunger and thirst will elude us.

Shall we call this pride on our part? There is, as a matter of fact, something of pride in it. We are inwardly resentful that the righteousness we pant after is God's and can come to us only from God. We should like to take the mighty thing into our own hands and under our own management, as we have done with so many other things. It seems quite desirable that the righteousness without which we cannot exist should be controlled by our own will, whatever kind of will that may really be. We arrogate to ourselves, unquestioningly, the right to take up the tumultuous question, What shall we *do?* as if that were in any case the first and most pressing problem. Only let us be quick to put our hand to reform, sanitation, methods, cultural and religious endeavors of all sorts! Only to do "real work"! And before we know it, the trumpet blast of conscience has lost its disturbing tone. The anxiety in which we found ourselves when confronted by the dominant world-will has been gently changed into a prosperous sense of normality, and we have arrived again at reflection, criticism, construction, and organization. The longing for a new world has lost all its bitterness, sharpness, and restlessness, has become the joy of development, and now blossoms sweetly and surely in orations, donor's tablets, committee meetings, reviews, annual reports, twenty-five-year anniversaries, and countless mutual bows. The righteousness of God itself has slowly changed from being the surest of facts into being the highest among various high ideals, and is now at all events our very own affair. This is evident in our ability now to hang it gayly out of the window and now to roll it up again, somewhat like a flag. *Eritis sicut Deus!* You may act as if you were God, you may with ease take his righteousness under your own management. This is certainly pride.

One might equally well, however, call it despair. And it is singular that in our relations with God these two contrasted qualities always keep each other company. We are fundamentally fearful of the stream of God's righteousness which seeks entrance into our life and our world. The safe citizen is startled enough when he hears of tuberculosis, the general strike, or war; but it is far more painful to him to think of that radical overturn of life which God might send to make an end not only of such results of unrighteousness but of unrighteousness itself. The same happy gentleman of culture who today drives up so briskly in his little car of progress and so cheerfully displays the pennants of his various ideals, will tell you apprehensively tomorrow, if the matter comes up, that men are small and imperfect and that one may not indeed desire and expect too much from them — that one may not be too decided about it, anyway. This will be his thought if he has once conceived or conjectured that, apart from the righteousness of God there is nothing to reflect upon, to reform, or to aim at; that, apart from the righteousness of God, all clever newspaper articles and well-attended conventions are completely insignificant; that the primary matter is a very decided Yes or No to a whole new world of life. We are apprehensive of the righteousness of God because we feel much too small and too human for anything different and new to begin in us and among us. This is our despair.

And because we are so proud and so despairing, we build a tower at Babel. The righteousness of God which we have looked upon and our hands have handled changes under our awkward touch into all kinds of human righteousness.

I think of the righteousness of our morality, of the good will which we all, I trust, develop and exemplify in certain excellent principles and virtues. The world is full of morality, but where have we really got with it? It is always an exceptional condition — I had almost said, an artificial dislocation of our will. It is no new will. Steadily or intermittently we apply ourselves to our morality — to our thrift, let us say, to thought for our family, to efficiency in our vocation, to our patriotism — and through it we lift ourselves above our own real level and that of our fellow men. We tear ourselves loose from the general unrighteousness and build ourselves a pleasant home in the suburbs apart — seemingly apart! But what has really happened? Is the unrighteous, self-seeking, capricious, world-will really struck at, much less overcome, by our withdrawing with our morality — seemingly — a little to one side? Is it not our very morality which prevents our discerning that at a hundred other points we are the more firmly fettered to that will? Does it not make us blind and impenitent toward the deep real needs of existence? Is it not remarkable that the greatest atrocities of life — I think of the capitalistic order and of the war — can justify themselves on purely moral principles? The devil may also make use of morality. He laughs at the tower of Babel which we erect to him.

The righteousness of the state and of the law. A wonderful tower! A most necessary and useful substitute to protect us in some measure from certain unpleasant results of our unrighteous will! Very suitable for quieting the conscience! But

what does the state really do for us? It can order
and organize the self-seeking and capricious vagaries of the human will. It can oppose certain hin-
drances to this will by its regulations and intimida-
tions. It can set up certain institutions — schools,
for instance — for the refining and ennobling of it.
A vast amount of respectable work goes into all of
this; for the building of this one tower of the state,
millions of valuable lives are offered and consumed
— to what end? The righteousness of the state, for
all its variety of form, fails to touch the inner character of the world-will at any point. By this will it
is indeed dominated. The war again provides the
striking illustration: were it really possible for the
state to make men out of wild animals, would the
state find it necessary by a thousand arts to make
wild animals out of men? The devil may laugh at
this tower of Babel, also.

Religious righteousness! There seem to be no
surer means of rescuing us from the alarm cry of
conscience than religion and Christianity. Religion
gives us the chance, beside and above the vexations
of business, politics, and private and social life, to
celebrate solemn hours of devotion — to take flight
to Christianity as to an eternally green island in the
gray sea of the everyday. There comes over us a
wonderful sense of safety and security from the
unrighteousness whose might we everywhere feel. It
is a wonderful illusion, if we can comfort ourselves
with it, that in our Europe — in the midst of capi-
talism, prostitution, the housing problem, alcohol-

ism, tax evasion, and militarism — the church's preaching, the church's morality, and the "religious life" go their uninterrupted way. And we are Christians! Our nation is a Christian nation! A wonderful illusion, but an illusion, a self-deception! We should above all be honest and ask ourselves far more frankly what we really gain from religion. *Cui bono?* What is the use of all the preaching, baptizing, confirming, bell-ringing, and organ-playing, of all the religious moods and modes, the counsels of "applied religion" "for the guidance of parents" (den Eheleuten zum Geleite), the community houses with or without motion-picture equipment, the efforts to enliven church singing, the unspeakably tame and stupid monthly church papers, and whatever else may belong to the equipment of modern ecclesiasticism? Will something different eventuate from all this in our relation to the righteousness of God? Are we even expecting something different from it? Are we hoping that something may happen? Are we not rather hoping by our very activity to conceal in the most subtle way the fact that the critical event that ought to happen has not yet done so and probably never will? Are we not, with our religious righteousness, acting "as if" — in order not to have to deal with reality? Is not our religious righteousness a product of our pride and our despair, a tower of Babel, at which the devil laughs more loudly than at all the others?

We are fixed firmly, very firmly, in human righteousness. We are alarmed by the cry of conscience,

but we have gone no further than to play sleepily
with shadow pictures of the divine righteousness.
It, itself, is too great and too high for us. And
therefore the need and anxiety caused by unrighteousness still remain with us. Conscience within
us continues to call. Our deepest longing is un-
stilled.

———

This then is the inner situation in which we come
upon the quite pointless question whether God is
righteous. The righteousness of God becomes pre-
posterously a problem and a subject for discussion. In the war it has become a "real question"
again. There is now hardly a community in all the
country round in which, noisily or quietly, roughly
or delicately, this question is not mooted; and it is
mooted, fundamentally, in us all: If God were
righteous, could he then "permit" all that is now
happening in the world?

A pointless question? Absolutely so, if it refers
to God, the living God. For the living God never
for a moment manifests himself in our conscience
except as a righteous God. When we see him as he
is and when he asks us to recognize and accept him
as he is, is it not pointless to ask, Art Thou righteous? A very pointed and correct and weighty
question it is, however, when we refer it to the god
to whom in our pride and despair we have erected
the tower of Babel; to the great personal or imper-
sonal, mystical, philosophical, or naïve Background

and Patron Saint of our human righteousness, morality, state, civilization, or religion. If it is he we mean, we are quite right in asking, Is God righteous? For the answer is soon given. It is our calamity, a calamity from which there is no possibility of rescue or release, that with a thousand arts we have made ourselves a god in our own image and must now own him — a god to whom one must put such comfortless questions and receive such comfortless answers. In the question, Is God righteous? our whole tower of Babel falls to pieces. In this now burning question it becomes evident that we are looking for a righteousness without God, that we are looking, in truth, for a god without God and against God — and that our quest is hopeless. It is clear that such a god is not God. He is not even righteous. He cannot prevent his worshipers, all the distinguished European and American apostles of civilization, welfare, and progress, all zealous citizens and pious Christians, from falling upon one another with fire and sword to the amazement and derision of the poor heathen in India and Africa. This god is really an unrighteous god, and it is high time for us to declare ourselves thorough-going doubters, sceptics, scoffers and atheists in regard to him. It is high time for us to confess freely and gladly: this god, to whom we have built the tower of Babel, is not God. He is an idol. He is dead.

God himself, the real, the living God, and his love which comes in glory! These provide the solution. We have not yet begun to listen quietly to what the conscience asks when it reminds us, in our need and anxiety, of the righteousness of God. We have been much too eager to do something ourselves. Much too quickly we have made ourselves comfortable in temporary structures. We have mistaken our tent for our home; the moratorium for the normal course of things. We have prayed, Thy will be done! and meant by it, Thy will be done not just now! We have believed in an eternal life, but what we took for eternal life and satisfied ourselves upon was really only temporary. And for this reason we have remained the same as we were. And unrighteousness has remained. And the righteousness of God has disappeared from our eyes. And God himself has become to us dubious, for in his place there has stood the questionable figment of our own thoughts.

There is a fundamentally different way to come into relation with the righteousness of God. This *other* way we enter not by speech nor reflection nor reason, but by being still, by listening to and not silencing the conscience when we have hardly begun to hear its voice. When we let conscience speak to the end, it tells us not only that there is something else, a righteousness above unrighteousness, but also — and more important — that this something else for which we long and which we need is God. He is right and not we! His righteousness is an eternal righteousness! This is difficult for us to hear. We must take the trouble to go far enough off to hear it again. We make a veritable uproar with our morality and culture and religion. But we may presently be brought to silence, and with that will begin our true redemption.

It will then be, above all, a matter of our recognizing God once more as God. It is easy to say recognize. But recognizing is an ability won only in fierce inner personal conflict. It is a task beside which all cultural, moral, and patriotic duties, all efforts in "applied religion," are child's play. For here one must give himself up in order to give himself over to God, that God's will may be done. To do his will, however, means to begin with him anew. His will is not a corrected continuation of our own. It approaches ours as a Wholly Other. There is nothing for our will except a basic re-creation. Not a reformation but a re-creation and re-growth. For the will to which the conscience points is purity, goodness, truth, and brotherhood as the perfect will of God. It is a will which knows no subterfuges, reservations, nor preliminary compromises. It is a will with character, a will blessed and holy through and through. It is the righteousness of God. In its presence the first need is for humility. Have we enough humility? May we take it for granted and go on to tower-building of various sorts? In taking it for granted, have we yet begun to practice it?

And then a second consideration: in place of despair a childlike joyfulness will come; a joy that God is so much greater than we thought. Joy that his righteousness has far more depth and meaning than we had allowed ourselves to dream. Joy

that from God much more is to be expected for
our poor, perplexed, and burdened life than with our
idealism, our principles, and our Christianity we had
dared to hope. More to be *expected!* We ought not
to scatter our emotions as we do to every wind. We
ought not so gratuitously to confuse our hearts by
the continual building of towers of Babel. We ought
not to waste our faith on these things — only to convince ourselves and others of our want of faith. We
ought not to put our most fruitful moments to
second-best uses in the belief that it is the way of
piety and wisdom to pursue men's thoughts rather
than God's. We ought to apply ourselves with all
our strength to expect more from God, to let grow
within us that which he will in fact cause to grow,
to accept what indeed he constantly offers us, watch-
ing and praying that we may respond to his originative touch. As children to take joy in the great God
and his righteousness, and to trust all to him! *Have*
we joy enough? Are the springs which might be
flowing really flowing so abundantly? Have we bare-
ly yet begun to feel the true creative joy of God's
presence?

In the Bible this humility and this joy are called
— faith. Faith means seeking not noise but quiet,
and letting God speak within — the righteous God,
for there is no other. And then God works in us.
Then begins in us, as from a seed, but an unfailing
seed, the new basic something which overcomes unrighteousness. Where faith is, in the midst of the
old world of war and money and death, there is born

a new spirit out of which grows a new world, the
world of the righteousness of God. The need and
anxiety in which we live are done away when this
new beginning comes. The old fetters are broken,
the false idols begin to totter. For now something
real has happened — the only real thing that can
happen: God has now taken his own work in hand.
"I beheld Satan as lightning fall from heaven."
Life receives its meaning again — your own life and
life as a whole. Lights of God rise in the darkness,
and powers of God become real in weakness. Real
love, real sincerity, real progress become possible;
morality and culture, state and nation, even religion
and the church now become possible — now for the
first time! One is taken with the vision of an immortality or even of a future life here on earth in
which the righteous will of God breaks forth, prevails, and is done as it is done in heaven. In such
wise the righteousness of God, far, strange, high,
becomes our own possession and our great hope.

The inner way, the way of simple faith, is the way
of Christ. A greater than Moses and a greater than
John the Baptist is here. He is the love of God,
glorified before the world was and forever glorified.
Can one say that humanity has exhausted the possibilities of his way? We have received from Jesus
many different truths. But the simplest of them all
we have the least comprehended — that he was the
Son of God and that we, if we will, may go with him
the way wherein one simply believes that the
Father's will is truth and must be done. One may

object that this method of squaring the circle is childlike and inadequate. I grant it. But this childlike and inadequate solution is the beginning of the vast plan of God. It remains to be seen whether the quaking of the tower of Babel which we are now experiencing will be violent enough to bring us somewhat nearer to the way of *faith*. Opportunity offers. We may take the new way. Or we may not. Sooner or later we shall. There is no other.

II

THE STRANGE NEW WORLD WITHIN THE BIBLE

W E are to attempt to find an answer to the question, What is there within the Bible? What sort of house is it to which the Bible is the door? What sort of country is spread before our eyes when we throw the Bible open?

We are with Abraham in Haran. We hear a call which commands him: Get thee out of thy country, and from thy kindred, unto a land that I will show thee! We hear a promise: I will make of thee a great nation. And Abraham believed in the Lord; and he counted it to him for righteousness. What is the meaning of all this? We can but feel that there is something behind these words and experiences. But what?

We are with Moses in the wilderness. For forty years he has been living among the sheep, doing penance for an over-hasty act. What change has come over him? We are not told; it is apparently not our concern. But suddenly there comes to him also a call: Moses, Moses! — a great command: Come now therefore, and I will send thee unto Pharaoh, that

---

This address was delivered in the church at Lentwil in the autumn of 1916.

thou mayest bring forth my people, the children of
Israel, out of Egypt!—and a simple assurance:
Certainly I will be with thee. Here again are words
and experiences which seem at first to be nothing but
riddles. We do not read the like either in the daily
papers or in other books. What lies behind?

It is a time of severe oppression in the land of
Canaan. Under the oak at Ophrah stands the farmer's son, Gideon. The "angel of the Lord" appears
to him, and says, The Lord is with thee, thou mighty
man of valor. He sees nothing amiss in protesting,
If the Lord be with us, why then is all this befallen
us? But "the Lord" knows how to bring him to
silence: Go in this thy might, and *thou* shalt save
Israel from the hand of the Midianites: have not *I*
sent thee?

In the tabernacle at Shiloh lies the young Samuel.
Again a call: Samuel, Samuel! And the pious priest
Eli, to whom he runs, wisely advises him to lie down
again. He obeys and sleeps until, the call returning
and returning, he can no longer sleep; and the
thought comes to the pious Eli: It might be . . . . !
And Samuel must hear and obey.

We read all this, but what do we read behind it?
We are aware of something like the tremors of an
earthquake or like the ceaseless thundering of ocean
waves against thin dikes; but what really is it that
beats at the barrier and seeks entrance here?

We remember how Elijah felt himself called of
"the Lord" to offer defiance to the whole authority
of his king, and then himself had to make the

acquaintance of this "Lord," not in the wind and
storm but in a "still, small voice" — how Isaiah and
Jeremiah wished not to speak but had to speak the
secrets of divine judgment and divine blessing upon
a sinful people — how, later, during the deepest
humiliation of this people there stood up strange and
solitary "servants of God" who struggled ever
more fiercely with the question, Where is now thy
God? and forever gave the answer, Israel hath yet
God for consolation! — how in the midst of all the
wrongdoing and misery of the people they could
but blare out, as it were, the announcement: Arise,
shine, for thy light is come, and the glory of the
Lord is risen upon thee! What does it mean? Why
do these men speak so? Whence is kindled all the
indignation, all the pity, all the joy, all the hope and
the unbounded confidence which even today we see
flaring up like fire from every page of the prophets
and the psalms?

Then come the incomprehensible, incomparable
days, when all previous time, history, and experience seem to stand still — like the sun at Gibeon —
in the presence of a man who was no prophet, no
poet, no hero, no thinker, and yet all of these and
more! His words cause alarm, for he speaks with
authority and not as we ministers. With compelling
power he calls to each one: Follow me! Even to the
distrustful and antagonistic he gives an irresistible
impression of "eternal life." "The blind receive
their sight, and the lame walk, the lepers are
cleansed, and the deaf hear, the dead are raised up,

and the poor have the gospel preached to them."
"Blessed is the womb that bare thee," cry the
people. And the quieter and lonelier he becomes,
and the less real "faith" he finds in the world about
him, the stronger through his whole being peals one
triumphant note: "I am the resurrection and the
life! Because I live — ye shall live also!"

And then comes the echo, weak enough, if we compare it with that note of Easter morning — and yet
strong, much too strong for our ears, accustomed as
they are to the weak, pitiably weak tones of to-day
— the echo which this man's life finds in a little
crowd of folk who listen, watch, and wait. Here is
the echo of the first courageous missionaries who
felt the necessity upon them to go into all the world
and preach the gospel to every creature. Here is the
echo of Paul: "The righteousness of God is revealed! If any man be in Christ, he is a new creature. And he which hath begun a good work in you
will finish it!" Here is the deep still echo of John:
"Life was manifested. . . . We beheld his glory
. . . Now are we the sons of God. . . . And this is
the victory that overcometh the world, even our
faith."

Then the echo ceases. The Bible is finished.

Who is the man who spoke such words and lived
such a life, who set these echoes ringing? And again
we ask: What is there within the Bible? What is
the significance of the remarkable line from Abraham to Christ? What of the chorus of prophets and
apostles? and what is the burden of their song?

What is the one truth that these voices evidently all
desire to announce, each in its own tone, each in its
own way? What lies between the strange statement,
In the beginning God created the heaven and the
earth, and the equally strange cry of longing, Even
so, come, Lord Jesus! What is there behind all this,
that labors for expression?

It is a dangerous question. We might do better
not to come too near this burning bush. For we are
sure to betray what is — behind *us!* The Bible gives
to every man and to every era such answers to their
questions as they deserve. We shall always find in it
as much as we seek and no more: high and divine
content if it is high and divine content that we seek;
transitory and "historical" content, if it is transitory and "historical" content that we seek — nothing whatever, if it is nothing whatever that we seek.
The hungry are satisfied by it, and to the satisfied
it is surfeiting before they have opened it. The question, What is within the Bible? has a mortifying way
of converting itself into the opposing question,
Well, what are you looking for, and who are you,
pray, who make bold to look?

But in spite of all this danger of making embarrassing discoveries in ourselves, we must yet trust
ourselves to ask our question. Moreover, we must
trust ourselves to reach eagerly for an answer which
is really much too large for us, for which we really
are not yet ready, and of which we do not seem
worthy, since it is a fruit which our own longing,
striving, and inner labor have not planted. What

this fruit, this answer, is, is suggested by the title of
my address: within the Bible there is a strange,
new world, the world of God. This answer is the
same as that which came to the first martyr, Stephen: Behold, I see the heavens opened and the Son
of man standing on the right hand of God. Neither
by the earnestness of our belief nor by the depth
and richness of our experience have we deserved the
right to this answer. What I shall have to say
about it will be only a small and unsatisfying part
of it. We must openly confess that we are reaching
far beyond ourselves. But that is just the point:
if we wish to come to grips with the contents of the
Bible, we must dare to reach far beyond ourselves.
The Book admits of nothing less. For, besides
giving to every one of us what he rightly deserves
— to one, much, to another, something, to a third,
nothing — it leaves us no rest whatever, if we are
in earnest, once with our shortsighted eyes and
awkward fingers we have found the answer in it
that *we* deserve. Such an answer is something but,
as we soon realize, not everything. It may satisfy
us for a few years, but we simply cannot be content
with it forever. Ere long the Bible says to us, in
a manner candid and friendly enough, with regard
to the ''versions'' we make of it: ''These may be
you, but they are not I! They may perhaps suit you,
meeting the demands of your thought and tempera-
ment, of your era and your 'circle,' of your religious
or philosophical theories. You wanted to be mir-
rored in me, and now you have really found in me

your own reflection. But now I bid you come seek *me*, as well. Seek what is here." It is the Bible itself, it is the straight inexorable logic of its on-march which drives us out beyond ourselves and invites us, without regard to our worthiness or un-worthiness, to reach for the last highest answer, in which all is said that can be said, although we can hardly understand and only stammeringly express it. And that answer is: A new world, the world of God. There is a spirit in the Bible that allows us to stop awhile and play among secondary things as is our wont — but presently it begins to press us on; and however we may object that we are only weak, imperfect, and most average folk, it presses us on to the primary fact, whether we will or no. There is a river in the Bible that carries us away, once we have entrusted our destiny to it — away from ourselves to the sea. The Holy Scriptures will interpret themselves in spite of all our human limitations. We need only dare to follow this drive, this spirit, this river, to grow out beyond ourselves toward the high-est answer. This daring is *faith;* and we read the Bible rightly, not when we do so with false mod-esty, restraint, and attempted sobriety, for these are passive qualities, but when we read it in faith. And the invitation to dare and to reach toward the highest, even though we do not deserve it, is the expression of *grace* in the Bible: the Bible unfolds to us as we are met, guided, drawn on, and made to grow by the grace of God.

What is there within the Bible? *History!* The

history of a remarkable, even unique, people; the history of powerful, mentally vigorous personalities; the history of Christianity in its beginnings — a history of men and ideas in which anyone who considers himself educated must be interested, if for no other reason than because of its effects upon the times following and the present time.

Now one can content himself for a time with this answer and find in it many true and beautiful possibilities. The Bible is full of history; religious history, literary history, cultural history, world history, and human history of every sort. A picture full of animation and color is unrolled before all who approach the Bible with open eyes.

But the pleasure is short-lived: the picture, on closer inspection, proves quite incomprehensible and flat, if it is meant only for history. The man who is looking for history or for stories will be glad after a little to turn from the Bible to the morning paper or to other books. For when we study history and amuse ourselves with stories, we are always wanting to know: How did it all happen? How is it that one event follows another? What are the natural causes of things? *Why* did the people speak such words and live such lives? It is just at the most decisive points of its history that the Bible gives no answer to our Why. Such is the case, indeed, not only with the Bible, but with all the truly decisive men and events of history. The greater a crisis, the less of an answer we get to our inquisitive Why. And *vice versa*: the smaller a man or an era, the more the "historians" find to explain and establish. But the Bible meets the lover of history with silences quite unparalleled.

Why was it that the Israelitish people did not perish in the Egyptian bondage, but remained a people, or rather, in the very deepest of their need, became one? Why? There was a reason! Why was it that Moses was able to create a law which for purity and humanity puts us moderns only to shame? There was a reason! Why is it that Jeremiah stands there during the siege of Jerusalem with his message of doom, an enemy of the people, a man without a country? Why Jesus' healing of the sick, why his messianic consciousness, why the resurrection? Why does a Saul become a Paul? Why that other-worldly picture of Christ in the fourth gospel? Why does John on the Isle of Patmos — ignoring the Roman Empire in its very heyday — see the holy city, new Jerusalem, coming down from God out of heaven, prepared as a bride adorned for her husband? There was a reason!

How much trouble the Bible makes the poor research workers! There was a reason (with an exclamation point)! is hardly an adequate answer for a history; and if one can say of the incidents of the Bible only There was a reason! its history is in truth stark nonsense. Some men have felt compelled to seek grounds and explanations where there were none, and what has resulted from that procedure is a history in itself — an unhappy history into which I will not enter at this time. The Bible itself, in any case, answers our eager Why neither like a sphinx, with There was a reason! nor, like a lawyer, with a thousand arguments, deductions, and parallels, but says to us, The decisive cause is *God*. Because *God* lives, speaks, and acts, there was a reason . . . !

To be sure, when we hear the word "God," it may at first seem the same as There was a reason! In the leading articles of our dailies, and in the primary history readers of our Aargau schools one does not expect to have events explained by the fact that "God created," or "God spoke!" When God enters, history for the while ceases to be, and there is nothing more to ask; for something wholly different and new begins — a history with its own distinct grounds, possibilities, and hypotheses.

The paramount question is whether we have understanding for this different, new world, or good will enough to meditate and enter upon it inwardly. Do we desire the presence of "God"? Do we dare to go whither evidently we are being led? That were "faith"! A new world projects itself into our old ordinary world. We may reject it. We may say, It is nothing; this is imagination, madness, this "God." But we may not deny nor prevent our being led by Bible "history" far out beyond what is elsewhere called history — into a new world, into the world of God.

We might also say, There is *morality* within the Bible. It is a collection of teachings and illustrations of virtue and human greatness. No one has ever yet seriously questioned the fact that in their way the men of the Bible were good representative men, from whom we have an endless amount to learn. Whether we seek practical wisdom or lofty examples of a certain type of heroism, we find them here forthwith.

And again in the long run we do not. Large parts of the Bible are almost useless to the school in its moral curriculum because they are lacking in just this wisdom and just these "good examples." The heroes of the Bible are to a certain degree quite respectable, but to serve as examples to the good, efficient, industrious, publicly educated, average citizen of Switzerland, men like Samson, David, Amos, and Peter are very ill fitted indeed; Rosa of Tannenburg, the figures of Amicis' "Courage" (*Il Cuore*), and the magnificent characters of later Swiss history are quite different people! The Bible is an embarrassment in the school and foreign to it. How shall we find in the life and teaching of Jesus something to "do" in "practical life"? Is it not as if he wished to say to us at every step "What interest have I in your 'practical life'? I have little to do with that. Follow after *me* or let me go my way!"

At certain crucial points the Bible amazes us by its remarkable indifference to our conception of good and evil. Abraham, for instance, as the highest proof of his faith desires to sacrifice his son to God; Jacob wins the birthright by a refined deception of his blind father; Elijah slays the four hundred and fifty priests of Baal by the brook Kishon. Are these exactly praiseworthy examples?

And in how many phases of morality the Bible is grievously wanting! How little fundamental information it offers in regard to the difficult questions of business life, marriage, civilization, and statecraft, with which we have to struggle! To mention only a single problem, but to us today a mortal one: how unceremoniously and constantly war is waged in the Bible! Time and again, when this question comes up, the teacher or minister must resort to various kinds of extra-Biblical material, because the New as well as the Old Testament almost completely breaks down at this point. Time and again serious Christian people who seek "comfort" and "inspiration" in the midst of personal difficulties will quietly close their Bibles and reach for the clearer-toned lyre of a Christian Fürchtegott Gellert or for the books of Hilty, if not toward psychoanalysis — where everything is so much more practicable, simple, and comprehensible. Time and again the Bible gives us the impression that it contains no instructions, counsels, or examples whatsoever, either for individuals or for nations and governments; and the impression is correct. It offers us not at all what we first seek in it.

Once more we stand before this "other" new world which begins in the Bible. In it the chief consideration is not the doings of man but the doings of God — not the various ways which we may take if we are men of good will, but the power

out of which good will must first be created — not
the unfolding and fruition of love as we may understand it, but the existence and outpouring of eternal
love, of love as God understands it — not industry,
honesty, and helpfulness as we may practice them
in our old ordinary world, but the establishment and
growth of a new world, the world in which God and
his morality reign.   In the light of this coming
world a David is a great man in spite of his adultery
and bloody sword: blessed is the man unto whom
the Lord imputeth not iniquity!   Into this world
the publicans and the harlots will go before your im-
peccably elegant and righteous folk of good society!
In this world the true hero is the lost son, who is
absolutely lost and feeding swine — and not his
moral elder brother!   The reality which lies behind
Abraham and Moses, behind Christ and his apostles,
is the world of the Father, in which morality is dis-
pensed with because it is taken for granted.   And
the blood of the New Testament which seeks inflow
into our veins is the will of the Father which would
be done on earth as it is in heaven.

We may have grasped this as the meaning of the
Bible, as *its* answer to our great and small questions, and still say: I do not need this; I do not
desire it; it tells me nothing; I cannot get anywhere
with it!   It may be that we really cannot get anywhere with it on our present highways and byways
— on our byways of church and school, for example,
and, in many instances, on the byway of the personal life which we have been traveling with such

perseverance. There are blind alleys of a thousand
types, out of which the way into the kingdom of
heaven can at first lead only backwards. And it is
certain that the Bible, if we read it carefully, makes
straight for the point where one must decide to
accept or to reject the sovereignty of God. This is
the new world within the Bible. We are offered the
magnificent, productive, hopeful life of a grain of
seed, a new beginning, out of which all things shall
be made new. One cannot learn or imitate this life
of the divine seed in the new world. One can only
let it live, grow, and ripen within him. One can only
believe — can only hold the ground whither he has
been led. Or not believe. There is no third way.

Let us seek our way out on still another side: let
us start with the proposition that in the Bible we
have a revelation of true *religion,* of religion defined
as what we are to think concerning God, how we are
to find him, and how we are to conduct ourselves in
his presence — all that is included in what today we
like to call "worship and service" (Frömmigkeit).
The Bible as a "source-book for godly living" —
how much has been said and written upon this theme
in the last years! And such the Bible is. It is
a treasury of truth concerning the right relation of
men to the eternal and divine — but here too the
same law holds: we have only to seek honestly and
we shall make the plain discovery that there is
something greater in the Bible than religion and
"worship." Here again we have only a kind of
crust which must be broken through.

We have all been troubled with the thought that there are so many kinds of Christianity in the world — Catholic Christianity and Protestant, the Christianities of the various communions and of the "groups" (Richtungen) within them, the Christianity of the old-fashioned and the Christianity of the modern — and all, all of them appealing with the same earnestness and zeal to the Bible. Each insists, *Ours* is the religion revealed in the Bible, or at least its most legitimate successor. And how is one to answer? Does it not require a generous bit of effrontery to say, We Protestants, or we members of such and such a communion or society are right, for such and such reasons; and all the others are wrong? When once one knows how easy it is to find "reasons," the pleasure of participating in this eternal game begins to pall.

Then shall we take the position that fundamentally we are all right? Shall we dip our hands into that from which the spirit of the Bible silently turns away, the dish of tolerance which is more and more being proclaimed, especially in our national church, as the highest good?

Or may we all, jointly and severally, with our various views and various forms of worship, be — wrong? The fact is that we must seek our answer in this direction — "Yea, let God be true, but every man a liar." All religions may be found in the Bible, if one will have it so; but when he looks closely, there are none at all. There is only — the "other," new, greater world! When we come to

the Bible with our questions — How shall I think
of God and the universe? How arrive at the divine?
How present myself? — it answers us, as it were,
"My dear sir, these are *your* problems: you must
not ask *me!* Whether it is better to hear mass or
hear a sermon, whether the proper form of Christianity is to be discovered in the Salvation Army or
in 'Christian Science,' whether the better belief is
that of old Reverend Doctor Smith or young Reverend Mr. Jones, whether your religion should be
more a religion of the understanding, of the will,
or of the feelings, you can and must decide for yourself. If you do not care to enter upon *my* questions,
you may, to be sure, find in me all sorts of arguments and quasi-arguments for one or another
standpoint, but you will not then find what is really
here." We shall find ourselves only in the midst
of a vast human controversy and far, far away from
reality, or what might become reality in our lives.

It is not the right human thoughts about God
which form the content of the Bible, but the right
divine thoughts about men. The Bible tells us not
how we should talk with God but what he says to
us; not how we find the way to him, but how he has
sought and found the way to us; not the right relation in which we must place ourselves to him, but
the covenant which he has made with all who are
Abraham's spiritual children and which he has
sealed once and for all in Jesus Christ. It is this
which is within the Bible. The word of God is
within the Bible.

Our grandfathers, after all, were right when they struggled so desperately in behalf of the truth that there is revelation in the Bible and not religion only, and when they would not allow facts to be turned upside down for them even by so pious and intelligent a man as Schleiermacher. And our fathers were right when they guarded warily against being drawn out upon the shaky scaffolding of religious self-expression.

The more honestly we search the Scriptures, the surer, sooner or later, comes the answer: The right forms of worship and service? — "they are they which testify of *Me!*" We seek ourselves — we find God; and having done so stand before him with our religions, Christianities, and other notions, like blundering scholars with their A B C's. Yet we cannot be sad about it but rejoice that we have found, among all lesser considerations, the chief one, without which every form of religion, even the most perfect, is only a delusion and a snare. This chief consideration contains, again, the living grain of seed out of which a right relation to God, a service of God "in spirit and in truth," necessarily must issue, whether we lay stress more upon this detail or that. The word of God! The standpoint of God!

Once more we have every liberty of choice. We may explain: "I cannot get anywhere with this: the conception of the 'word of God' is not part of my philosophy. I still prefer the old ordinary Christianity of my kind of 'worship' and my own particular standpoint." Or we may be willing to hear

what "passeth all understanding"; may desire in
the power of God and the Saviour to let it grow and
ripen within us according to the laws of the great
life process set forth in the Bible; may obey the
spirit of the Book and acknowledge God to be right
instead of trying to prove ourselves right; may
dare — to believe. Here we find ourselves faced
once more by the question of faith. But without
anticipating our answer to it, we may rest assured
that in the Bible, in both the Old and the New Testaments, the theme is, so to speak, the religion of God
and never once the religion of the Jews, or Christians, or heathen; that in this respect, as in others,
the Bible lifts us out of the old atmosphere of man
to the open portals of a new world, the world of God.

But we are not yet quite at an end. We have
found in the Bible a new world, God, God's sovereignty, God's glory, God's incomprehensible love.
Not the history of man but the history of God! Not
the virtues of men but the virtues of him who hath
called us out of darkness into his marvelous light!
Not human standpoints but the standpoint of God!

Now, however, might not a last series of questions
arise: Who then is God? What is his will? What
are his thoughts? What is the mysterious "other,"
new, greater world which emerges in the Bible beyond all the ways of men, summoning us to a decision to believe or not to believe? In whom did
Abraham believe? For whom did the heroes fight
and conquer? Whom did the prophets prophesy?
In whose power did Christ die and rise again?

Whose name did the Apostles proclaim? The contents of the Bible are "God." But what is the content of the contents? Something "new" breaks forth! But what is the new?

To these questions there is a series of ready answers, serious and well-founded answers taken from the Bible itself, answers to which we must listen: God is the Lord and Redeemer, the Saviour and Comforter of all the souls that turn to him; and the new world is the kingdom of blessedness which is prepared for the little flock who escape destruction. Is not this in the Bible? . . . Again: God is the fountain of life which begins its quiet murmuring when once we turn away from the externalities of the world and bow before him in silence; and the new world is the incomparable peace of such a life hid with Christ in God. Is not this also in the Bible? . . . Again: God is the Lord of the heaven which awaits us, and in which, when our journey through the sorrows and imperfections of this life is done, we are to possess and enjoy our citizenship; and the new world is just this blessed other life, the "still eternity" into which the faithful shall one day enter. This answer also comes directly from the Bible.

These are true enough answers. But are they *truth?* Are they the whole truth? Can one read or hear read even as much as two chapters from the Bible and still with good conscience say, God's word went forth to humanity, his mandate guided history from Abraham to Christ, the Holy Spirit descended in tongues of fire upon the apostles at Pentecost, a Saul became a Paul and traveled over land and sea — all in order that here and there specimens of men like you and me might be "converted," find inner "peace," and by a redeeming death go some day to "heaven." Is *that* all? Is *that* all of God and his new world, of the meaning of the Bible, of the content of the contents? The powerful forces which come to expression in the Bible, the movements of peoples, the battles, and the convulsions which take place before us there, the miracles and revelations which constantly occur there, the immeasurable promises for the future which are unceasingly repeated to us there — do not all these things stand in a rather strange relation to so small a result — if that is really the only result they have? Is not God — greater than that? Even in these answers, earnest and pious as they may be, have we not measured God with our own measure, conceived God with our own conceptions, wished ourselves a God according to our own wishes? When we begin to read the Bible carefully, must we not grow beyond these answers, too?

Must we not also grow beyond the strange question, Who is God? As if we could dream of asking such a question, having willingly and sincerely allowed ourselves to be led to the gates of the new world, to the threshold of the kingdom of God! There one asks no longer. There one sees. There one hears. There one has. There one knows. There one no longer gives his petty, narrow little answers.

The question, Who is God? and our inadequate answers to it come only from our having halted somewhere on the way to the open gates of the new world; from our having refused somewhere to let the Bible speak to us candidly; from our having failed somewhere truly to desire to — believe. At the point of halt the truth again becomes unclear, confused, problematical — narrow, stupid, high-church, non-conformist, monotonous, or meaningless. "He that hath *seen* me hath *seen* the Father." That is it: when we allow ourselves to press on to the highest answer, when we find God in the Bible, when we dare with Paul not to be disobedient to the heavenly vision, then God stands before us as he really is. "Believing, ye *shall* receive!" God is *God*.

But who may say, I believe? — "Lord, I believe; help thou mine unbelief." It is because of our unbelief that we are so perplexed by the question, Who is God? — that we feel so small and ashamed before the fullness of the Godhead which the men and women of the Bible saw and proclaimed. It is because of our unbelief that even now I can only stammer, hint at, and make promises about that which would be opened to us if the Bible could speak to us unhindered, in the full fluency of its revelations.

Who is God? The heavenly Father! But the heavenly Father even upon *earth,* and upon earth really the *heavenly* Father. He will not allow life to be split into a "here" and "beyond." He will

not leave to death the task of freeing us from sin and
sorrow. He will bless us, not with the power of the
church but with the power of life and resurrection.
In Christ he caused his word to be made flesh. He
has caused eternity to dawn in place of time, or
rather upon time — for what sort of eternity were
it which should begin "afterwards"! He purposes
naught but the establishment of a new *world*.

Who is God? The Son who has become "the
mediator for my soul." But more than that: He
has become the mediator for the whole world, the
redeeming Word, who was in the beginning of all
things and is earnestly expected by all things. He
is the redeemer of my brothers and sisters. He is
the redeemer of a humanity gone astray and ruled
by evil spirits and powers. He is the redeemer of
the groaning creation about us. The whole Bible
authoritatively announces that God must be all in
all; and the events of the Bible are the beginning,
the glorious beginning of a new *world*.

Who is God? The Spirit in his believers, the
spirit

> .... by which we own
> The Son who lived and died and rose;
> Which crystal clear from God's pure throne
> Through quiet hearts forever flows.

But God is also that spirit (that is to say, that
love and good will) which will and must break forth
from quiet hearts into the world outside, that it may
be manifest, visible, comprehensible: behold the
tabernacle of God is with men! The Holy Spirit

makes a new heaven and a new earth and, therefore, new men, new families, new relationships, new politics. It has no respect for old traditions simply because they are traditions, for old solemnities simply because they are solemn, for old powers simply because they are powerful. The *Holy* Spirit has respect only for truth, for itself. The Holy Spirit establishes the righteousness of heaven in the midst of the unrighteousness of earth and will not stop nor stay until all that is dead has been brought to life and a new *world* has come into being.

This is within the Bible. It is within the Bible for us. For it we were baptized. Oh, that we dared in faith to take what grace can offer us!

I need not suggest that we all have need of this. We live in a sick old world which cries from its soul, out of deepest need: Heal me, O Lord, and I shall be healed! In all men, whoever and wherever and whatever and however they may be, there is a longing for exactly this which is here within the Bible. We all know that.

And now hear: "A certain man made a great supper, and bade many; and sent his servant at supper-time to say to them that were bidden, Come, for all things are now ready! . . . "

III.

BIBLICAL QUESTIONS, INSIGHTS, AND VISTAS

𝕿HE question we have now to consider is, What does the Bible offer us toward an understanding of the meaning of the world? It is a question which, as we have noted before, has a disconcerting way of turning about, facing us who ask it, and inquiring whether or how far we are capable of understanding its answer.

The immediate answer to our question is, of course, that the Bible offers us a knowledge of God: we look to it not so much to give us knowledge about this particular or that, as to indicate to us the beginning and the end, the origin and the limit, the creative unity and the last problem of all knowledge. "In the beginning God created the heaven and the earth" and "Amen. Even so, come, Lord Jesus" Such is the meaning of the world according to the Bible. It is our part to confirm it in our own lives by laboring to relate ourselves, our daily task, and our hour of history to God the Creator and Redeemer. It is not a meaning apart from other meanings, for in it all others—the meanings of natural

This address was delivered at the Aarau Student Conference in April, 1920.

science, of history, of esthetics, and of religion —
are at once included and concluded; and this meaning in the last analysis will be found to be identical
with that of philosophy, so far as philosophy understands itself. It is the meaning *par excellence,* without rivals, without challengers, the meaning *sub
specie aeterni.* What more can we desire?

This we can say: but the knowledge of God is so
simple and so comprehensive that it is also very
perplexing. On the one hand, our question as to
what the Bible offers is an idle one, for we already
have the answer: all the knowledge that we possess
takes its start from the knowledge of God. We are
not outside, as it were, but inside. The knowledge
of God is not a possibility which we may, or at
worst may *not,* apply in our search for a meaning
of the world; it is rather the presupposition on the
basis of which consciously, half-consciously, or unconsciously all our searchings for meaning are made.
On the other hand, we are far from being equal to
that knowledge. If we were, we should not be asking what the Bible offers. As a matter of fact, instead of being the document of the axiomatic, the
Bible tends to become to us a document of objective
historical information; we come to maintain a questioning attitude toward it, as if it could tell us something that we do not in our heart of hearts already
know; and the knowledge of God, instead of being
the presupposition which gets *us* somewhere, as the
phrase goes, comes to be a philosophical or mytho-
logical problem which one must try to get some-

where *with*. And thus we give evidence that the
simplicity and comprehensiveness which would
make us capable of understanding the Bible as it
understands itself, and as it alone can be understood, are at least to some degree wanting in us.
We give evidence that we are not wholly qualified
for or equal to the knowledge of God. We give
evidence by our questioning of the Bible that the
Bible's answer, which we know before we ask, perplexes us.

It perplexes us, I say, and not more and not less.
The question we ask becomes a question asked of us,
in face of which we are thrown into a strangely
embarrassing position, midway between Yes and
No, No and Yes. This is a confession we must make
at the very outset, and it will bear amplification.

We are inside and not outside, we said; the
knowledge of God and of the last things, of which
the Bible speaks, is the premise of all our life and
thought. The simplicity and comprehensiveness
which the Bible offers us do correspond, to a certain degree, to a like simplicity and comprehensiveness in ourselves. "It is the spirit that beareth
witness that the spirit is truth."

But this is apparently contradicted by our dark,
enigmatical, inexplicable sense of being outside and
of lacking a premise. The last things loom ahead
of us distant, strange, problematical, immense. The
complexity of our lives, of our this-and-that culture,
revolts against the simplicity of the knowledge of
God: our individualism revolts against its compre-

hensiveness. The unredeemed mind of man, split off from the mind of the Creator, denies its Origin, denies itself.

Now how does it happen that there is no resolving of this contradiction? The No from the earliest days has had on its side much greater power to convince than the Yes has had; what is the reason it cannot once for all submerge the Yes? Why is it that we never break through to the clear and final conclusion that our sense of being inside is mistaken? The answer is hinted at in the very inevitableness of our continued asking for a knowledge of God: we belong to the Yes and not to the No. Our quest for God cannot be due to the influence of theology and the church, for *theology* and the *church* from the beginning of the world have done more in this particular to narcotize than to stimulate. It cannot be due to our *simple-mindedness,* for it really needs more intelligence to believe in God in simplicity, in face of the whole smothering power of the No in us all, than it does to consider the question about God closed. Were it actually our simple-mindedness which has kept the question open, this would speak well for the intelligence in that simple-mindedness, but would not meet the pressing and actual dead weight of the question itself. And our quest cannot be due to the natural strength of our so-called *religious emotion,* for the religious emotion may turn men aside from God as well as toward him. Religion and thought concerning God have never meant the same thing.

It is evident that the question about God is a *last inevitability*, that it contains its own answer, that we are caught and taken captive by a presupposed and original Yes which we would not attempt to deny if it did not cause us such unrest. We cannot quite forget the soul's provenance: we cannot quite forget its unity with God in the beginning. We cannot reach and recognize the boundaries of mortality without being mindful at the same time of what lies beyond. We should not seek had we not already found. Why then should we not admit our knowledge of God?

But we have only expressed our perplexity! When we admit our knowledge of God, we apparently admit something else besides. When we hold to our partly inside position, we are apparently at the same time establishing a position partly outside. We set up for ourselves a duality, a dualism. We admit our knowledge of God only as an antithesis to other knowledge.

Knowledge of God as an antithesis to other knowledge! How does it happen that we honestly do not seem to get further than this absurd inconsistency? How is it that even our Yes cannot win its way to a place of rest, fulfillment, confirmation? Why do we not break through into the clear conclusion that our sense of being outside, our naturalism, our soulless historism, and our estheticism are mistaken? Whence arises the opposing fact that we are always in part refusing to ask after God? It is not due to the *triumph* of philosophical enlightenment, ancient or modern, *over dogmatism;* for when the human soul becomes actually conscious of its autonomy and freedom, the gravity of the question about unity, the question about God, is not lessened but increased. Our refusal is not due to our *progress in the theoretical and practical conquest of nature,* for it is five or ten thousand years older than modern science and its applications; and the frank materialism of the modern sciences is not a denial but an affirmation of the truth that our existence hangs on the hinges of a beginning and ending which point beyond themselves. It is not due, either, to the natural weakness of our *religious emotion* — most men being weak in this regard — for if the strength of the emotion cannot explain the thought about God, its weakness cannot explain the lack of it. There have often been frankly unreligious men who felt the whole importance and gravity of the question about God much more keenly, and expressed it much more poignantly, than the most deeply and zealously pious. I think of the remarkably unsentimental Immanuel Kant. I think of the outspoken and apparently unavoidably religious Philistinism of almost all the founders and leaders of socialism. I think of the theologian who did not wish to be one, the skeptic, Franz Overbeck. With or without emotion, they veritably lived the question about God. How does it happen then to a great degree, that with or without emotion, we veritably can *not* live it?

It is evident that our refusal to do so is no chance

circumstance to be explained on historical and psychological grounds, but is itself a *last inevitability*. We sometimes ask after God in such a way as to make it evident that we are not really in earnest, but keep asking only in order to escape hearing an answer we cannot understand or do not want to understand — which is one and the same thing. We succeed at times in ignoring what we know, in forgetting the original unity of the soul. We contrive for a little to be satisfied to have our knowledge split into a thousand parts, each man clinging with jealous eagerness to his own fragment, the spiritual bond being cast to the winds — you take your biology! you take your history! I have my religion! — you in your small corner and I in mine! It is a fact as inexplicable as it is undeniable that there is also a presupposed original No which holds us captive, and that sometimes in the alleged interest of threatened religion and sometimes, *vice versa,* in the alleged interest of threatened culture, we feel we must oppose a special truth about the world to a special truth about God; but this is to establish a system of double-entry bookkeeping which converts the knowledge of God offered in the Bible into what it is not. For the fear of the Lord which is offered us in the Bible is not something apart from other things: it is the beginning of wisdom.

With the Yes and the No, the No and the Yes in which we find ourselves, we are thrown into the perplexity, into the crisis, of the Scriptures. He that hath *ears* to hear, let *him* hear. Give no credence to any *secondary* reasons and explanations for this perplexity. When we ask the Bible what it has to offer, it answers by putting to us the fact of *election*. What we call religion and culture may be available to everybody, but the belief, simple and comprehensive, which is offered in the Bible, is not available to everybody: not at any time nor in any respect can any who will, reach out and take it. Simplicity has nothing about it so simple as that. Comprehensiveness, universality, is not generality. The thesis upon which all things rest is never a *datum*. The ultimate presupposition is never one supposed truth among other truths. The axiomatic is never the obvious. The knowledge which the Bible offers and commands us to accept forces us out upon a narrow ridge of rock upon which we must balance between Yes and No, between life and death, between heaven and earth. "Work out your own salvation with fear and trembling. For it is God which worketh in you both to will and to do of his good pleasure."

The really vital core, the secret both of history and of our existence, is our response to the fact of election. This, as a doctrine, was too quickly and drastically adapted by Augustine and the Reformers to meet the requirements of the *psychological* unity of the individual; and the rigid laws of nature were once and for all stamped upon each man's salvation or damnation. As a matter of fact, however, the idea of election is well adapted to the requirements of individual *freedom*: our responses cannot be determined once and for all: they are constantly to be made anew. Indeed, opposite responses are awakened *simultaneously* in a single individual. There is never so decisive a Yes that it does not harbor the possibility of the No: there is never so decisive a No that it is not liable to be toppled over into the Yes. There is no certainty of election today which may not become a sense of reprobation tomorrow, and, similarly, no sense of reprobation which may not become a certainty of election. The only eternal election is God's: the dispositions of history and of the individual mind are secondary and temporal.

What the Bible has to offer us, above all, is insight to the effect that the knowledge of God is the eternal problem of our profoundest personal existence, that it is the starting-point at which we begin and yet do not begin, from which we are separated and yet are not separated. From the Bible we may learn to soften the affirmations of our belief or unbelief, and perhaps to keep silence, until we perceive the true relation between God and ourselves:

> Who may Him name?
> And who proclaim,
>   I believe in Him!
> And who may dare
> Straight to declare,
>   I believe not in Him!

We are dust and ashes with our Yes and No. No one compels us to turn from the quiet pursuit of our so-called religious or so-called cultural duties to the Bible; but once we have done so, there is nothing for it but that we should find ourselves in perplexity, and in fear and trembling come to respect the necessity under which, as we shall realize, we were living *before* we asked our question or heard the answer.

We have undertaken the task of Christian thinking today by asking what the Bible offers. We must be conscious that it is a dangerous and two-sided task, that there is no task which lays a fate upon the one who undertakes it as does this. Except in terms of the vexing thought of election, no word can be spoken and no word heard of what the Bible has to say to us regarding the glory of God in the face of Jesus Christ.

The Bible is the literary monument of an ancient racial religion and of a Hellenistic cultus religion of the Near East. A human document like any other, it can lay no *a priori* dogmatic claim to special attention and consideration. This judgment, being announced by every tongue and believed in every territory, we may take for granted today. We need not continue trying to break through an open door. And when now we turn our serious though somewhat dispassionate attention to the objective content of the Bible, we shall not do so in a way to provoke religious enthusiasm and scientific indignation to another battle against "stark orthodoxy" and "dead belief in the letter." For it is too clear that intelligent and fruitful discussion of the Bible begins when the judgment as to its human, its historical and psychological character has been made and *put behind* us. Would that the teachers of our high and lower schools, and with them the progressive element among the clergy of our established churches, would forthwith resolve to have done with a battle that once had its time but has now *had* it! The special *content* of this human document, the remarkable *something* with which the writers of these stories and those who stood behind them were concerned, the Biblical *object* — this is the question that will engage and engross us today.

With the historians and psychologists we first come upon the fact that evidently there once lived men of a quite extraordinary mental attitude and interest. There are doubtless varying degrees of this peculiarity within the Bible. The Biblical documents have margins, and on the margins the distinctive characteristics of its people merge into the attitudes of other men. One must not miss, however, a certain surprising sameness of orientation here. It is true that instances of it are not confined to the Biblical world. But along this one historical line — of which the beginning is lost in the darkness of the ancient East and the end in the twilight of the modern West, its enigmatical middle point being the turning-point in our reckoning of time — this one attitude and interest appear with a frequency, intensity, unified multiplicity, and multiplied unity which are not the less remarkable because traces of something similar are to be found also in Greece, in the wonderland of India, and in the German Middle Ages. I take a few examples at random. What is the key to the mind in which a book of such "subdued enthusiasm" as Ecclesiastes could have been conceived? What is the secret of the man — call him a copyist who will! — who could baffle a historical dissecting expert by the genius he used in combining the two major sections of the two books of Isaiah into *one?* How could any one be capable of thinking such a chapter as the fifteenth of First Corinthians and putting it down on paper? What sort of public was it of whom the devotional reading of epistles of the caliber of Romans or Hebrews was evidently once expected? What conception of God and of the world was it which made it possible for men to refuse to accept the Old and New Testaments upon the same basis, but to understand one in the light of the other?

We all know the curiosity that comes over us when from a window we see the people in the street suddenly stop and look up — shade their eyes with their hands and look straight up into the sky toward something which is hidden from us by the roof. Our curiosity is superfluous, for what they see is doubtless an aeroplane. But as to the sudden stopping, looking up, and tense attention characteristic of the people of the Bible, our wonder will not be so lightly dismissed. To me personally it came first with Paul: this man evidently sees and hears something which is above everything, which is absolutely beyond the range of my observation and the measure of my thought. Let me place myself as I will to this coming something — or rather this present something — no, rather, this coming something — that he insists in enigmatical words that he sees and hears, I am still taken by the fact that he, Paul, or whoever it was who wrote the Epistle to the Ephesians, for example, is eye and ear in a state which expressions such as inspiration, alarm, or stirring or overwhelming emotion, do not satisfactorily describe. I seem to see within so transparent a piece of literature a personality who is actually thrown out of his course and out of every ordinary course by seeing and hearing what I for my part do not see and hear — who is, so to speak, captured, in order to be dragged as a prisoner from land to land for strange, intense, uncertain, and yet mysteriously well-planned service.

And if ever I come to fear lest mine is a case of self-hallucination, one glance at the secular events of those times, one glance at the widening circle of ripples in the pool of history, tells me of a certainty that a stone of unusual weight must have been dropped into deep water there somewhere — tells me that, among all the hundreds of peripatetic preachers and miracle-workers from the Near East who in that day must have gone along the same Appian Way into imperial Rome, it was this one Paul, seeing and hearing what he did, who was the cause, if not of all, yet of the most important developments in that city's future. And this is only one of the Biblical company, "Paul" by name.

Near by him in the Bible, spellbound by what he
sees and hears, is one whose name is John. His
position is unique and yet not dissimilar to Paul's.
Next to him is one with an eye original enough to
combine the old and the new — the author of the
First Gospel. Then Paul's friend and pupil, the
physician — in more than the "social gospel"
sense — Luke. Then a seer and hearer whose simple
moral sobriety makes him the more disturbing —
James; and behind these are other figures in Jerusalem and farther back on the shores of the Galilean
Sea, whose names and faces may not be distinguished. But always there is the same seeing of
the invisible, the same hearing of the inaudible, the
same incomprehensible but no less undeniable epi-
demic of standing still and looking up. "These
twelve Jesus sent forth." Or was it seventy, or five
hundred? Who belonged? Who did not belong?
It is enough that even if they speak in tongues
strange to us we cannot fail to see that their eyes
are very strangely open, their ears are very remarkably sensitive. And the same kind of eyes and
ears, in despite of all historical causality, are in
evidence before this, in the fullness of the time before the fullness of the time. People like others,
surely, were the people of Israel and Judah, but
they were people among whom lofty things were
being seen and heard continually, a people among
whom attention to a Wholly Other seems never
wholly to have lapsed.

Or are we suffering from a historical hallucination when we say this? One glance at those mysteriously moved and mobile people, the Jews and Jewish Christians, as they live in our midst today, may serve to teach us that their race must once, certainly, have seen the beginning of new and striking developments.

Whether it be the prophets in the prolific middle line of Biblical descent, or the priests nearer to the margin where the Bible ceases to be Bible, whether they speak in psalms, proverbs, or in the comfortable flow of historical narrative, their theme in all its variations is equally astonishing. What matters it whether figures like Abraham and Moses are products of later myth-making — believe it who can! There were once, a few centuries earlier or later, men who lived by faith like Abraham, who were strangers in the promised land like Isaac and Jacob, who declared plainly that they were seeking a country, who like Moses endured as seeing him who is invisible. There were once men who dared. We may believe what we can and will concerning the something which encouraged them to dare, which moved these seers and hearers, but the movement itself into which they all, the named, the unnamed, and the pseudonymous, were drawn, we can no more deny than we can deny the rotation of the stellar firmament around an unknown central sun. This movement meets us in the Bible in an unescapable way. We think of John the Baptist in Grünewald's painting of the crucifixion, with his strangely pointing hand. It is this hand which is in evidence in the Bible.

Yet this calls for interpretation. When we describe the pointing hand as religion, worship, experience, or the like, even if we do so with utmost practical knowledge and the truest spirit of love, we do not offer any interpretation of it. Its true interpretation is found in the very fact that the categories of the science of religion cannot exhaustively describe the turning of man to God, much less contribute anything toward an understanding of it. In the Biblical experience there is a final element to which nothing in psychology corresponds, which cannot be reproduced in feeling, which cannot be demonstrated in experience. Biblical piety is not really pious; one must rather characterize it as well-considered and definite refusal to regard anything as sacred. Biblical religious history has the distinction of being in its essence, in its inmost character, neither religion nor history — not religion but reality, not history but truth, one might say. But we will not anticipate.

We mark here the distinctive feature of the Bible in contradistinction to everything else we call religious history. Everything we are wont to describe as "religion" contains, to be sure, the ultimate ingredient of an inner tendency to stay clear of history, to live in another world, whence things may be taken objectively and not sacredly. At all times and in all places religion has meant and means content and not only form, movement and not only a function of motion, life and not only a consecrated part of life, the divine and not only the human.

But always and everywhere, along with this inner tendency, there is traceable a strain of untruth: religion forgets that she has a right to exist only when she continually does away with herself. Instead, she takes joy in her existence and considers herself indispensable. She deceives herself and the world as to her true character; and she *can* do this by virtue of her wealth of sentimental and symbolical associations, of interesting nooks for the soul, of dogma, cultus, and morality, of ecclesiastical circumstance. She does not tolerate her own relativity. She has not the patience to wait; she lacks that spirit of the stranger and pilgrim, which alone justifies her coming into the world. She is not satisfied with hinting at the x that is over the world *and* herself. She acts in her lofty ecclesiastical estate as if she were in possession of a gold mine; and in the so-called "religious values" she actually pretends to give out clinking coins. She takes her place as a competitive power *over against* other powers in life, as an alleged superior world *over against* the world. She sends missionaries as if she herself could give them a mission. The extraordinary attitude of the men of the Bible becomes easy, familiar, not impracticable, and therefore not even unusual. Confidence in God is commended to the astonished world as a completely attainable and quite useful requisite for life, and is thoughtlessly asserted on the slightest pretext. The pointing hand of John the Baptist is not a strange sight — in pulpits. The experience of Paul is here and there *duplicated* by earnest young people. Prayer, that last possibility grasped at by spirit-imprisoned souls in their deepest need or joy, becomes a more or less familiar part of bourgeois housekeeping and church-keeping. One speaks, without blushing, of "Christian" morals, families, clubs, and organizations. "God in us" — then why not also I in you and you in me? Religious arrogance permits itself simply everything. A metaphysics is developed along the lines of physics, as if this were the necessary way. Form believes itself capable of taking the place of content. Experience becomes its own enjoyment, its own sufficiency, its own end. Motion becomes emotion. Man has taken the divine into his possession; he has brought it under his management.

No one notices, no one cares to notice, that the whole business rests upon supposition, upon an enormous "as if" and *quid pro quo*. How did it originally happen? Who was responsible? Was it the people who broke out in the cry for gods because they felt themselves deserted in the wilderness, or was it Moses' unavoidable brother, the priestly Aaron, who knew only too well how to tell the people the way that gods are made? Suffice it to say that the history of religion got started somehow, or, rather, the history of the untrue in religion, in contrast to what religion really is. For *at the moment when religion becomes conscious of religion, when it becomes a psychologically and historically conceivable magnitude in the world, it falls away from its inner character, from its truth, to idols. Its truth is its other-worldliness, its refusal of the idea of sacredness, its non-historicity.* I see the decisive characteristic of the Bible — as opposed to the history of religion, of which obviously the history of the Christian church is a chief part — in that the Bible displays a quite striking continuity of faithfulness, constancy, patient hopefulness, and objective attention toward the incomprehensible, unpsychological, and unhistorical truth of God. The human attempt to betray and to compromise the secret of which all religion dreams has no standing in the Bible.

Biblical *piety* is conscious of its own limits, of its relativity. In its essence it is humility, fear of the Lord. It points beyond the world, and points at the same time and above all beyond itself. It lives absolutely by virtue of its Object and for its Object.

In Biblical *experience* nothing is less important than experience as such. It is an appointment and a commission, not a goal and a fulfillment; and therefore it is an elementary thing, hardly conscious of itself, and necessitating only a minimum of reflection and confession. The prophets and apostles do not *wish* to be what they are; they *have* to be. And therefore they *are*.

At the central point of typically religious interest, at the point of the *personal relation of men to God* — in contrast to myth and mysticism, with their wealth of rainbow colors of suppressed sexuality — the Bible is astonishingly staid, sober, and colorless. It is evident that the relation to God with which the

Bible is concerned does not have its source in the
purple depths of the subconscious, and cannot be
quite identical with what the deep-sea psychical research of our day describes, in the narrower or
broader sense, as *libido* fulfillment.

One also observes in this connection the Bible's
circumspect and distant treatment of the conception of *sacrifice,* so important to all history of religion.   Even the Old Testament continually points
beyond sacrifice to a last fact which will not be done
away by the greatest and purest sacrifice, and which
will finally make all sacrifice superfluous.   It is not
sacrifice that God desires but — what? the religious
folk of that time may well ask!   Obedience, righteousness, love, open ears, thanksgiving, a contrite
spirit and broken heart — these are the enigmatical,
negative answers which precede the dawn of the New
Testament truth that by *one* sacrifice all sacrifices
are done away: "Where remission is, there is no
more offering for sin."   The narrative of Stephen
is the only one of its kind in the whole flood of
Christian martyr stories.   From that point on in the
Bible there is nothing more said of redemption by
sacrifices which *we* must make.

The polemic of the Bible, unlike that of the religions, is directed not against the godless world
but against the *religious* world, whether it worships
under the auspices of Baal or of Jehovah; and
against the heathen only in so far as their gods are
relativities, powers, and authorities which they have
raised into metaphysical absolutes and which are

therefore an abomination unto the Lord and abolished in Christ.

Moreover, in the Old and New Testaments a whole succession of *heathen* declare a faith such as is not found in Israel, and so demonstrate *ad oculos* how much the man of the Bible is without father, without mother, always a beginner, a first fruit, and in contrast to all history dependent only upon himself and God — Melchizedek, king of Salem, being his classical prototype.

Note also the surprisingly meager interest of the Bible in *biography,* in the development of its heroes. There is no gripping history of the youth and conversion of Jeremiah, no report of the edifying death of Paul. To the grief of our theological contemporaries there is above all no "Life of Jesus." What we hear of these men they never tell themselves; we do not read it in their "life and letters." The man of the Bible stands and falls with his task, his work.

For the same reason the Biblical *idea of the creation* is never expanded into a cosmogony. It is intended for a solemn marking of the distance between the cosmos and the Creator, and precisely not for a metaphysical explanation of the world. God said, Let there be! That is all. All being waits upon a word of God, all things perishable upon something imperishable, all time upon eternity — though the word of God, the imperishable, the eternal, is no In-Itself, no something apart from other things. "Where shall wisdom be found? and where is the place of understanding? Man knoweth not the price thereof; neither is it found in the land of the living. The depth saith, It is not in me: and the sea saith, It is not with me." "God" in the Bible is the boundary, the origin, and the problem of the world, "the King of kings, and Lord of lords; who only hath immortality, dwelling in the light which no man can approach unto." And in consequence and for this very reason let everything that hath breath praise the Lord!

Biblical *history* in the Old and New Testaments is not really history at all, but seen from above is a series of free divine acts and seen from below a series of fruitless attempts to undertake something in itself impossible. From the viewpoint of ordered development in particular and in general it is quite incomprehensible — as every religious teacher who is worth his salt knows only too well.

The *church* of the Bible is significantly the tabernacle, the portable tent. The moment it becomes a temple it becomes essentially only an object of attack. One gathers that for the apostles the whole of the Old Testament is summarized in Stephen's apology. Undeniably the central interest of both Testaments is not in the building of the church but in its destruction, which is always threatening and even beginning. In the heavenly Jerusalem of Revelation nothing is more finally significant than the church's complete absence: "And I saw no temple therein."

It is the peculiarity of Biblical *thought and speech* that they flow from a source which is above religious antinomies. The Bible treats, for instance, of both creation and redemption, grace and judgment, nature and spirit, earth and heaven, promise and fulfillment. To be sure, it enters now upon this and now upon that side of its antitheses, but it never brings them pedantically to an end; it never carries on into consequences; it never hardens, either in the thesis or in the antithesis; it never stiffens into positive or negative finalities. It has no understanding of what our ponderous age calls an "honest either-or" (ein ehrliches Entweder-Oder). It always finds as much and as little in the Yes as in the No; for the truth lies not in the Yes and not in the No but in the knowledge of the beginning from which the Yes and the No arise. Its thought and speech are concerned with the original; they issue from the whole and point toward the whole. They will be found to agree admirably with every philosophy worthy the name, but never with any collection of psychologisms, crude or subtle, masquerading as philosophy. What the Bible is interested in never loses its importance but is never captured in a word. It desires not to be accepted but understood, πνευματικοῖς πνευματικά, spirit by spirit. It is through and through dialectic. *Caveant professores!* Biblical dogmatics are fundamentally the suspension of all dogmatics. The Bible has only *one* theological interest and that is not speculative: interest in God himself.

It is this that I call the Bible's other-worldliness, its unhistoricalness, its antipathy to the idea of sacredness. *God* is the new, incomparable, unattainable, not only heavenly but more than heavenly interest, who has drawn the regard of the men of the Bible to himself. He desires their *complete* attention, their *entire* obedience. For he must be true to himself; he must be and remain holy. He cannot be grasped, brought under management, and put to use; he cannot serve. He must rule. He must himself grasp, seize, manage, use. He can satisfy no other needs than his own. He is not in another world over against this one; he submerges all of this in the other. He is not a thing among other things, but the *Wholly Other,* the infinite aggregate of all merely relative others. He is not the form of religious history but is the Lord of our life, the eternal Lord of the world. *He* it is of whom the Bible speaks. And is he spoken of elsewhere? Certainly. But whereas elsewhere consideration of him is left to the last, an imposing background, an esoteric secret, and therefore only a possibility, in the Bible he is the first consideration, the foreground, the revelation, the one all-dominating theme.

To be sure, for every characteristic of the people in the Biblical line of descent there is also a Biblical example of the opposite. The Biblical line is not identical with the Bible. Unprotected even in the Bible it runs through the midst of the general history of religion; and there is hardly a point where it is not cut by other heterogeneous lines. Those margins of the Bible where the Biblical men seem very similar not only to *other* men but to *religious*

men are often perplexingly broad, especially in the
Old Testament, and they are not by any means lacking even in the New. The abundance of variations makes one, at times, almost forget the theme.
That even the Bible, therefore, should be thought
to be only a part of our general religious chaos
is comprehensible. But not likely! Not likely at
least in a time when we know the difference between false and true Christianity as we do today —
when the failure of the relative type, consisting of
experience, metaphysics, and history, is so palpably,
so unmistakably before our eyes, and the demand for
a *new* something, the *Wholly* Other, the reality of
God, is so definitely upon our lips. The only likelihood is that we may misunderstand the character
and aim of the Bible by reading into it our own
vacillations.

A thoroughly enlightened ecclesiastical council of
the time of the Reformation, the Bernese synod of
1532, had as its motto the very unecclesiastical
Pauline utterance, ''Though we have known Christ
after the flesh, yet now henceforth know we him no
more.'' This suggests that Biblical insight, in spite
of its obscuration through the history of the Christian church, has not faded away entirely, even in
the later centuries.

Let Grünewald speak again. Near the steadily
pointing figure of his John are the words, *Illum
oportet crescere, me autem minui.* The prophet, the
man of God, the seer and hearer, ceases to be, as that
to which he unwaveringly points begins to be. The

object, the reality, the Divine Himself takes on new meaning; and the meaning of piety as such, of the function of the church as such, falls away. We may call this the characteristic insight of the Bible.

He must increase! But who can fail to feel an underlying fear in speaking and hearing of him who, as the men of the Bible see and as perhaps we also distantly see, must increase? When we turn our backs upon the gay fête of the history of religion, we find ourselves in something of the sheer, oppressive, awe-inspiring stillness and solitude of the wilderness — where for good reason so much of the action of the Bible takes place. It can in truth be no less than a *mysterium tremendum* that draws the men of the Bible before our eyes out and on to the edge of all experience, thought, and action, to the edge of time and history, and impels them to attempt to leap off into the air, where obviously no man can stand. Would it not be better for us and for our peace of mind, to turn back here? Shall we dare turn our eyes in the direction of the pointing hand of Grünewald's John? We know whither it points. It points to Christ. But to Christ the crucified, we must immediately add. That is your direction, says the hand. "He shall grow up before *us* as a tender plant, and as a root out of a dry ground: he hath no form nor comeliness; and when we shall see him, there is no beauty that we should desire him. He is despised and rejected of men; a man of sorrows, and acquainted with grief: and we hid as it were our faces from him; he was despised, and we esteemed him not.'' The only source for the real, the immediate, revelation of God is *death*. Christ unlocked its gates. He brought *life* to light out of *death*.

Out of *death!* The word cannot be spoken significantly enough. The meaning of God, the power of God, begins to shine upon the men of the Bible at the boundary of mortality, there

"Where thought and thinking leave me (like a light
That flickers and goes out) within the night."

The human correlate to the divine aliveness is neither virtue, nor inspiration, nor love, but the *fear* of the Lord, mortal fear, the last, absolute, perfect fear. I have in mind what is expressed in Michelangelo's figures of the prophets. "Our God is a consuming fire." "Who is there of all flesh, that hath heard the voice of the living God, and lived?" Men may kill the body, but he is able to destroy both soul and body in hell. He falls upon Jacob like an armed enemy. Before him one covers his face, and even the reflection of his glory on the face of Moses is overpowering. Moses, Isaiah, Jeremiah, and Jonah refuse to serve him, not, in truth, on mere moral or psychological grounds but because of a last constraint in the presence of him, to fall into whose hands is a *fearful* thing. "The lion hath roared, who will not fear? the Lord God hath spoken, who can but prophesy?" "O Lord, thou hast deceived me, and I was deceived: thou art stronger than I, and hast prevailed. . . . . I said, I will not make mention of him, nor speak any more in his name. But his word was in mine heart as a burning fire shut up in my bones, and I was weary with forbearing, and I could not stay.''

So it happens between God and his own. It is for this reason that they are all such distraught, humanly unsatisfactory figures, uncertain of their souls and of their practical success, the direct opposite of heroes, their life stories unconcluded, their life work unfinished. So far from founding any *institutions,* the criteria of the *historical* worth of things, they do not even attempt it! Whether we think of Jacob or David or Jeremiah, or of Peter or Paul, there is no form nor comeliness in any aspect of them; there is a vital witness not to humanity but to the *end* of humanity. In the case of more than one of these men of God, one has the impression, to speak honestly, that he personally must have been quite unendurable.

It is for this reason that the epochs of the history of Israel are each as unclassical as the others, being merely different phases of human insufficiency, or sickness as Hosea called it — the sickness of Israel before Jehovah, Israel's God. Between the promise, I will take you to me for a people and I will be to you a God, and the fulfillment of that promise, there intervenes the actuality of the destruction of that people. Over the entrance to the wisdom of Solomon is fixed the minatory tablet: Vanity of vanities, all is vanity! The unmistakable undertone of the piety of the Psalms which people so much admire and still insist they find inspiring, is "Lord, make me to know my end, and the measure of my days, what it is; that I may know how frail I am. Behold, thou hast made my days as an handbreadth; and my age is as nothing before thee: verily every man at his best state is altogether vanity." And the divine answer in response to Job's request for the theodicy, for the vindication of God's righteousness in the world, and in response to Job's friends' apologetic care for his soul — the answer "out of the whirl-wind" that brings to him both knowledge and re-pentance and brings to the friends a gratifying silence — is only a revelation of the ultimate and absolute mysteriousness, incomprehensibleness, and darkness of all natural existence. And as crown witnesses to this, as convincing as they are grue-some, the hippopotamus and the crocodile, behemoth and leviathan, march powerfully up. "I have heard of Thee by the hearing of the ear," Job confesses: "but now my eye seeth Thee." He now *knows* the righteousness of God!

After this it is natural that the Prince of Peace of the last day, the Servant of God among the peo-ples, the heaven-descended Son of Man of the Old Testament, who comes to occupy the central place of the New Testament, should be *crucified*. The New Testament proves itself, when one observes this correlation, to be really the quintessence of the Old. "The axe is laid unto the root of the trees," *consum-matio mundi*, the dissolution of all things, the crumbling away of all being, the passing of this

age — this is the meaning of the "kingdom of God"
as it is preached not only by the Baptist but by
"Jesus of Nazareth," by Paul, and by the Apocalyp-
tist. The work of Christ, according to the consistent
synoptic, Pauline, and Johannine witness, is a type
of obedience to the will of the Father that leads him
straight toward death. The kingdom of God comes
in violently, and after a short application and trial
reaches the last question, the last doubt, the last uncertainty, the last boundary, where all things cease,
and where there is only one thing to say of the future
of the Son of Man: heaven and earth shall pass
away! At that point even the question, My God,
my God, why hast thou forsaken me? is possible
and necessary; at that point there is nothing more
to know, nothing more to believe, nothing more to
do; at that point the only thing to do is to *bear* the
sin of the world; at that point only one possibility
remains, but that lies *beyond* all thinking and all
things — the possibility: *Behold, I make all things
new! The affirmation of God, man, and the world
given in the New Testament is based exclusively
upon the possibility of a new order absolutely beyond human thought; and therefore, as prerequisite
to that order, there must come a crisis that denies
all human thought.*

To understand the New Testament Yes as anything but the Yes contained in the No, is not to
understand it at all. Life comes from *death!* Death
is the source of all. *Thence* comes the New Testament's knowledge of God as the Father, the Original,

the Creator of heaven and earth. Thence comes its
grace, which is the first and last word, the decisive,
the perfect, the inexpressible word, for the kingly
and conquering relation of God to estranged
humanity. Thence comes its at once fundamental
and far-sighted attack upon the law, upon the moral
and religious human righteousness of Judaism —
an attack which assures the universality of grace.
Thence comes its more than intuitive vision, "I beheld Satan as lightning fall from heaven." Thence
comes its unprecedented prolepsis, "You *were* dead
in trespasses and sins; wherein *in time past* ye
walked according to the course of this world."
Thence comes the decision of Christ not to break
through the death-limited reality of this world by
miracle, but to hold up the world as a whole and to
display its limitation publicly, "to preach the gospel to the poor, to heal the broken-hearted, to preach
deliverance to the captives, and recovering of sight
to the blind, to set at liberty them that are bruised,
to preach the acceptable year of the Lord." Thence
come the new, the impossible, standards for judging
the difference between good and bad, happy and
unhappy, beautiful and ugly; that which is highly
esteemed among men is abomination in the sight of
God, but blessed are the poor, the meek, they that
mourn, they which do hunger and thirst after righteousness! Thence comes the warning against mammon — certainly not meant in a sociological sense —
the warning against having a god before God, who,
as a materiality deceptively similar to death, tends

to veil from us the reality of life. "Thou fool, this night thy soul shall be required of thee: then whose shall those things be, which thou hast provided?"

Thence comes the Saviour's call to the weary and heavy-laden to exchange their small yoke for the great yoke of meekness and lowliness of heart, and to find the ease, the rest which is hid from the wise and prudent and revealed unto babes. Thence comes the call to repentance which has nothing to do with penitence, penance, or the arts of sacrifice, but consists in a radical change of mind, in a revaluation of all practical values, in becoming like a child, in beginning at the beginning, in remembering that in us dwelleth no good thing, that a camel does not go through the eye of a needle, that there is none good save God. Thence comes the call of the Master to the disciples — a call laden with impressive warnings against hasty acceptance: — You unto whom it is given to know the mysteries of the kingdom of heaven, to leave all, to deny yourselves, and to lose your lives for my sake, follow me!

Thence! From the last boundary! or rather from the obliteration of the last boundary of all things!

The Messiahship of Jesus must be kept secret. It is better that his mission should be known to no one than that it should be conceived *apart* from the "thence" of crisis. It is not a possibility of the *old* order: it is not a *religious* possibility. Jesus will be understood wholly or not at all. He does not confess his Messiahship until the moment when the danger of founding a religion is finally past. His

confession in the trial before Caiaphas is at the
same time his own death sentence. Now for the first
time his words have their rightful content: Jesus
consents to be acknowledged as Messiah only when
he is delivered up to death. *"Hereafter* shall ye see
the Son of man sitting on the right hand of power,
and coming in the clouds of heaven." Flesh and
blood cannot inherit the kingdom of God, and they
should not; for unto them that are without, all these
things are done in parables. Flesh and blood did
not reveal even to Simon Peter that Jesus was the
Christ the Son of the living God, but Jesus' Father
in heaven; and on the rock of this knowledge coming
thence, out of the blue, is built the church against
which the gates of hell shall not prevail. But when
this same Peter calls in question Christ's going to
his death, he speaks no longer from thence, divinely,
but in the rôle of Satan, humanly. A thorough
awakening to the relativity of all secondary
thoughts and things, a readiness for *last* questions
and answers, an awaiting and a hastening toward
last decisions, a listening for the sound of the *last*
trump which makes known *the* truth which is beyond
the grave — this is God in consciousness, come to
light in the New Testament as the finality and totality of the Old. Overbeck called this "the wisdom of,
death" (Todesweisheit). So be it — the wisdom of
death, which consists in knowing that in the sacrifice of Christ the sacrifice demanded of us is *made*
once and for all, that we ourselves *are* sacrificed
with Christ, and that we therefore have no more

sacrifices to *bring;* and just because it is the wisdom of death, it is at the same time the most comprehensive wisdom of life. I quote Kierkegaard:
"The bird on the branch, the lily in the meadow, the
stag in the forest, the fish in the sea, and countless
joyful people sing: God is love! But under all these
sopranos, as it were a *sustained* bass part, sounds
the *de profundis* of the sacrificed: God is love."

Really *love?* Can the sacrificed really *sustain*
their part? Is there something else to be expected
from the boundaries of mortality beside doubt and
dissolution? May absolute fear be fruitful, generative, creative? Is it *knowledge,* knowledge of God,
which rises victoriously out of its concealment in the
great negation, when that negation comes upon us?
Is it true that *life* comes from death? We may
fancy ourselves to be standing at the point where,
as in Buddhism, the deepest meditation and loftiest
endeavor find their last word in conscious resigna-
tion and scepticism. The *Mater Dolorosa,* the Mary
Magdalene, and the disciple John, who in Grünewald's altar piece form the companion picture to
the pointing John the Baptist, seem to indicate
that it is possible to remain standing before the
secret of the cross in perplexity, terror, and despair.
Whence has the artist his authority to declare despair both possible and impossible, to place the
Lamb of God, who shed his blood for many, between
the knowing and the unknowing, and finally to open
his crucifixion scene literally, as doors are opened,
and to show us on the back not only the gracious

annunciation to Mary and the resurrection of Christ
on the third day, but in the center, as a glimpse of
the new world that waits behind the gruesome wall
of death, the adoration of the new-born child by men
on earth and by angels singing hosanna — with a
vista beyond toward the glory of God the Father
throned in limitless heights? The evolutionary
rhythm — from life into death, from death into life
— which seems to meet us at the central point of
the Bible, where the New Testament, in fulfillment
of the Old, speaks of the sufferings and the glory of
the Messiah — is this rhythm credible, rational,
real?

Let us not be too hasty in answering this question positively: our positiveness might be wanting in
specific gravity! Let us not contrast ourselves too
quickly with those to whom the cross is a stumbling-
block and a foolishness, for as a matter of fact we
all belong with them. Let us not fail to see that the
people of our times stand in anxiety and need *before*
the closed wall of death, hardly aware in any way of
the new world that may be waiting behind it, and
that in any case we do not do well to hurry on before
them, building our speculative dreams, attending to
our much business of evangelism or social service,
and asserting the immediacy of our religious experience. For the sake of the suffering of the millions,
for the sake of the blood shed for many that cries
against us all, for the sake of the fear of God, let
us not be *so* sure! Such sureness is only a synonym
for smugness. If any utterance at all is in need

of substantiation, attestation, and demonstration in corresponding moral, social, and political action, it is the Biblical utterance that death is swallowed up in victory. But if we really believed this, our actions would manifest the possibility that lies beyond human thought: Behold, I make all things new. And if we were only aware *how* little that possibility *is* manifested in our conventional and self-reliant lives, we should assuredly take the utterance upon our lips only with the greatest shame, confusion, and restraint.

The only real way to *name* the theme of the Bible, which is the Easter message, is to have it, to show it, to live it. The Easter message becomes truth, movement, reality, as it is expressed — or it is not the Easter message which is expressed. Let us be satisfied that all Biblical questions, insights, and vistas focus upon this common theme. But let us not for a moment conceal from ourselves the fact that obedience to this vision — our actual acceptance of what the Bible proposes — is a step into space, an undertaking of unknown consequences, a venture into eternity. Better first to stop and count the cost, than to leap too short! Better to hear everywhere only the No than to hear an unreal, unconfirmed, merely religious Yes. Better to go away sorrowful while there is time, because we have too great possessions, than to follow in company with the innumerable great folk of religion and the church — even the greatest in history — for to follow with them is not to follow at all. Religion's blind and vicious habit of asserting eternally that it possesses something, feasts upon it, and distributes it, must sometime cease, if we are ever to have an honest, a fierce, seeking, asking, and knocking.

With this conscious reservation, that we are saying something that we do not know, that *is* true only when it *becomes* true, let the page now be turned, and the Bible's final suggestion be taken up (as a suggestion!).

The God of Moses and Job, the fearful God of Gethsemane and Golgotha, is love. Wind and earthquake and fire proceed from the Lord, but the Lord is not in the wind, not in the earthquake, not in the fire. "After the fire a still small voice." *After* the fire? Yes. That which for God is at the beginning comes into the consciousness of Elijah the man at the *end*. *The divine first is on the further side of the human last.* As the wheat brings forth fruit from the corn that dies in the ground, as the child is born in the suffering womb, as thought and law arise from a chaos of viewpoint and experience resulting in something wholly new, by which alone, in fact, experience is made possible and actual, so the divine first lies beyond the human last, its fulfillment, its confirmation, and at the same time its subversion, its annulment. The fear of the Lord is the beginning of wisdom. He who makes the patriarchs strangers and pilgrims and allows them no rest is also their shield and their exceeding great reward. Those who give themselves to be prophets of judgment and evil are by the very act legitimized and accoutred as messengers of grace and salvation. He who cries to the Lord out of the depths finds courage to say, "I will abide in thy tabernacle forever." When Job looks into the face of behemoth and leviathan his captivity is turned. It is only the last intense disquietude that contains the first actual quiet. The last and most fundamental question calls forth the first real answer. It is in the last mortal terror that for the first time one can hear with certainty the words, Peace be unto thee. The last day of man is the first day of God. *At the sound of the last trump,* says Paul, it shall come to pass that the dead shall be raised incorruptible and they shall be changed.

Resurrection — the Easter message — means the *sovereignty of God.* Resurrection, the sovereignty of God, is the purport of the life of Jesus from the first day of his coming. "Jesus is the conqueror!" sang Blumhardt, and it is so. He is the herald of the divine will, the champion of the divine honor, the authoritative bearer of divine power. Jesus simply had nothing to do with religion. The significance of his life lies in its possessing an actuality which no religion possesses — the actuality of the unapproachable, incomprehensible, inconceivable — the realization of that possibility which passes human consideration, "Behold, *I* make all things new." There is hardly a word of Jesus that did not bear witness to the vehemence of this consciousness. Jesus' death reveals the absolutely fundamental character of it. "He must reign, till he hath put all

enemies under his feet. The last enemy that shall
be destroyed is death.'' He stands at the boundary
of our existence, where it is clear that since existence is bounded by God, it must be comprehended,
determined, governed by God. So truth turns
toward the reality of existence, to unfold it. Reality,
therefore, is not ignored, not set aside, not disqualified, not dismissed, but is accepted in its own quality,
understood in its idea, restored to its definition.
Truth gives up its distant, reserved, transcendent
attitude toward reality. It ''rejoices'' again in the
habitable part of the earth, as the eighth chapter of
Proverbs describes it; it rejoices as the living dialectic of all the reality of the world when it questions
the world's alleged answers and answers the world's
real questions. The spirit in everything spiritual,
the human in humanity, the generative impulse in
the cosmos, the omnipotence of God — all this understood as power to create crisis, as redemption in
action, as increasing clarity of interpretation, as
knowledge pressing forward and winning meaning
— this is the meaning of Easter, and therefore the
meaning of the Bible.

Resurrection means *eternity*. Since it is the sovereignty of God which gives significance to time, it is
for that very reason not in time. It is not one temporal thing among others. What is in time has not
yet reached the boundary of death, has not yet been
taken under the government of God. It must yet die
in order to enter into life. The moment when the
last trump is sounded, when the dead shall be raised

and the living shall be changed, is not the last moment of time, but is time's τέλος· , its non-temporal limit and end. It comes ἐν ἀτόμῳ , says Paul, in an indivisible, non-temporal, eternal now. Is it yesterday, tomorrow, today? Is it ever? Is it never? In each case we may answer Yes and No. For, though our times are in God's hands, God's times are not in ours. To everything there is a time, but to everything there will also be an eternity. Abraham of old saw the day of days, the day of Jesus Christ. However it may be with the historical Jesus, it is certain that Jesus the Christ, the Son of the living God, belongs neither to history nor to psychology; for what is historical and psychological is as such corruptible. The resurrection of Christ, or his second coming, which is the same thing, is not a historical event; the historians may reassure themselves — unless, of course, they prefer to let it destroy their assurance — that our concern *here* is with an event which, though it is the only real happening *in* is not a real happening *of* history. The Logos, if misunderstood, will stand in shame in the corner, as a myth. Better to do this than to be shorn of its character of timelessness by being explained historically. The dawn of the new time, of the sovereignty of him which is and which was and which is to come — this is the meaning of Easter.

Resurrection means the *new world*, the world of a new quality and kind. Our discovery of the significance of the world we live in, that its life comes from death, our knowledge that *its* origin is in God because our *own* is in God, is not a continuation of anything that has been or is, either in the spiritual or the natural realm, but comes to our mind spontaneously as a new creation. Reality as we have known it, even if it be understood in the optimistic way of the reformers as a process of growth, is neither verified nor explained by this new truth; but in the light of this truth, it is seen to be clothed upon with new reality. *Qualiter? Totaliter aliter!* "That which is born of the flesh is flesh; and that which is born of the spirit is spirit." There are no transitions, intermixings, or intermediate stages. There is only crisis, finality, new insight. What the Bible brings us from beyond the grave is the perfect, the absolute miracle. The *many* miracles of the Bible are only illustrations of this, *the* miracle; the more they tell the more we are aware of the range of the possibility of the one miraculous new order. And they illustrate what the resurrection illustrates supremely, that it is beside the point even to ask whether they are historical and possible. They make no claim to being either. They signalize the unhistorical, the impossible, the new time that is coming. Least of all are they relative miracles, exceptions to or rare special cases of the laws we know. The Bible without the *absolute* miracle is simply *not* the Bible. Some day people will smile at the pictures of Jesus which we have made acceptable to the cultured by purging them of miracle, even more than our eighteenth and nineteenth centuries have smiled at the miracle stories.

The highest expression of the *totaliter aliter* which the Bible utters is the teaching of the forgiveness of sins. To me — let me say incidentally — this fact of "forgiveness" is even more astonishing than the raising of Lazarus. It is a new and unprecedented factor in the practical reckoning of life. In the midst of the field of moral and political reality the moral subject is constituted anew by virtue of his interconnection with the order of the kingdom of heaven, by virtue of his being counted unto God; the beginning of good is perceived in the midst of bad; the royal freedom of man is established by virtue of the royal freedom of God; the possibility is given of understanding all things in the light of God, of doing the greatest and the smallest deeds to the glory of God, of prizing the good man not too much and damning the bad man not too much, but seeing both as brothers united in the reconciling light of God. Man, for all his limited, constrained, and ephemeral existence, is at the same time "in an all-exclusive way" dependent upon God, animated by God, and supported by God. The simplicity and comprehensiveness of grace — who shall measure *it?* Is *it* to be derived, proved, and demonstrated psychologically? It is outside of all history, an absolute *novum* and original *datum,* wherever its traces are discernible. Just *this* — the unattainable *novum* beyond proof, understood as an entering, προσαγωγή, as a promise, as a movement of our being toward the Perfectly Other — this is the meaning of Easter.

Resurrection means a *new corporeality*. We must at least indicate this rarely mentioned but necessary implication. If there is *one* Creator of all things visible and invisible there will be one *redemption* of all things, a redemption even of our body. The groaning of creation cannot remain unheard by him. As it participates in the incomprehensibility, the vexatiousness, and the darkness of our existence, it must also participate in the new possibility beyond the boundary of our existence. The Spirit is the Creator and the Redeemer in one. It was in the power of the spirit that Christ rose from the dead. It is on account of the spirit, on account of the unity of God, that the Bible speaks of the corporeality of the resurrection and the new world. A change of predicates takes place between the sowing in corruption and the raising in incorruption (or, otherwise expressed, the raising into a consciousness of God). The subject remains the same. But since the subject is born anew, that is, "from above," ἄνωθεν, and is conscious of itself in God, *ultimately* there can remain in it no "below" whatever. Everything awaits its eternity. Corruption doth not inherit incorruption, but all corruption is streaming toward incorruption and there is no smallest hair of our head that will be counted out. *This* corruptible *must* put on incorruption as surely as it is corruptible, as surely as it *must* die. The dependence of our *whole* existence upon God, our ultimate understanding of the meaning of breadth and length and depth and height, our acceptance of appearances not as *mere* appearances but as appearances of the idea, as works of the Creator who will sustain what he has made — the whole again being understood as intelligence in motion, consciousness at work, faith in action — this is the meaning of Easter.

One thing more remains to be said: resurrection is the *one experience of man.* I trust I may not be misunderstood. Actual experience begins where our alleged experiences cease, in the crisis of our experiences, in the fear of God. In God, however, the individual discovers not only his duty but his right. "He that loseth his life for my sake shall find it." Biblical history is natural history, spiritual history, and world history only in so far as it is first and foremost the history of *man.* God is the subject of this history and he alone; but it is a God beyond and above *man,* who is the element in which *man* originally lives, moves, and has his being, who is to be sought and found by *man,* who will lend to *man* the first fruits of the spirit. In Christ as the Son of *man* all things, the heavenly and the earthly, are comprehended. Eternity is set in the heart of *man,* and it is the new *man* who is to be put on, made in the image of God. It is not the cosmos, not history in general, not even so-called humanity, organized or unorganized, not even the articulate or inarticulate masses of nations, classes, or parties; but it is always the single man, the suffering, working, and knowing subject of society, carrying its need and rejoicing in its hope, and therefore aware of God in his nature and in his life — it is the *God-fearing*

individual who is the first to be touched. *Thou* art
the man — *thou* art marked for it — it is *thy* concern — to *thee* it is promised and in *thee* it will be
fulfilled — *thou* must believe — *thou* must venture
— of *thee* is ὑπομονή, perseverance, demanded —
thou art the arena where the issues of resurrection,
the issues of God, are determined. Observers of
God there are none, as surely as there are no offi-
cious collaborators with God. There may, however,
be children of God who are what they are by his
grace. These our God-given selves, which do *not yet*
appear what they shall be, this our experience, yours
and mine, which may always *become* the experience
of *God* — this is the meaning of Easter.

Have we said too much? We know that every
word that we have said upon this theme may have
been too much. But the most fundamental and comprehensive words upon it might have been too little.
The Bible tells us more, or less, according to the
much or little that we are able to hear and translate
into deed and truth. We began with the question of
election. It appears that we must also close with it.
In any case it is necessary, as we come to the last
Biblical vista, to renew our insight into the problem
of our own existence. But the source even of our
sense of problem is in God. Our searching as well
as our mistaking the way, our standing as well as
our falling, our remembering as well as our forgetting, our Yes as well as our No, is compassed
about and upheld by him. He knoweth our frame;
he remembereth that we are dust. We *are* known

before we *know*. This is saying neither too much nor too little. And this is certainly the *ultimate* Biblical vista.

IV.

THE NEED AND PROMISE OF CHRISTIAN PREACHING

THE friendly invitation extended to me for today's session by the general superintendent, Dr. Jacobi, contains the request that I give you an "introduction into an understanding of my theology." It makes me a little embarrassed to hear "my theology" spoken of so seriously. Not, to be sure, because I think that what I am working at is something more or better than plain and honest theology. From the children's disease of being ashamed of theology, I think I have to some degree recovered. Some of you have had it too, perhaps — and recovered. It is rather because I have to ask myself with some perplexity what really is that theology of mine into an understanding of which, as though it were a cathedral or a fortress, I might now — with the aid of a ground plan — "introduce" you.

I am regretful enough that it is so; but I must frankly confess to you that what I might conceivably call "my theology" becomes, when I look at it closely, a single point, and that not, as one might

<hr>

This address was delivered at a Ministers' Meeting in Schulpforta in July, 1922.

demand as the least qualification of a true theology, a *stand*point, but rather a *mathematical* point upon which one cannot stand — a *view*point merely. With theology proper I have hardly made a start. Whether I shall ever get on with it or whether I shall even wish to get on with it, I do not know. I really do not presume to place beside the work that has been done and is being done by the great and venerable creators of theological systems anything equal or commensurable. Do not think that I make my contribution to theological discussion, today or any day, in rivalry with the fundamentalist, liberal, Ritschlian, or history-of-religion type of theology. Take it rather as a kind of *marginal note*, a gloss which in its way agrees and yet does not agree with all these types — and which, I am convinced, loses its meaning the moment it becomes more than a note and takes up space as a new theology next to the others. So far as Thurneysen, Gogarten, and I really may be said to form a "school" in the familiar sense of the word, our work is superfluous. I think that every one, however important may be the contents of his marginal note, may well *remain* in his own school and with his own masters, if only as a *corrective*, as the "pinch of spice (biszchen Zimt) in the food," as Kierkegaard says. "My theology" is related to the theologies proper somewhat as the Community of Moravian Brethren is related to the communions and churches proper: it has no wish whatever to form a new type of its own.

And now I must make a second request: I trust

that you will not ascribe it to pride and self-conceit that I venture to take this particular position. I am aware that one cannot stand on the air, but that whether he will or no he must touch the earth somewhere, if only with one foot. I am aware that I am not the first and not the only one to follow longingly after the ideal of a *theologia viatorum* which takes its way through the existing possibilities, to the left of some, to the right of others, and through the midst of others, understanding them all, embracing them all, and surpassing them all. Who would not wish today somehow to be "above the schools" (über den Richtungen)? And I am also aware that no one of these true or alleged *theologi viatores* — if the gods did not love him so much as to let him die young — has succeeded in finishing his course without having somewhere erected, if not a cathedral or fortress, at least a gypsy's tent — which, whether he wished it or not, has been taken not as a gloss but as a text, a *new* theology. This was the case even with that most venturesome of the knights on the chessboard, Kierkegaard himself. So also "we" must necessarily expect that in the eyes of many it is only another somewhat singular theology which is entering the arena, to take up spiritual space, to gain historical breadth. It will be questionable enough, among its old and new and so much statelier neighbors. It may be taken for a kind of mystical or even Biblicistic neo-supernaturalism, not to say neo-Marcionitism! We cannot help having it appear so: we can only assure any one who may happen to desire an understanding of it that it did not come into being as a result of any desire of ours to form a school or to devise a system; it arose simply out of what we felt to be the *"need and promise of Christian preaching"* — and this is the subject upon which I wish to speak to you today.

May I make a brief personal explanation? It is relevant to the subject. For twelve years I was a minister, as all of you are. I *had* my theology. It was not really mine, to be sure, but that of my unforgotten teacher Wilhelm Hermann, grafted upon the principles which I had learned, less consciously than unconsciously, in my native home — the principles of those Reformed Churches which today I represent and am honored to represent in an official capacity. Once in the ministry, I found myself growing away from these theological habits of thought and being forced back at every point more and more upon the specific *minister's* problem, the *sermon.* I sought to find my way between the problem of human life on the one hand and the content of the Bible on the other. As a minister I wanted to speak to the *people* in the infinite contradiction of their life, but to speak the no less infinite message of the *Bible,* which was as much of a riddle as life. Often enough these two magnitudes, life and the Bible, have risen before me (and still rise!) like Scylla and Charybdis: if *these* are the whence and whither of Christian preaching, who shall, who can, be a minister and preach? I am sure that you all know this situation and this difficulty. Many of you know it perhaps much more deeply, vividly, and vitally than I and are silent about it. To *you* today, I have really nothing essential to say; you are already introduced to my theology. While you have kept silence I have been speaking. There is a time to keep silence and a time to speak. I do not overrate the value of speaking, and I also have wished to keep silence. But it simply came about that the familiar situation of the minister on Saturday at his desk and on Sunday in his pulpit crystallized in my case into a marginal note to all theology, which finally assumed the voluminous form of a complete commentary upon the Epistle to the Romans; and events have taken a similar course with my friends.

It is not as if I had found any way *out* of this critical situation. *Exactly not that.* But this critical situation itself became to me an explanation of the character of all theology. What else can theology be but the truest possible expression of this quest and questioning on the part of the minister, the description of this embarrassment into which a man falls when he ventures upon this task and out of which he cannot find his way — a cry for rescue arising from great need and great hope? What better can theology do to fulfill its *cultural* task — and it has such — and its *pedagogical* task, as it faces the unsuspecting and much suspecting youth who have decided to "study minister," as they say with us — what better can it do as it sets forth its traditional, historical, systematic, and practical material than to be constantly aware that in its essential and innermost idea it must be the description of an embarrassment? Embarrassment is certainly the situation most characteristic of the profession for which theology desires to prepare. Why then does it apparently prepare so meagerly for just *this* situation?

Why, I had to ask myself, did those question marks and exclamation points, which are the very existence of the minister, play really no rôle at all in the theology I knew, so that I had to be surprised by the truth as by an armed man after I became a minister? Was my question only my own, and did others *know* a way out, which I had not found? I saw the ways they took, but I could not recognize in any of them a way out. Why then did the theologians I knew seek to represent the minister's perplexity, if they touched upon it at all, as a condition superable and sufferable, instead of *understanding* it at all costs, instead of facing it — and thereby perhaps discovering in it, in its very insuperableness and insufferableness, the real theme of theology?

Would it not pay, I asked myself further, to satisfy one's self how much light might be shed upon theology from *this* viewpoint? Would it not be for theology's own good if it attempted, as I have said, to be nothing more than this knowledge of the quest and questioning of the Christian preacher, full of need and full of promise? Must not everything else result from this knowledge? Oppressed by the question — and I asked myself again, Is it merely my own chance question? — I finally went to work

upon the Epistle to the Romans, which first was to
be only an essay to help me to know my own mind.
Naturally and evidently there are many subjects
mentioned in the book — New Testament theology,
dogmatics, ethics, and philosophy — but you will
best understand it when you hear through it all, the
minister's question: What is preaching? — not How
does one do it? but How *can* one do it? Contained
in it there is a reflection of the light, though not the
light itself, toward which I saw that I was pointed
and wished to point. And so there grew what
threatens now to broaden out somewhat into "my
theology," or, let us say, a "corrective theology"
(Theologie des Korrektivs).

I have told you all this not to enlighten you with
my biography but to show you that my intention is
not to create a new theology: I have wished simply
to throw a light upon theology from outside, so to
speak, and to throw it from the very point at which,
perhaps not as theologians, but certainly as ministers, you find your own selves standing. I take it
for granted that you will be willing to overlook any
incidental vagaries of my own; and I am sure that
we cannot help understanding each other if you will
bear in mind this one consideration: I do not really
come to you armed with a new and astonishing theology, but I want to take my place *among* you with a
theology — which may also be your own — which consists simply in an understanding of and sympathy
for the situation which every minister faces. Understand clearly therefore that I speak to you today

more as a minister to colleagues than as a professor. The facts involved make this the only reasonable way to follow out your order. If then I have not only a *view*point, but something also of a *stand*point, it is simply the familiar standpoint of the man in the pulpit. Before him lies the Bible, full of mystery: and before him are seated his more or less numerous hearers, also full of mystery — and what indeed is more so? *What now?* asks the minister. If I could succeed in bringing acutely to your minds the whole content of that "what now?" I should have won you not only to my *stand*point, which indeed you occupy already, but also to my *view*point, no matter what you might think of my theology.

On Sunday morning when the bells ring to call the congregation and minister to church, there is in the air an *expectancy* that something great, crucial, and even momentous is to *happen*. How strong this expectancy is in the people who are interested, or even whether there are any people whatever who consciously cherish it, is not our question now. Expectancy is inherent in the whole situation.

Here is an ancient and venerable *institution*, capable of change and yet constant, ancient and usually modern as well (though it does not like either word), often and severely attacked from outside and still more often and more severely compromised from within, but possessed of an inexhaustible ability to live or at least to exist. Abundantly equal to the severest intellectual, political,

social, and even religious shocks in the past, why
should it not continue so in the future? Its existence is grounded upon a claim that seems to stand
in grotesque contradiction to the facts, and yet
there are actually only a few people — and very
few important people — who dare loudly and un-
equivocally and wholly to deny its right to make such
a claim. Here is a *building,* old or new, of which the
very architecture, even apart from the symbols,
paintings, and appointments which adorn it, betrays
the fact that it is thought of as a place of extraordinary doings. Here are *people,* only two or
three, perhaps, as sometimes happens in this country, or perhaps even a few hundred, who, impelled
by a strange instinct or will, stream toward this
building, where they seek — *what?* Satisfaction of
an old habit? But whence came this old habit?
Entertainment and instruction? Very strange
entertainment and instruction it is! Edification?
So they say, but what is edification? Do they know?
Do they really know at all why they are here? In
any case here they are — even though they be
shrunk in number to one little old woman — and
their being here points to the event that is expected
or appears to be expected, or at least, if the place
be dead and deserted, was once expected here.

And here above all is a *man,* upon whom the expectation of the apparently imminent event seems to
rest in a special way, not only because he has studied
the technique of the event and is supposed to have
mastered it, not only because he is paid and em-

ployed by the community or is tolerated almost
without opposition in the function evidently associated with the event, but also because freedom is
displayed here as well as law: the man himself chose
this profession, God knows from what understanding or misunderstanding of it, and he has now for
better or for worse wedded his short, his only life
to the expectation of the event. And now before the
congregation and for the congregation he will *pray*
— you note: pray — to God! He will open the *Bible*
and read from it words of infinite import, words that
refer, all of them, to God. And then he will enter
the pulpit and — here is daring! — *preach;* that is,
he will add to what has been read from the Bible
something from his own head and heart, "Biblical"
ideas, it may be, according to his knowledge and conscience, or ideas which fly boldly or timidly beyond
the Bible; yesterday one prepared a "fundamentalist" (positive), and another a "liberal" (liberale)
sermon. But does it make so much difference which
it was, when the subject is considered? Every one
must apparently, perhaps *nolens volens,* speak of
God. And then the man will have the congregation *sing* ancient songs full of weighty and weird
memories, strange ghostly witnesses of the sufferings, struggles, and triumphs of the long departed
fathers, all leading to the edge of an immeasurable
event, all, whether the minister and people understand what they are singing or not, full of remi-
niscences of God, always of God. "God is present!"
God *is* present. The whole situation witnesses, cries,

simply shouts of it, even when in minister or people there arises questioning, wretchedness, or despair. Then perhaps it is witnessed to best of all — better than when the real problem is obscured or concealed by abundant human success.

But what does the situation mean? To what kind of event does the expectancy reflected in it point? What does "God is present" mean? Evidently not quite the same in this connection as it does when we use it of a blossoming cherry tree, Beethoven's ninth symphony, the state, or even our own or others' honest daily work. Else why the superfluous appurtenances? Why the unique features here, if they do not point to a unique, specific, bolder meaning of "God is present?" Is it not true that when people come to church, they consciously or unconsciously leave *behind* them cherry tree, symphony, state, daily work, and other things, as possibilities somehow exhausted? The answer, God is present, which is doubtless given, in a way, in all of these things — the content of truth in them, their witness to a meaning in life — has evidently itself become a question, become the great riddle of existence. The impenetrable muteness of the so-called nature that surrounds us, the chance and shadowy existence of every single thing in time, the ill fortune and ill fate of nations and individuals, the basic evil, death — thoughts of these things come to us, disquiet us, and crowd out all that might assure us God is present. The question will no longer down, but breaks out in flame: *is it true?* Is it true, this sense of a unity in diversity, of a stationary pole amid changing appearances, of a righteousness not somewhere behind the stars but within the events which are our present life, of a heaven above the earth — not only *above* the earth, that is to say, but above the *earth?* Is it true, this talk of a loving and good God, who is more than one of the friendly idols whose rise is so easy to account for, and whose dominion is so brief? What the people want to find out and thoroughly understand is, *Is it true?* And *so* they reach, not knowing what they do, toward the unprecedented possibility of praying, of reading the Bible, of speaking, hearing, and singing of God. *So* they come to us, entering into the whole grotesque situation of Sunday morning, which is only the expression of this possibility raised to a high power.

They want to find out and thoroughly understand: they do not want to hear mere assertions and asseverations, however fervent and enthusiastic they may be. And they want to find out and thoroughly understand the answer to this one question, *Is it true?* — and not some other answer which beats about the bush. Let us not be surprised that this want of theirs seldom or never meets us openly with such urgency as I have indicated. People naturally do not shout it out, and least of all into the ears of us ministers. But let us not be deceived by their silence. Blood and tears, deepest despair and highest hope, a passionate longing to lay hold of *that* which, or rather of *him* who, overcomes the world because he is its Creator and Redeemer, its beginning and ending and Lord, a passionate longing to have the *word* spoken, *the* word which promises grace in *judgment,* life in *death,* and the beyond in the *here and now, God's* word — this it is which animates our church-goers, however lazy, bourgeois, or commonplace may be the manner in which they express their want in so-called real life.   There is no wisdom in stopping at the next-to-the-last and the next-to-the-next-to-the-last want of the people; and they will not thank us for doing so.   They expect us to understand them better than they understand themselves, and to take them more seriously than they take themselves.   We are unfeeling, not when we probe deeply into the wound which they carry when they come to us for healing, but rather when we pass over it as if we did not know why they had come.   We are misled not when we assume that they are brought to us by the last and profoundest questions, but rather when we think that when they come to us they may really be put off with next-to-the-last and less profound answers.

They are often put off, to be sure, for the time being; even when they do not find what they are actually seeking, they are touched, delighted, gratified by the forms of their worship (broadly religious, Christian, or Fundamentalist-Christian) — though they might find better forms in other churches.   Catholicism, for instance, illustrates on a grand scale how, if need be, people can successfully be put off, lulled to sleep, and made to forget their real want by being entertained in a manner both felicitous and, for the time being, final. But let us not deceive ourselves: *we* are not Catholic, nor are our congregations. With us, in spite of all appearances of retrogression, the situation has advanced to a point where the dispensing of even the best chosen narcotics can only partly, or only for a little time, succeed. Do not believe the kind-hearted, who assure us that we have done our work well, even on those occasions when we have shown skill only in avoiding the true meaning of the situation! Do not hearken to the timid who despairingly warn us not to let the situation become too serious, not to change from our customary broadsides to sharpshooting! It is *not* the voice of the church of God that speaks in them.

The serious meaning of the situation in our churches is that the people want to hear the *word,* that is, the answer to the question by which, whether they know it or not, they are actually animated, *Is it true?* The situation on Sunday morning is related in the most literal sense to the *end of history;* it is eschatological, even from the viewpoint of the people, quite apart from the Bible. That is to say, when this situation arises, history, further history, is done with, and the *ultimate* desire of man, the desire for an *ultimate* event, now becomes authoritative. If we do not understand this ultimate desire, if we do *not* take the people seriously (I repeat it, more seriously than they take themselves!) at the point of their life perplexity, we need not wonder if a majority of them, without becoming enemies of the church, gradually learn to leave the church to itself and us to the kind-hearted and timid. Is it psychologically strange that the more wide-awake sons of ministers and theologians continue to join this silent army of deserters? Do they not do so because they know from close observation that people will hardly find in our churches what they are really seeking? Am I not at least partly right when I say that people, educated and uneducated alike, are simply *disappointed* in us, unspeakably disappointed? Have they been too often — perhaps for centuries — *put off?* Has the church, in spite of its very best of intentions to meet their needs, too often indulged in secondary utterances?

And instead of continuing to make new plans for putting off the disappointed, out of alleged love for people, would it not be better for us to pay attention to the fact that the sole and simple reason for their staying in the church is that in the vast and ceaseless unrest of their lives they may be taken *seriously* and *understood* — taken *more* seriously and *better* understood than in the church (in contrast to Methodist, communistic, or anthroposophic meetings) they usually are? By allowing us at least to baptize, confirm, marry, and bury them, they still show that they place expectancy in us — and this is miraculous enough. It is miraculous enough that there are still so-called congregations and parishes. It would perhaps be better for us if there were none, in order that we might at least perceive that the hour had struck. At any rate, we should not depend upon the patience of God, which meets us frequently in the patience, not to say drowsiness, of our audience, to save us from the penitence which is the first need of our generation.

But this is only one side of the situation on Sunday morning. The other is still more important. Outwardly it is symbolized by the opening of the *Bible,* at least in our Protestant churches.

It is worth while to stop here a moment to see what immeasurable consequences follow upon the Reformers' proclamation that the word of God expressed in the Holy Scriptures is the foundation and final aim of the church. No one who has never bemoaned this act of the Reformers has a right to rejoice in it with Reformation joy; for by it — so far as we and our congregations are concerned — a door of conscience was bolted against the attempt to temporize with Reality.

How incomparably more securely, uninterruptedly, and confidently the other church goes its way, having wisely left this dangerous principle of the Word undiscovered! We have absolutely no occasion, however, to curl our lip at the sense of certainty displayed by Catholics. I think of what a Benedictine from Alsace once told me. It was during the war. One evening, being choirmaster of his monastery, he was chanting the Magnificat with his confrères, when suddenly a French shell crashed through the roof and exploded in the nave of the

church. But the smoke thinned away and the Magnificat continued. I ask you whether a Protestant
sermon would have been continued. At those times
when the task of being *verbi divini ministri,* as we of
the Reformed churches say, has worried and oppressed us, have we not all felt a yearning for the
"rich services" (schönen Gottesdiensten) of Catholicism, and for the enviable rôle of the priest at the
altar? When he elevates the Sanctissimum, with its
full measure of that meaning and power which is enjoyed by the material symbol over the symbol of the
human word as such, the double grace of the sacri-
ficial death and the incarnation of the Son of God is
not only preached in words but consummated under
his hands, and he becomes a *creator Creatoris* before
the people. I once heard it announced literally at a
first mass, *"Le prêtre un autre Jésus Christ!"* If
only we might be such too! Even at the mass the
Bible is displayed; but how unimportant, how indifferent a matter is the delivery of the sermon based
upon it — and yet, again, how completely the poor-
est of sermonettes is transfigured by the saving ra-
diance of the eucharistic miracle! For the sake of
this miracle people actually come alone to church.
How evident, obvious, well-ordered, and possible is
the way of God to man and of man to God which
leads from this center — a way which the Catholic
priest may daily walk himself, and indicate to
others! How brilliantly the problem is solved
there; the need of the people being perfectly understood, it is possible to put them off by a far-reaching

and, for the time being, final act; the equilibrium of the soul and the world being seemingly disturbed with great violence, it is unnecessary to disturb it actually; and the final word of redemption is spoken!

We do not wish to cast a shadow on the Gospel content and effect of the Catholic altar sacrament by suggesting that *we* possibly have something better. Yet it is very clear that the Reformation wished to see something better substituted for the mass it abolished, and that it expected that that better thing would be — our preaching of the Word. The *verbum visibile,* the objectively clarified preaching of the Word, is the only sacrament left to us. The Reformers sternly took from us everything but the Bible.

Today we are apparently preparing to turn the clock backwards a bit — to the days before the Reformation at least. We refrain from quoting Question 80 of the Heidelberg catechism, which boldly dubs the papal mass a "denial of the one sacrifice and passion of Jesus Christ and a cursed remnant of idolatry." Is this because of our increased tolerance and delicacy of feeling or because of the waning of our sense of mission? And what is indicated by our present-day efforts to *broaden* the narrow, fearfully narrow, basis of Protestant Christian preaching? Is it not simply a faint-hearted yearning for something that is not Protestantism? And what could more clearly prove the direction we are traveling than the positively facetious proposal to fill the aching void in the church of the *Word* by a so-called "sacrament of — *silence?*" And is not the deep impression made upon us by Heiler's oppressive book on prayer more remarkable than the book itself? And what is one to think when he hears serious men seriously speak of going back even *behind* Catholicism to introduce the dance into the church?

The perplexity out of which all this arises is only too easy to understand. The door the Reformation bolted against us is not easy to open; after four hundred years the situation has not changed and, though obscured by the incense smoke which divers folk would like today to see again ascending, it actually can never change; the frontier that separates the land of Jehovah from the land of Baal, if not, as the *figura* indicates, hermetically closed, is none the less effectually closed; and the preaching of the Biblical word of God is laid upon us with the whole dead weight of a historical reality and cannot be shaken off. We are confronted by the difficulty that, instead of lingering in the bright light of the Middle Ages, such as shines from the close of the second part of Goethe's Faust, we are compelled to live in the dusky shadows of the Reformation, though only as Epigoni. This is indeed a difficulty, but no more a difficulty that that other, of which we were speaking a little while ago — that our hearers and erstwhile hearers expect to hear from us and from our church the Word, the answer to the question, *Is it true?* Scylla and Charybdis! — facing each other from opposite sides, between which we must find our way.

But we must look more closely at the side of the situation symbolized on pulpit and altar by the open Bible. What makes it so difficult for us to remain true to the scriptural principle of the Reformation? We must answer honestly. It is not the age of the Bible, not its remoteness or strangeness (that is, the strangeness of its "philosophy"). It is not the rivalry of Goethe and Schiller, of Buddha and Nietzsche, which tempts us away from it. And as a rule it is not that the abundant flow of our own inspiration, if confined to the ideas of the Bible, would seem a little cramped. No, it is because the Bible has a somewhat uncanny way of bringing into the church situation its *own* new and tense and mighty *(mightier!) expectancy*. If the congregation brings to church the great *question* of human life and *seeks* an *answer* for it, the Bible contrariwise brings an *answer*, and *seeks* the *question* corresponding to this answer: it seeks questioning *people* who are eager to find and able to understand that its seeking of them is the very answer to their question. The thoughts of the Bible touch just those points where the negative factors in life preponderate, casting doubt over life's possibilities — the very points, that is, where on the human side we have the question arising, Is it true? The Bible, with uncanny singleness of interest, omits all the stages of human life where this crisis is not yet acute, where a man in unbroken naïveté can still take comfort in the presence of God in the cherry tree, the symphony, the state, or his daily work;

but it does become concerned with him, and with
weird intensity, at the stage — shall we call it the
highest or the lowest? — where doubt has seized him.
Even praise and thanksgiving and jubilation and
certainty have their place in the Bible not on the
hither but on the farther side of the point where man
begins to seek, to ask, and to knock; where that last
perplexed craving has seized him and leads him, let
us say, to church.

To give only one typical illustration — notice
where the Bible touches human life in the *Psalms*.
Here it comes to men who are clearly conscious of
guilt, who are sick, who are oppressed by enemies
personal and national, who are aware of their remoteness from God and the things of God, who are
in doubt and despair, and faced by vicissitude and
death.

The Bible responds without ado to the man who
has awakened to a consciousness of his condition
and to whom certainty has everywhere begun to
waver; and its way of answering him is to ask with
him, in its own way, — think of the forty-second
Psalm, think of Job — *Is it true?* Is it true that
there is in all things a meaning, a goal, and a God?

In two respects the Bible's question differs from
and alters that of the awakened man. In the first
place, it gives *his* question its first real depth and
meaning — and in a way that leads even the most
frightened, the most humbled, and the most despairing man on to the edge of a worse abyss than he has
dreamed of; in a way that makes gladness and grief,

good and bad, light and darkness, Yes and No as
we know them, the contradictory elements of our
existence, suddenly draw very close together, and
our most instant and urgent question seem trivial
and die away; in a way that shows us that all our
previous questioning has really been preparation
and practice for the question of questions which now
arises, Are we asking in dead *earnest?* Are we asking after *God?*

When the patient Job pours out his grief, he is
thinking evidently of a grief which, humanly speaking, has no end. When Paul speaks of sin he means
not the puppet sins with which we torment ourselves, but the sin of Adam in which we are begotten
and with which we are born, the sin of which we
shall not rid ourselves as long as time shall last.
The darkness of this world to which the writings of
John refer is not merely the darkness of a night in
which and through which there are various friendly
candles burning for every one except the most rab-
idly pessimistic; the reference is properly to that
darkness in which the question whether one ought
rather to be an optimist or a pessimist is quite
beside the point. And when Jesus Christ dies on the
cross he asks not simply, Is it true? but "My God,
my God, why hast Thou forsaken me?" People have
attempted to absolve Jesus from blame for this
utterance by the argument, difficult to substantiate,
that it was not an expression of real despair — and
the fact has been quite overlooked that it was not
less but *more* than doubt and despair: as our old

dogmatists knew, it was *derelictio,* a being lost and abandoned. To suffer in the Bible means to suffer because of *God;* to sin, to sin against *God;* to doubt, to doubt of *God;* to perish, to perish at the hand of *God.* In other words, that painful awareness of the boundary of mortality which man acquires with more or less certainty in life's rise and fall becomes, in the Bible, the order of the God of holiness; it is the message of the *cross,* and from it, in this life, there is no escape. The cross is the demand of God that we ask about him, about God: it is his declaration that as long as we live, though all other questions may finally be answered, we may not tear ourselves loose and be free from *this* one. Clearly and ever more clearly through the Bible, through both the Old and the New Testaments, this message struggles for a hearing and becomes unambiguous and unmistakable in Jesus Christ. The Bible seeks people who can and will ask about God. It seeks those who are capable of letting their *little* questions — and which of them is *not* little in comparison? — merge in the *great* question about the cross, that is, about God. "Come unto me, all ye that labor and are heavy laden." For what purpose? To "take *my* yoke upon you." It is not obvious, even to the most awakened seekers, that they labor and are heavy laden to the end that they may take *his* yoke, *Christ's* yoke, upon them. Though we may have understood this a thousand times, it is still impossible to understand.

There is a second crucial change which the Bible

makes in the awakened consciousness. Our questions
about human life, even in their highest forms, are
mere questions to which the answers sought are
additional and must be matched to them. But as the
Bible takes these questions, translating them into
the unescapable question about *God,* one simply cannot ask or hear the "question" without hearing the
answer. The person who says that the Bible leads
us to where finally we hear only a great No or see a
great void, proves only that he has not yet been led
thither. *This* No is really Yes. *This* judgment is
grace. *This* condemnation is forgiveness. *This*
death is life. *This* hell is heaven. *This* fearful God
is a loving father who takes the prodigal in his arms.
The crucified is the one raised from the dead. And
the explanation of the cross as such is eternal life.
No other additional thing needs to be joined to the
question. The question is the answer.

This equation is the essence of the whole Bible,
but by what truth, what fact, can it be proved? I
know no other than the reality of the living God, who
is what he is, who is self-proved. The Bible dis-
claims all proofs of God. It witnesses to revelation:
we beheld his glory and we beheld it as the answer
in the *question.* How could we find out and understand the answer in any other way? But the *answer*
is the essence of it. It would be no question if it
were not the answer. It is only in order that it may
really *be* an answer to man that it must meet him as
a question. God is the Yes in its fullness: it is only
in order that we may *understand* him as *God* that

we must pass through his No. The strait gate leads
to life; it is only because it is *this* gate that it must
be so narrow. "I will give you rest." "My yoke
is easy, and my burden is light." It is only in order
that we may know this to be *true* that we must take
the yoke and the burden upon us. "When ye shall
search for me with all your heart, I will be *found* of
you, saith the Lord." Only the *Lord* can speak so:
only he can reduce seeking and finding, question and
answer, to one. But the Bible is witness that he
does so.

This is what the *other* side of the situation in the
church comes to. Have I put it correctly? It is the
greater expectancy that the *Bible* brings into the
situation. It is expectant of people who *in* its question will recognize their own question as well as
God's answer — a final answer, which redeems, re-
creates, enlivens, and makes happy; an answer
which casts the light of eternity upon time and upon
all things in time; an answer which generates hope
and obedience. It is expectant of people who have
eyes to see what eye hath not seen, ears to hear what
ear hath not heard, and hearts to understand what
hath not entered into the heart of man — people who
will and can receive the Holy Spirit as security for
what has *not yet* appeared even to the children of
God, and has *not yet* appeared to them *because* they
are children of God — people who will and can believe in the *promise* in the midst of their need. *God*
expects, *God* seeks, such people. In the Bible it is not
we who seek answers to questions about *our* life, *our*

affairs, *our* wants and wishes, but it is the *Lord* who
seeks laborers in *his* vineyard. The expectancy
brought to the situation by the *congregation,* intense
as it may be, is in truth small and insignificant in
comparison to that expectancy, as mute as the other
but far more real, which comes from the side of the
open *Bible.* If the awakening of the people in this
situation is significant and striking, it is so only in
the light of what *God* expects there. The reason the
human expectancy is to be taken seriously, and cannot be taken seriously enough, is because it is an
adumbration of the great expectancy with which
God arrives first upon the scene. This is an uncanny situation; who would not recognize it? It is
easy to understand why we should like to avoid it.
But we cannot kick against the pricks; we are held
fast from the very side from which the uncanny element comes originally into the situation, from the
Bible side; *we* are held fast, I repeat, by what came
over Christianity four hundred years ago.

The event toward which this expectancy is directed from both sides is Christian preaching. And
the man who stands, perhaps not at the center but
certainly in the foremost and most exposed position,
is the Christian preacher, the minister. As the
minister of the people who come or do not come to
church on Sunday, he must be the first to give them
the *answer;* and as the minister of the Bible he must
be the first to be prepared to submit to God's *question* by asking the question about God, without

which God's answer cannot be given. If he answers the *people's question* but answers it as a man who has himself been *questioned by God,* then he speaks — the word of God; and this is what the people seek in him and what God has commissioned him to speak. For being truly questioned by God and truly questioning about God, he will know God's answer and so be able to give it to the people, who with *their* question really want *God's* answer, even when they do not realize it. When he does do *that,* what event in the world is more momentous and decisive than Christian preaching?

The whole situation in the church suddenly becomes intelligible if it is seen to be the framework of *this* event; the existence of the minister is justified if he makes himself the servant of this event; and the very act which in Protestantism should form the crux of its service, the sermon as the exposition of Scripture, becomes fraught with meaning, when it is a preaching of the word of God. It is simply a truism that there is nothing more important, more urgent, more helpful, more redemptive, and more salutary, there is nothing, from the viewpoint of heaven or earth, more relevant to the real situation than the speaking and the hearing of the *Word* of God in the originative and regulative power of its truth, in its all-eradicating and all-reconciling earnestness, in the light that it casts not only upon *time* and time's confusions but also beyond, toward the brightness of *eternity,* revealing time and eternity *through* each other and *in* each other — the

Word, the Logos, of the Living God. Let us ask ourselves — and, as we do so, think of Jesus Christ — whether the will of God does not drive us, and the plight of man, modern man, here in Germany in 1922, does not call us, toward this event?

What Christian preaching ours would be, if it *were* this event! And that it is, is the promise contained in it: if we do our full work as ministers we can but confirm this promise, for it is *implicit* in our taking seriously the situation in which we find ourselves between the congregation and the Bible. And taking it seriously can be nothing more nor less than seizing upon, believing and trusting in, and being obedient to God's promise, which lies behind it all.

But we must not stop here. *Speaking the word of God* is the *promise* of Christian preaching. Promise is not fulfillment. Promise means that fulfillment is guaranteed us. Promise does not do away with the necessity of believing but establishes it. Promise is *man's* part, fulfillment is *God's*. We can only believe that what is God's is also man's. "*We* have this treasure in *earthen* vessels." No confusing of God's part with man's, of the treasure with the earthen vessel! No one indeed seems to confuse these two so easily as we theologians and careless philosophers, the very ones who ought to know better! But it is clear that even we can speak God's word if we can only believe. The word of God on the lips of a man is an impossibility; it does not happen: no one will ever accomplish it or see it accomplished. The event toward which the expectancy of heaven and of earth is directed is none the less *God's* act. Nothing else can satisfy the waiting people and nothing else can be the will of God than that he himself should be revealed in the event. But the word of God is and will and must be and remain the word of *God*. When it seems to be something else, however brilliant, however Christian, however Biblical that something else may be, it has ceased to be itself. A too early fulfillment robs us even of the promise.

And now mention must be made of the great *peril* which inheres in the situation of which we have been speaking. Is there not every likelihood that men will seem to have undertaken and — who knows? — accomplished the feat of taking God's word on their lips as their own? To be sure, the more we seem to have done so and the more threatening the actual peril is, the more complete and successful our sermons may appear — and the fuller our churches — and the better blessed and more satisfying our activity. But what does blessing mean? And what, in the ministry, is satisfaction? Do the prophets and apostles, not to speak of Jesus Christ, give us the impression of being people who have succeeded, who could at the end look back upon a blessed and satisfying life? Strange that we do so much better than they! What can it mean? It means above all that we should feel a fundamental alarm. What are you doing, you man, with the word of *God* upon *your* lips? Upon what grounds do you assume the rôle of mediator between heaven and earth? Who has authorized you to take your place there and to generate religious feeling? And, to crown all, to do so with results, with success? Did one ever hear of such overweening presumption, such Titanism, or — to speak less classically but more clearly — such brazenness! One does not with impunity cross the boundaries of mortality! One does not with impunity usurp the prerogative of God!

But does not the profession of the ministry inevitably involve both? *Is* not the whole situation in the church an illustration of man's chronic presumption, which is really worse here than in any other field? Can a minister be saved? I would answer that with men this is impossible; but with God all things *are* possible. *God* may pluck us as a brand out of the fire. But so far as *we* know, there is no one who deserves the wrath of God more abundantly than the ministers. We may as well acknowledge that *we* are under judgment — and I mean judgment not in any spiritual, religious, or otherwise innocuous sense but in the utmost realism; Moses and Isaiah, Jeremiah and Jonah knew of a certainty why they did *not* want to enter into the preacher's situation. As a matter of fact, the church is really an impossibility. There can be no such thing as a minister. Who dares, who can, preach, knowing what preaching is? The situation of crisis in the church has not yet been impressed upon us with sufficient intensity. One wonders if it ever will be.

Is there any one of the many objections which today are raised against the church and against

Christianity by their detractors, both educated and
uneducated, which does not simmer down to the very
objection which we should have to raise against ourselves if we were more clearly conscious of what as
ministers we are daring to do? Whether the objections are fair or unfair, shrewd or silly, ought we
not in a way to accept them, as David did the stone-
throwing of Shimei the son of Gera, with the thought
that there is a reason behind them — rather than to
rush to defend ourselves against them in the armor
of a subtle but questionable apologetic? Would it
not be wiser to let certain storms which threaten
quietly work out upon us their purifying strength
than to meet them at once with an ecclesiastical
counterstorm? Would it not be better for us, instead of reading ministerial, theological, and similar
periodicals, to take up Feuerbach, for example, and
to read him without trying continually to escape
from his snares? If God has chosen us — miracles
being *possible* with *him* — and if he will justify us
as ministers even *in* the church situation, we may
be certain that he will do so only *when* we come
under *judgment,* when the church comes under
judgment, and when our ministry comes under
judgment. For it is not until then that we can obtain the promise, that we can believe.

It is ours to take upon ourselves the great question of God, the question which utterly humbles and
even kills all flesh, and to do so not in a comfortable,
expansive way as men in general might, but — since
nobody is a man in general — in our very capacity

as priests, as mediators. It is not until then that
we shall be capable of being "priests" (Geistliche),
that is, of hearing God's *answer* and then answering the question of *men*. Not until our preaching
arises from need will our work become a *mission*.
Mission alone can legitimize preaching.

There is a lesson for us in the sixteenth chapter
of Leviticus: it was the law that on the great day
of atonement the high priest should bring a bullock,
kill it, and offer it as a sin offering to "make an
atonement for *himself*, and for *his* house" *before*
offering the goat as a sin offering for the people.
Would it not be wise for us to offer up the bullock —
and in the meanwhile at least to let the goat live?
Have we not been refusing to admit that judgment
must begin at the house of God? Have we not been
refusing to acknowledge that we and our calling and
our church belong where all flesh must belong?
Ought this not to have been the point at which we
always *began*, of which we always thought *first, from*
which our work in the study and the pulpit took its
departure? Have we not been wishing, secretly or
openly, for worldly or for Christian reasons, to
escape the utter disillusion this entailed? Ought
we, taking our stand against the world, against un-
christian views of life, and against the unreligious
masses, to have been flinging out accusations which
we had not first applied in their full weight to our
own selves — and applied so forcibly as to have
squeezed out of us what breath we had for condemning others? Ought we to have been speaking of

the sin *Eritis sicut Dei,* without first having said
each to himself: *Thou* art the man, thou *more* than
all others? And if we ought not, how can we but
be under the judgment from which only the word of
God can extricate and save us, as it can extricate
and save *all* flesh? Our refusal to examine ourselves first can mean only that we are *not* satisfied
with the promise, that we will *not* believe. How
then can we hear and speak the word of *God* or our
congregations learn to know and live it? How can
any one believe us? How can we preach the forgiveness of sins, the resurrection of the body, and
the life everlasting — not merely in words but in
reality?

We are *worthy* of being believed only as we aware
of our unworthiness. There is no such thing as *convincing* utterance about God except as Christian
preaching feels its *need,* takes up its *cross,* and asks
the *question* which God demands in order to be able
to answer it. From this need we may not hope to
flee.

The charge that young Luther brought against
the Catholicism of the Middle Ages was that it desired to be *free* from this need. Almost every page
of his exposition of the Psalms and the Epistle to
the Romans speaks of the sense of alarm which
seized him when he made the discovery that what
the Scholastics and the Mystics were cultivating,
as he put it in the Heidelberg Disputation of 1518,
was a *theologia gloriae,* a naïve religious will to be
edified, a *flight* from the question which God de-

mands in order to be able to give his answer. *Here*
he entrenched himself; and his theology, which became that of the Reformation and which we claim
as the basis of our own, he defined as a *theologia
crucis.* This arises at the point where man has
sacrificed his highest and best — *just* that, — where
he has delivered it up to be judged and *so* has laid
hold of the promise; and this he does on the strength
of his faith and on the strength of his *faith alone,*
because he himself has been laid hold of by the un-
substantiated, self-substantiated mercy of God, because *Christ* the *crucified* is, in his *derelictio,* the
bearer of the promise. "It is he that hath made us
and not we ourselves: we are his people and the
sheep of his pasture." But how are the people to
hear this in the Christian preaching of the church,
if the church itself has not yet heard it?

Is our own basically a *theologia crucis?* This, it
seems to me, is the question of destiny which our
Protestant churches face today; and today, in bitter
truth, we have occasion to observe what the cross is.
We need today ministers who take their work
seriously; but this seriousness must concern itself
for the *inwardness* of the church and in no sense for
the church itself. The ministers who are concerned
for the church are no longer equal to the almost
infinite seriousness of our present condition. We
need ministers who are *efficient,* but not necessarily
efficient in *business.* Ministration of the word is not

*ad*ministration, however smoothly it may go. Its efficiency will have to prove itself in situations into which in business only the inefficient are usually drawn — in failure and ineffectualness, in the most severe isolation, and in conclusions which seem forever negative. We need ministers who are *devout* — provided devotion means obedience to the call, Follow *me,* which may perhaps lead us away from everything that the conservative or the liberal call devotion.

What ought seriousness, efficiency, and devotion to mean in a basic *theologia crucis?* For us they must mean in any case a resolute leave-taking of everything that partakes of the nature of the Catholic altar sacrament. In this most ingenious symbol of its sovereignty, the church depicts its fancied *escape* from judgment, though its escape is actually from *grace;* it is not satisfied with the promise but must possess, enjoy, and experience the fulfillment — to *experience* it, as if the way to the experience of fulfillment did not lie through the death of all human sovereignty, and first of all that of the church! Under no circumstances and in no sense ought we to desire to be *creatores Creatoris.* Ours is not to give *birth* to God but to give *testimony* of him. Whatever is of the nature of the altar sacrament is a *flight* from the need of Christian preaching, and therefore a flight from its *promise.* Let us not deceive ourselves; there are many things of this nature which for some time have seemed not at all Catholic but very evangelical and even very modern. I leave it to you to consider whether something of this nature has not penetrated into our most ordinary homiletic and pastoral activities, into our *traditional* church forms, and even more into our *newer,* and most of all into our *newest* efforts in the realm of form — not to mention a penetration, a deep penetration, into our systematic and historical presentation of theology of all types. It enters everywhere that an asset appears which is not also a liability, everywhere that there is haste without waiting, giving without taking, possessing without dispensing, knowing without not-knowing, doing right without doing wrong, sitting still without rising up, or a present kingdom of heaven without the "poor in spirit." No one can really arrive by this means at certainty and victory. For God, from whom certainty and victory come, is one who dwells in a light which no one can approach unto, and he desires to be recognized and worshiped as such. This is the crisis of Christian preaching.

You will note that in speaking of this fatal tendency I make no direct charge against any one. The matter lends itself ill to the making of charges. For I am aware that much may be said and done which at first glance seems to come within a hairbreadth of this fatal tendency, but which none the less arises from the need and therefore shares the promise of Christian preaching. All praise to whatever possesses this character, be it said or done today by the Right or the Left, by low churchmen or high churchmen, by old or young! *Fiat, fiat!*

"One fate is not decreed for all.
    Let each man, on his separate way,
    Let each man labor as he may,
And standing, guard him lest he fall."

The matter cannot be settled by setting up, in opposition to this or that, a new affirmative, or even a negative. It can be settled only by allowing *thought* to enter into what is said and done — thought concerning the one thing needful and inescapable which confronts us pastors and theologians, and our churches with us, in greater reality today than ever before. And thought means *recollecting* the *meaning* of what we say and do. When thought enters in, perhaps this or that will cease to be said and done or begin to be said and done otherwise than heretofore. Perhaps the same thing will need to be said and done with another meaning than it has had. Thought means fundamentally neither affirmation nor negation, but only — a marginal note, a "pinch of spice." Thought, in any case, need not separate us from each other, even if its theoretical and practical results are not the same with all of us. I hold therefore that it must be fundamentally possible in the long last to come to an agreement in thought even with a Catholic theologian, and even over the subject of the altar sacrament — without any accompanying desire to take it from him. The need and promise of Christian preaching, the divine judgment and divine justification, are in the last analysis the life even of the church of the Council of Trent. There is so much of the Catholic in us

Protestants that we cannot suppose that the ideals of the Reformation are totally dead in the other church. Little entitles us to suppose so. Supposing so only makes a *rapprochement* between us the more difficult. But that *rapprochement* is made no less difficult by our supposing that the ideals of the Reformation are somehow obvious in us and to us. They are obvious *neither* in us *nor* to us. One can *not* take it for granted that we know them and that they are alive in us. Today, tomorrow, and continually, they must be revivified in us. Reformation is truly no less possible and necessary today than it was four hundred years ago. Reformation takes place where thought takes place.

If today you feel the longing for reformation more as a bitter anxiety than as anything else, remember that it may not be otherwise. According to the eighth chapter of Romans, there is more hope when one sighs *Veni Creator Spiritus,* than when he exults as if the spirit were already his. You have been introduced to "my theology" if you have heard this sigh. If you have heard it and understood it — and understood it perhaps better than you cared to — then you will also understand why I should like to close with a confession of *hope.* It consists of a few sentences taken from Calvin's commentary on Micah 4:6 ("In that day, saith the Lord, will I assemble her that halteth, and I will gather her that is driven out, and her that I have afflicted"). "Although the church," Calvin comments, "is at the present time hardly to be distinguished from a

dead or at best a sick man, there is no reason for
despair, for the Lord raises up his own suddenly, as
he waked the dead from the grave. This we must
clearly remember, lest, when the church fails to shine
forth, we conclude too quickly that her light has died
utterly away. But the church in the world is so
preserved that *she* rises *suddenly* from the dead.
Her very preservation through the days is due to a
succession of such miracles. Let us cling to the re-
membrance that she is not without her resurrection,
or rather, not without her many resurrections.
*"Tenendum est, ecclesiae vitam non esse absque
resurrectione, imo absque multis resurrectionibus."*

V

THE PROBLEM OF ETHICS TODAY

*T*HE problem of ethics is concerned with man's conduct, that is, his whole temporal existence. It arises from crisis. Man finds himself seeking the inner meaning and law of his conduct, the truth about his existence. For that meaning and law and truth he becomes aware that he is responsible.

So far as truth is expressed in any way by human life, it becomes problematical in the light of the ethical question. The seeming facts change to tasks. Things conceived as they are, with a claim to highest dignity and worth, enter the shadow of other and superior things-as-they-might-be. What is true — even what is truest — must submit itself to the question of crisis, whether it is also *good*. The competence of this question is established by the very fact that it is asked. Logic asks the truth of things as they are, and for its own purposes even *its* question is not accidental and arbitrary but inevitable; it is not the object but the presupposition of thought; to a certain degree it is substantiated not by something else but by itself. This is the

---

This address was delivered at a conference of ministers at Wiesbaden in September, 1922.

case, however, only to the degree that it accepts the counter-question regarding the truth about truth, that is, the ethical question. In this the idea of things as they might be and ought to be lays claim to the whole of human life. It is only when the logical question, about things as they are, is merged in the ethical question, about things as they might be, about the good, that it becomes ultimate and partakes of the nature of crisis.

Absolutely nothing therefore can come of submitting the question about the good to the question about the truth in the logical sense — as if it were not the very ground upon which the latter substantiates itself. Nothing can come of converting the question about duty and right, about the moral subject, into the question about the reality and practical possibilities of man as the object of our thought — as if man himself as such were not called in question by the consideration of what ought to be. Above all, nothing can come of our facing the ethical question from the viewpoint of spectators — as if the question did not arise out of the very fact that we can *not* find complete satisfaction in playing the part of spectators in matters of life and conduct, and that we are compelled to conceive ourselves as living doers.

We must not for one moment think we can escape being part of the world in which we live, in which we can do no more than demonstrate our existence, and within which tne ethical good can *not* be found — for to find or to be able to find a thing here is to

prove that it can *not* be the good. But at the same
time the fact remains that our demonstrated existence in this world is measured upon a standard
which is not at all a part of existence as we know it
or conceive it. The fact remains that man as man is
irresistibly compelled to acknowledge that his life
is the business for which he is responsible, that his
desires require examination, and that the might-be
is sometimes the ought-to-be which is the *truth*
about truth, the ultimate governor of conduct.

The historical and psychological happenings in
which man becomes aware of the ethical question,
and the particular ideal in which yesterday, today,
or tomorrow he may think he discerns the answer
to it — these may be derivable from existence as we
conceive or may conceive it, from contingent,
secondary, non-causative causes, from fate or
nature, from caprice or chance, from hunger or love;
but the problem of ethics itself does not stand or
fall with its expressions within the world of existing things, and certainly not with yesterday's,
today's, or tomorrow's attempt at solving it. Its
roots reach beyond its temporal beginnings and beyond all its actual and possible temporal solutions;
in its origin as in its goal it stands in its own right,
in its own dignity. It is not touched by the skepticism to which all ethical systems are exposed, for
the reason that long before skeptics arose, it, itself,
was the pitiless crisis which produced all ethical
systems.

The problem of the good calls in question all

actual and possible *forms* of human conduct, all
temporal *happenings* in the history both of the individual and of society. *What* ought we to do? is
our question; and this *what,* infiltrating and en-
trenching itself everywhere, directs its attack
against all that we did yesterday and shall do tomorrow. It weighs all things in the balance, constantly
dividing our manifold activities into good and bad —
in order the next moment to do the same thing over
again, as if for the first time since the world began.
It continually breaks out in crisis, causing us to re-
examine what but now we thought to be good, as
well as what but now we thought to be bad.

When the ethical problem arises, we begin to perceive what the perfect life may mean; but, for us,
what can it mean except death? We begin to build
that life, but how can it be completed except by
progressive destruction? Perfect timelessness
opens up, but it is a timelessness which might better
be defined as the time-limit of all things. And when
men venture to ask themselves the simple question,
What ought we to do? they take their place before
this perfection and put themselves at its disposal, in
its service; they enter into relationship with it — a
relationship in comparison to which all other inter-
course with the heavenly or demonic powers of the
supersensual world fades to insignificance. For
this question asks how man ought to live and move
and have his being not only in this but in all possible worlds. When he makes it his own, he not
only acknowledges that he sees an Eye looking at

him from beyond all the worlds, but that he *also* sees
what this eternal Eye sees, that every act of his life
is weighed in the balance, that his conduct is wholly
and constantly in crisis. Not only is he asked but he
must *himself* ask the question by which, in so far as
he understands it, he annihilates himself. For by
the question, he proves his peculiar connection with
the One who regards him from the viewpoint of
eternity, and so he bids an unavoidable farewell to
all viewpoints peculiarly his own. By the question,
he proves his relationship to *God,* and takes upon
himself the immense, the abysmal consequences
which that relationship must have for him. For all
we could say of a man who gave himself to the
ethical question with a seriousness corresponding to
its counsel of perfection would be that he was committed to God and lost in God. How could we think
of him but as deliberately and willfully *dying?* And
how could a counsel of perfection seriously call upon
man (as we know man) deliberately and willfully to
die? The problem of ethics contains the secret that
man as we know him in this life is an impossibility.
This man, in God's sight, can only perish.

We must still be clear upon one fact: we have no
choice as to whether or not *we* will take up the ethical problem, as to whether we will accept or reject
the crisis which accompanies all our choices, or as
to whether we will approve or disregard our underlying relationship with God. The ethical problem
does not wait upon any ethical theorizing we may
indulge in, nor the crisis upon our becoming critical

— nor our relationship to God upon our so-called religious experiences. The ethical problem dominates; it is fundamental, *first, a priori* in the situation; it takes *us* up. We *live* within this crisis and relationship; and our theory and criticism and so-called experience are possible only as we bow continually before a truth which stands firm without our aid — only as we face the fact that the problem is *given* us and that we must *accept* it. There is no moment in which we may hope to be free from the burden of it.

We *live* from moment to moment. And living means *doing,* even when doing means doing nothing. Of living which was not doing we could have no awareness; it would not be *our* kind of living. But all doing, all conduct, since it must be related to its goal, is subject to the question as to its truth, as to its inner meaning and law. And our question is *not* answered when we perceive the inner meaning and law which relates our conduct to this or that proximate and finite goal For this or that goal must look toward its own goal, and so on toward the ultimate goal of all goals — and so our question reaches toward a good which lies beyond all existence. Every random and temporal What shall we do? contains a What to which no random and temporal That can give a satisfying answer, because it is a last and eternal What. And with the question, the crisis in our lives continues, and with the crisis, our relationship to God. We *live* in this relationship. Let us look well to our responsibilities in it!

Why is the topic assigned us, "The Problem of
Ethics *Today?*" It is evidently intended that we
should be reminded that in this problem we are concerned not with a view of life, a philosophy, or any
other matter similarly innocuous, but rather with
our very existence, with our own instant situation
at this moment: we are dealing with an actual problem from which we cannot dream of escaping so long
as we see it as it really is and not as something that
it is not. We are faced not with *a* problem but with
the problem. When we speak of the problem of
ethics *today,* we mean as far as possible to eliminate any time element which might separate us from
and cause us to be spectators of the problem in its
reality.

But we should be reminded, on the other hand,
that we cannot eliminate the time element entirely.
For we know no present that does not branch off
directly into the past and the future, and no present
that is not itself a time, *our* time. The problem of
ethics today can be no other than it has been in all
the yesterdays and will be in all the tomorrows.
When we regard the eternal problem of time in the
light of a definite time, *our* time, we take upon ourselves a responsibility that has no end. We enter
into a history in which there is no development and
into a relation in which there is no change. The
only thing for us to do is what Jacob did: struggle
with the Lord — I will not let Thee go except Thou
bless me! We can apply ourselves to this problem
in no more timely way than by taking it up in its

timeless, say rather time-long, significance. Today, for example, we must guard ourselves from the temptation of accepting either a philosophy of revolution or a philosophy of reaction. But this particular duty cannot exempt us, although we are men of *our* time and no other, from facing the whole ethical question, mindful that our *time* is a *now*, an eternity "between the ages" (zwischen den Zeiten). We may not be exempted from the question, for we cannot separate ourselves from *our* time; we are the ones who both face and are faced with the question; we are the definite people to whom it is put and who are disturbed and perplexed by it. And we are definite people because we are people of *our* time. As surely as the problem of ethics is recognized by man to be the cardinal question of his existence, so surely does he recognize it in the light of a definite time, *his* time, and so surely must he come to an understanding with it in a *peculiar* way which answers to his time. But, we add, this peculiar way can be nothing more nor less than the way which is the same for all times. Its peculiarity lies only in the emphasis we give it.

To come down to facts, the peculiarity of our own time is that, in much greater measure than the time just preceding, it presents the problem of ethics as a real concern, that is, as a true *problem*. The whole nation is beginning to ask, What ought we to do? And the whole nation is beginning to see that it is no question for an idle hour, but is the question which haunts every hour, forever demanding answer

and forever remaining unanswered. I would spare
you the hearing, and myself the reciting, of any
"oral journal of the days we shudder to be living
in." When the Negro is on the Rhine and Lenin on
the throne of the Czar, and when the dollar stands
at over two thousand marks, it needs no words from
me to prove to you that the question as to what we
ought to do in our immediate circumstances comes
to us with something more of gravity than it did at
the beginning of the century, when the brilliant and
confident age of the Hohenzollerns was at its height.
But there is a deeper problem underlying our immediate circumstances which has become for us difficult, bitter, and painful. I will not say that it was
not also difficult, bitter, and painful to those who
went before us. But one cannot possibly avoid
thinking that we face it in a more perplexed, embarrassed, and uncertain way than the generation
of 1914 did. Surely we divine more clearly the unavoidable and *ultimate* character of the perplexity,
embarrassment, and uncertainty under which man
is placed by the ethical question. And without
wishing to deny that our predecessors also divined
it, we marvel that they betrayed so little of it in
what they said and what they did.

Let me indicate the contrast at a few points.
There was a time when the ethical problem, at least
for the theologians and philosophers, was the kind
ordinarily called academic. Whatever pessimists,
grumblers, *literati,* and other excited ones might
find objectionable in the productions of Nietzsche,

Ibsen, or Tolstoy, here was yet a human culture
building itself up in orderly fashion in politics,
economics, and science, theoretical and applied,
progressing steadily along its whole front, interpreted and ennobled by art, and through its morality
and religion reaching well beyond itself toward yet
better days. The naïve belief in those better days
essentially simplified the question about the good,
or at least made its difficulties less instant. It was
then a pleasure to study ethics. Fundamentally, it
was a matter not of asking *what* to do, as if that
were not known, but rather of finding out whether
philosophy or theology, Kant or Schleiermacher,
provided the more illuminating formula for the obvious — for it was obvious that what to do was to
further this infinitely imperfect but infinitely per-
fectible culture. How to avoid or neglect the opposition of the New Testament to such a conception
only made the times more interesting, especially to
the theologians. The ethics of the *Ritschlian* school
are the ethics of the bourgeoisie growing prosperous
in the time of the consolidation of the Bismarkian
empire. The ethics of *Troeltsch,* with his great
Both-And, are the ethics of the new German economic civilization, which did not wholly abandon
its Christianity, especially in its social hope, and
was able to find a prophet in Friedrich Naumann.
Here are two examples; and in what other recognized ethics of those days do we find the question,
What ought we to do? leading up to anything but
an almost perfectly obvious answer, We ought to

do *this* — something which, in the state, in society, or in the church, was already being done before the question was asked?

With the reeling, rocking, and ruin of this culture *we* have lost a good part, at least, of the courage to answer the ethical question with any such *this*. We think we see less of the good in the world which would make the question easier to answer. Our what? has become hollower, emptier. We realize that we are not to be spared *asking* in bitterest earnest — as men who know not how to answer — What ought we to do?

There was a time when with Kant or, let us say, with the cheerful Fichte, people took the ethical problem to be the expression and witness of the peculiar greatness and dignity of man. They were not disturbed and embarrassed but felt an exaltation and delight when their thought led them from things as they are to things as they ought to be, from facts to norms, from nature to history. Here was the absolute distinction between man and the animals, not to say between civilized man and the savages. Here they even thought themselves to have found the *pou sto* from which any godless, despairing, materialistic view of life might be lifted from its foundations.

Today we are beginning to fear that the patent of nobility to which they confidently thought man was entitled by virtue of his awareness of the transcendental origin of the ethical problem is not so easily obtainable as they believed it to be. We are

forced to regard this problem as nothing else than
the *problem* of man. The question about the good
seems always and everywhere to entail a *judgment*
about man as we know him — even about *moral* man
as we know him. It is our acquaintance not with
savage and unmoral man so much as with moral
man that makes us none too proud of his achieve-
ments. We are reminded by the third chapter of
Genesis that man's ability to distinguish between
good and evil and his consequent greatness and
dignity may indicate his fall from God as well as
his ascendancy over nature.

There was a time when people considered dogmatics a difficult and ethics a relatively easy undertaking. They regarded the Epistle to the Romans
as weighted down and obscured by the history of
the times, while the Sermon on the Mount seemed
lucid as daylight and well adapted to modern preaching. They considered it a gain when the superfluous
metaphysical labors of the church fathers and
scholastics were rejected, and the gospel seemed to
be successfully reduced to a few religious and moral
categories like trust in God and brotherly love.
They reckoned Christianity to be essentially a religious ethic, and thought that by urging it as such
they could commend it to our generation.

But since Christianity is now proved impossible
as an *ethic*, or rather, since the ways of European
man are now proved impossible in relation to the
ethic of Christianity, we are faced with a need and
placed before questions which make us think that

the difficult asseverations of the Christian dogma of
the old style correspond far more closely to the
actual situation than does our predecessors' confident assertion that "following Jesus" is a simple
task.

Shall I go further? There once were those who
thought that God, the spirit, and the future life
stood in need of apology, but who derived aid and
comfort from the outlook which the ethical problem
opened up into the future. But to us this is only a
source of anxiety. It troubles us, it troubles us
sorely, that that problem, in pointing into the future
so inexorably, points beyond all our present ideas —
above all, beyond our dearest, our religious, ideas.
Now that the ethical problem threatens *man,* it is
not so easy, in reverse of the former situation, for
us to save ourselves with an apologetic.

There was once a Schleiermacher, a Rothe, a
Troeltsch who hardly knew what to do to take care
of the profusion and variety of the facts of life.
They felt they must be impartial at all costs to the
whole of creation and to every creature; and they
became so generously impartial, that Christianity,
having no special privileges with them, found itself
the unhappy victim of a housing-shortage. But we
no longer see in the European of the present day
the rich man of the parable; we see only the poor
Lazarus. For us the urgent ethical questions are
reduced to one: how we may be impartial to the
truth of the *Creator!* For us the field of human
conduct has assumed the aspect of a modern battlefield; the whole no-man's-land in front of our lines
of advance has become vacant and terrible.

To Ritschl and his school the work of a God-
fearing man in his profession — and therefore in
the kingdom of God — was invested with a heavenly
light; but to us that light is darkness. Instead of
the much commended "Commit thy way . . . !" we
are more likely in this connection to fall back upon
the words of the Epistle to the Hebrews: it is a
fearful thing to fall into the hands of the living God.

Further illustrations are hardly necessary. Those
I have given are not important taken separately, but
common to them *all* there is evidence that the present problem of ethics is disquieting, perplexing,
aggressive. Into the bright circle of our lives it
makes its uncanny and disturbing entrance like a
strange guest of stone. Whoever wishes seriously
to ask and to answer the question, What ought we
to do? whether or not he is imbued with Dostoevski
and Kierkegaard, must have remarked something of
the difference between today's situation and yesterday's. It is foolish to go on talking with glibness
and certainty as if nothing had happened. The era
of the *old* ethics is *gone* forever. Whoever now desires certainty must first of all become *uncertain.*
And whoever desires to speak must first of all be
silent. For something *has* happened. The world
has not been destroyed, to be sure, and the old man
has not been put off, in spite of what many may have
thought, under the first impact of these devastating
times. It is simply that over against man's confidence and belief in himself, there has been written,
in huge proportions and with utmost clearness, a
mene, mene, tekel.

We are not of course skeptical of the authority and urgency of the ethical problem, for we think we see better than ever how imperative it is. And neither indeed are we skeptical of the connection between the ethical problem and our relation to God. Quite the opposite. It is the very fact of this relation that frightens us today, and makes us wholly skeptical of *ourselves,* of *man,* and of man's ideas as to moral personality and the moral goal.

This is *our* situation; we cannot abstract ourselves from it. And how can we separate the ethical problem from it, when the simple fact that it is both *our* situation and a problem makes it ethical. We are not, however, generalizing for all time on the basis of our temporary moods and impressions. Like everything else in history, they are relative. It is possible that our children and children's children may look at life more composedly and naïvely than we, but they must first see, and see at least as clearly as we and more clearly than our fathers, that the problem of ethics is not only the sickness of man but is a sickness unto *death.* Do not think this merely a passing impression of the after-war period; for all its temporal and limited form, it is an insight which is laid upon us by reality, and which, however glad we should be to do so, we are not likely to forget. It is broadly grounded, as we have seen; and it must be broadly realized. But we acquire it only as men of *our* time. We can grasp the principle which holds for *all* time only in the form of the particular, only as it makes itself known to *us.*

Allow me one more observation. When I say that the ethical problem is the crisis of man, the sickness of man unto death, and that the peculiarity of the present is that it points us *away* from all more comfortable conceptions to *this* one, I would beg that this peculiarity be not neutralized by a *theological* and *philosophical* process with which indeed I am familiar and which is at all times quite possible and proper in itself. I have heard that crisis is a dialectic conception which not only allows but calls for its opposite — that this negation, which *removes* from human conduct all false value, may *restore* to it new value, may return to it its original value — that the question may be its own *answer*, and the argument against man be the argument *for* him. We shall have more to say later regarding this process. But for the moment I simply warn you against taking refuge in dialectic, for all that it would seem to make for logical symmetry and completeness. I simply ask whether the process actually corresponds with *reality*. Who can transform the *No* of the ethical problem in which we find ourselves to-day into a *Yes?* Who is bold enough and omniscient enough to resolve our difficulty from a height above the Yes and the No? That such a thing may ultimately be done (but not by us!) is a possibility which has its definite and appointed place among other possibilities; but so far as we are concerned, it lies "deeper in the No than in the Yes." The problem of ethics may sometime paradoxically resolve itself into justification and new possibility, but to *us* it reveals more clearly the negative of life, the judgment upon humanity — for we cannot be blind to the facts of our own day. Even if I could find a logical reason for doing so, I would not speak more confidently — so great is the need and perplexity of the millions and so great is our own confusion. Let us accept the truth from the angle at which it comes to *us,* and comes to the man in the street, in *our* time, knowing that *when* we do so and *only* when we do so are we dealing with the *whole* truth.

―――――――――

But we turn back now to the fundamental consideration which alone can be decisive. I say that the problem of ethics is a responsibility that cannot be borne: a deadly *aggression* against man. Either it puts to man a question to which for *him* there are only such answers as themselves become questions; or it gives him an answer for which he cannot ask. But he cannot live upon nothing but questions, forever new questions. And he cannot live upon an answer which is so final that for him it is no answer at all.

―――――――――

That this aggression is a fact and an unescapable fact may be seen, first, in its relation to the asking *subject;* and it may therefore best be studied in the ethics of Kant, where this relation is brought out with peculiar vividness. Kant grounds the conception of the moral personality on the idea of the autonomous will, but he teaches that the only will that can be called good is one that governs itself according to a law which is *pure form* without content. That law alone can be good which is superior to any self, universally applicable, and capable of being accepted as a law for all humanity. A *material* will determined by the desire for this or that *object* shows itself to be individual, self-loving, heteronomous. Good will turns away from all finite goals, moves on beyond all desire for them, and pays its pure and direct respect to the *final goal,* which is identical with the categorical *imperative* of duty. Kant sees the man whose will is so determined grounded in the intelligible world of freedom; and this world has its own causality, above that of nature. The moral personality is the author both of the conduct with which the ethical question is concerned and of the question itself.

Plainer words than Kant's concerning the unescapable significance of the ethical question have seldom been spoken. But if we grant that the man who asks the question and is the subject of ethical conduct is grounded in the world of freedom, it is difficult to connect him logically with the actual world where he must answer his question and live his *life*: does this free subject bring with him, as it were, into the world of nature where he does his actual living as the man we know, the causality of the world whence he comes? Is *this* subject then to be identified in objective experience with the man we know? And is the will of the man we know therefore determined by his pure respect for the law and not at all by his desire for this or that object? Is the will, is the conduct, of the men whom we venture to call I and we directed only toward a final goal — which is not a goal like others but is the infinite aggregate of all goals? Kant — and it is this that makes his ethics so credible — resolutely refused to make any positive statement anent these questions.

We know that no personality whose will is governed by the idea of humanity and is therefore a *pure* and *autonomous* and *good* will — we know that no such *moral* personality has ever stepped into *our* world over the threshold of the world of freedom. No such man has ever lived or will ever live. It is impossible to dream or to think of a man without interests, or of a man with an interest in the moral law as such. There is no such thing in time or space as a human will determined by pure practical reason.

Freedom, according to Kant, is a *presupposition* confirmed by the fact that man is conscious of an Ought which is *not* the same as his own desire — not the same, that is, as his own will, in the ordinary sense. But what does this presupposition thus confirmed then indicate? Kant guarded against speaking with that Titanism in which Fichte later declaimed, "One decision — and I am superior to nature!" As if, to achieve that superiority, it needed only a kind of leap of the soul, a thrust of the conscience! As a matter of fact, when we venture to make freedom the source of the causality of *our* will and of *our* conduct, we are dealing with the

most invincible type of presupposition, a permanent
a priori. Although in a real sense we may have an
idea of this freedom, we have not the slightest
knowledge of it, for we know no motive in our own
wills or any imaginable will which could seriously
be thought of as free or making for freedom. We
have *knowledge* of motives only in so far as they
are desires, but as such they neither derive from
freedom nor lead to freedom. The only man we can
know is one who proves by his desires that he is not
a personality grounded in the world of freedom. All
that we can *conceive* of the categorical imperative
is its inconceivability.

The Kantian ethics, therefore, reaches its peak
in the doctrine of the *postulates*: the postulate of
God, or of a final unity in what we must continue to
see as duality, namely, morality and happiness, the
kingdom of freedom and the kingdom of nature; the
postulate of *freedom,* or of our ability to think,
inferred from our ability to learn; and the postulate
of *immortality,* or of the harmonizing of our real
character with the moral law in a process of sanctifi-
cation that goes on forever. These postulates, all
three alike, can mean only one thing: Kant sees man
amazingly claimed by a demand upon his natural
will which he is wholly unable to realize except by a
still more amazing act of faith. In that act he must
assume, *first,* that God is the guarantor of this demand which contradicts the reality of man; *second,*
that he himself is able to make this demand his own;
and *third,* that in his will and his conduct he is at

least capable (an infinite regress being presupposed) of approaching the content of that demand.

This theory of postulates, I repeat, demands an act of faith that is less reasonable than the moral demand which it is supposed to support. I am not sure that Kant adequately reckoned with this difficulty. But whether he did or not, if this act of faith, which is directed away from everything finite, is the sole ground and essence of the moral personality, one must ask what becomes of the "I" or "we" to which we are continually referring. What becomes of the real person, the one we know, if the only person who is good is a mere object of *faith?* Does not the good person represent the annulment of all predicates which man, as we know him, can possess? Is not *his* conduct the negation of all *real* action in history? Is not the standard of *his* conduct the dissolution of all *possible standards?* From this viewpoint — and this is the *only* viewpoint — what *answer* to the ethical question can escape the fate of conversion into a new *question?* How can any idealistic ethic be developed except as a *criticism* of all ethics? What can its ultimate presupposition be but a recognition of the *bondage* which prevents the human will from achieving the good — the *servum arbitrium?*

And if questions and always new questions are all that man can find as answers to the ethical question, how can he *live?* Can he live on nothing but questions? Can he? By resigning himself to the situation like a Stoic, perhaps? Or by falling down at

God's left hand, inspired by the words of Lessing:
truth is for Thee alone! Or how?

One may also observe the situation in its relation
to the ethical *objective*. Consider therefore the apparently, but only apparently, remote conception
of the *millennium*. For many of our contemporaries
— and I confess that I belong with them — this conception has taken the definite form of the socialistic
ideal. It plays its part even in Kant, and cannot
indeed be avoided by anyone who takes the ethical
problem seriously (Article 17 of the Augsburg Confession with its *damnant* to the contrary notwithstanding). It is concerned with the *goal of earthly
history* — and this without prejudice to the hope of
eternal life in another world. The ethical question,
as we have just seen, though an individual question,
is not a question concerning individuals, but is concerned rather with the universally applicable law
of humanity. It therefore contains within itself a
more or less distinct question as to the historical
ideal, as to the *goal* which lies, and is capable of
being realized, not outside of time but within it, as to
the order of human *society* which is to be grounded
in what our stammering paraphrases call truth and
righteousness, intelligence and love, peace and freedom. This question is manifestly embodied in the
"we" of the larger question, "What ought we to
do?" When the individual regards himself as the
subject of the ethical question, he conceives himself
in association with his *fellow* men, he regards him-

self as the *subject* of *society;* but this means that more or less consciously he regards what he does, his moral *objective,* as a goal of *history.* Ethics can no more exist without millenarianism, without at least some minute degree of it, than without the idea of a moral personality. The man who claims he is happily free from this *judaica opinio* has either not yet learned or has forgotten what the ethical problem really is. When we take the question, What ought we to do? with sufficient seriousness, happenings in time, outward happenings as well as inward, cease to be a foregone conclusion: they become a problem and continue to be one.

Some may attempt to draw the teeth of the problem by maintaining at the outset, as if it were self-evident, that its solution lies beyond time; but those who take it seriously know that it must be concerned first with the events of *time.*

And how can one limit ethics to the right thought or to the personal morality of the individual? It is one thing to enquire whether an *answer* may be found for this particular person or that particular group, but what right and what reason have we to place limits upon the *question* as it comes to us? It points us as irresistibly to the idea of a totality of good conduct as it does to the idea of a pure will, and it is evidently this totality which, so far from being denied, is really denoted by the idea of the millennium and its derivatives.

In this connection I can but interpose a word for my countryman *Ragaz,* from whom in other matters

I seem to differ not a little. We may well ask ourselves, as he asks us, if it is really a sign of moral
maturity to be an impassive, unenthusiastic, and
thorough-going *dis*believer in the social state and in
world peace. From the viewpoint of the question
as to what ought to be — from the ethical viewpoint
— such skepticism has certainly no grounding. As
a matter of fact, many of Ragaz' critics have an ideal
for the future which differs from his own only in
that their field of vision, being perceptibly shortened,
has a somewhat different coloring. If they find
satisfaction in believing, for instance, in the future
of Germany or the church or missions, may they
not, must they not, go on to draw the circle of their
hopes with a somewhat longer radius or from a
slightly different center and so include in their
vision the League of Nations, let us say, or some
similar next step toward the millennium? *All* ideas
as to the goal of history are "imaginative" and so
are all of today's ideas as to the next steps which
might lead thither. The *essential* elements in both
the near and the distant goals, so far as they are
ethical, *must* be very much the same. It is only a
question — and this is what we should learn from
Ragaz — whether one can really visualize the ethical
problem without taking such ideas in earnest. The
religious socialists of Switzerland are not to be dismissed so easily as *Althaus,* or so very easily as
Schlatter in the "Furrow" (Furche), thought they
might. But this is only by the way.

The fact now to be observed is that the motivating

idea in the millennial expectation is not the eudae-
monistic dream of a return of a golden age of universal bliss but the vision of the reality of that
infinite aggregate of all goals, upon which the humdrum purposes of every day implicity depend for
validation. According to the twentieth chapter of
Revelation, the millennium is by no means an island
of the blest, but the kingdom of saints and martyrs
built over the bottomless pit in which the old dragon
is chained. According to Kant it is the kingdom of
the practical reason. It is as a task and not as an
object of desire, as a goal and not as a termination
of the moral struggle, that enthusiastic, idealistic,
communistic, anarchistic, and, it is well to remember (all true Lutheran doctrine to the contrary
notwithstanding), even *Christian* hope envisages
reality here on earth. The cry of Western humanity
is one: let freedom in love and love in freedom be
the pure and direct motive of social life, and a community of righteousness its direct objective! Let
paternalism cease, and the exploitation and oppression of man by man! Let class differences, national
boundaries, war, and, above all, violence and unre-
strained power be done away! Let a civilization of
the spirit take the place of a civilization of things,
human values the place of property values, brotherhood the place of hostility! Some may paint the
goal in bright, others in more subdued colors, some
may think the way thither to be short, others may
think it longer, some may fix their attention upon
the goal itself, others rather upon the way thither

— upon the temporarily indispensable national state, for instance; — but it is certain that the question about the good cannot be asked seriously apart from some idea, inchoate or well-developed, fantastic or practicable, as to how the good is to be realized in history. Plato is not without the Platonic state: Calvin is not without the *Cité de Dieu* on the Lake of Geneva: Kant is not without the idea of eternal peace. It was an unhappy hour when Schiller wrote his "Words of Unbelief," exaggerating the *abstract* side of idealism and denying what moral thought can not and may not deny.

It is true that when we ask, What ought we to do? we call in question our conduct *here* in *time*, but it is equally true that we cannot free ourselves from the thought of a something which is to be effected here in time, of a moral objective in which the two lines, morality and *history*, meet. For this, no promise of heaven and no so-called inward experience can ever be a sufficient substitute. Such expedients, as every one knows, have had only the effect of letting the question as a *question* languish and finally die.

What then does this unescapable millenarian anticipation mean? What is freedom? What is the meaning of love, of the spirit, of peace, of brotherhood . . . . of all those words which provoke thought but which none of the various pictures of the future seem to be able to embody in any final way — of all those words in which, under the perplexity of being asked and of asking the ethical question, man falteringly expresses what he feels

must eventually be done, if his answer is seriously to
meet the seriousness of the question? We may
imagine man establishing world peace by building
up the social state — perhaps even with a corresponding religious league of humanity — but how
shall we picture him as having achieved what is
signified by our word freedom, for instance? And
what becomes of the whole picture of the future if
we can *not* achieve what is signified by this word
and our other words? Is it not indeed the tacit and
bitter secret of all morality which consciously pur-
sues its aim and desires to be creative — as the
issue of all enthusiastic, revolutionary movements
makes painfully evident — that the more singly and
surely the eye of man is directed to his pictures of
the future, visionary or practical, and to the thought-
provoking words which they attempt to embody, and
the more fully he is aware that what we ought to do
is to become free and make free, to love each other,
to be men of the spirit and men of peace — just
that! — the more remote and ever more remote he
feels his picture to be, and the more impossible those
words, the *work* that they demand of him, and he
himself as the *doer* of the work, appear?

Happy therefore is the man who, for all the remoteness, acquires and maintains a sure and single
eye for the reality of the millennium, who becomes
clear and remains clear upon it that those words
alone can give his pictures meaning. Happy he who
at least gives himself no illusions over his own
ability to realize what he sees there, who does not

underestimate the distances, falsify the high words, and in order to fit the ideal to his limited possibilities trim and shorten it — who does not gamble away or squander his moral thoughts, as such, for the sake of a mess of pottage! And happy he who perceives that he, *man,* is powerless and impossible, and who does not breathe out words of unbelief, denying and reviling his hope as if *it* had deceived him, as if *it* were impossible! Happy, in a word, the man who at least goes down with colors flying, without capitulation or compromise, true to himself and to what he desires! Ignominy lies in wait for man from the time that he begins to notice what the moral object means for him. But with either honor or ignominy (usually with both!) man *makes shipwreck* and cannot save himself. For one has only to conceive the idea of an infinite aggregate of goals as the object of human endeavor in order sooner or later, as a first step in thought or as a last step in life, to recognize the distinct and irreconcilable difference between all temporary goals — which are the only kind he can desire — and that ultimate goal.

What *can* we desire and what *can* we do?

First of all, we can eat, drink, and sleep, beget and bear children, and live our physical lives: this is the broad foundation which it is generally fashionable for ethics to pass over or to "explain" in a few commonplaces. As if it were child's play to explain this sphere of ends which claims almost the entire interest of at least ninety per cent of the people and is not without some claim upon all of us! As if it were easy to bring all this into relation to the things of righteousness and the spirit!

Resting upon this foundation there is a considerably thinner layer of theoretical and applied science, politics, and art. It may be said that these pursuits embody purposes which make for the highest purpose, the good. In theological ethics they are complacently accepted as being in the "service of the kingdom of God"—which is supposed to be something more than the millennium! They might indeed do service in that kingdom, if only they were separated from *people!* if only they were not always and everywhere the purposes which *we* desire! As such, however, they are nothing but the more extraordinary puffs of our own genius, and may be applied—I need only to recall the rôle of science in the war—to ends utterly absurd. And even apart from such misuses, is not the absurdity to which they may lead made abundantly clear in those men who "lose themselves" in pure science, pure art, or pure politics?

Above this there is another layer—a still thinner layer—of *moral* purposes. But these also are our own. And therefore there is a bourgeois, a bolshevist, a Negro morality. For the moment pass over morality conceived as the uncertain reflection of certain infinitely great purposes; consider it in its ordinary meaning, and what is it but a *man* standing up to his own height? And how can such a proceeding conduce to the enjoyment and satisfaction, not to say the peace and well-being, of his fellow men — especially when it becomes a self-conscious ambition. Is there a more effective negation of the kingdom of freedom and love than a man whose will is supposed to be sheer morality?

Perhaps there is, for above the moral layer there is another — the topmost and thinnest of all — that of *religious* purposes. Man can seek God, worship, and pray in all the keys of all the religions and confessions. Even that! One hears religion commended as the indispensable ferment of civilization. We are overjoyed when now and then a scientist or a statesman bestows this praise upon it. He may be right, but if he is, we must explicitly understand that the civilization he refers to is one of the *lower* layers we have mentioned, and *not* the kingdom of love, *not* the final goal. Consider Luther or Ignatius Loyola or Kierkegaard or any other religious genius: does the religious man as such, with his eccentricity, his fanaticism, his conceit, his almost unavoidable tendency toward refined Pharisaism, his high audacious Titanism — for religion viewed as human desire and conduct *is* nothing else — does *he* lend himself to being understood as a guide to the kingdom of love? May not the very tragedy of the situation lie in the fact that he is the greatest hindrance to its coming, and the religious goal the most distant of all from the final goal?

All that *man* can desire is things, and things are not the spirit. All that man can do is to express himself to his capacity, but self-expression is not love. All that man can hope to develop in history is a community of one of two possible types: either a company of highly individual members, from which the crying wrongs that go with such a membership are never absent; or a kind of barracks, ruled by constraint, tediousness, and stupidity, wherein right is wrong — but neither of these is freedom in love and love in freedom. Man's only possible love is Eros. The righteousness possible to man is *justitia civilis*. Even the prayer possible to man (*vide* Heiler!) is the superabundance of a feeling, which is a feeling like others, and not a very sympathetic one, either. There is nothing in the whole range of human possibilities, from popular indifference to mystical absorption in the All, which is capable of realizing the moral objective, the goal of history. Our range of possibilities is certainly capable of being increased and broadened, but its relation to the final goal must continue to be as 1 : ∞. Man desires to *live;* that is all; and this desire to live admits fundamentally neither of being spiritualized, nor explained, nor, as the phrase goes, "applied to the service of God." It is just what it is, no more. It stamps man as a *creature*. And the seal it uses is the fact that all men must *die,* one after another, without having seen the goal of history. Man cannot begin to answer the ethical question in actual life. He can only continue to recognize that he is wholly incapable of commanding an answer. The conception of the moral objective offers us only a sense of what the Bible describes as the *fall* of man, which precedes and determines all history.

But man can evidently not live, either, by any answer he is incapable of making. Can he? By choosing ignominy, compromise, capitulation, perhaps, and so escaping the sense of sin? By learning to close his eyes? Or how?

Keeping this situation in view, let us return to a consideration of the *dialectic of the thought of God.* I should like to set before you, as far as possible in my own words, the teaching of Paul, Luther, and Calvin — a teaching which is paralleled in many ways, I should say, by that of Plato.

That teaching begins with an unconditioned affirmation of the truth we have now arrived at from two different points of departure: that man condemns himself to death by his question about the good, because the only certain answer is that he, man, is *not* good, and from the viewpoint of the good, is powerless. But this insight, this all-inclusive critical negation under which we and our world exist, this fear of death into which the insight leads the upright conscience, is the narrow way and the strait gate that lead to truth, to the real, to the redeeming answer. The first demand is that we stand firm to the negative insight, face it squarely, and avoid it, *not* by making light of the basic seriousness of our question, *nor* by discounting something of the transcendent quality of the origin and end of truly moral conduct, *nor* by giving ourselves any illusion, when confronted by Scylla and Charybdis, as to our own ability to escape them. We are to understand the whole unbearable human situation, espouse it, take it upon ourselves. We are to *bend* before the doom revealed in the problem of ethics.

It is through the unescapable severity of this doom that we come upon the reality of *God*. It is this that proves that the problem of ethics, when it becomes our own, is the bond that relates us to God. We apply our hearts unto wisdom when we number our days, for by this very act we arrive at a world which is superior both in quality and kind to this in which we live. The impassable frontier of death, the unbridgable chasm before which we are called to a halt, is the boundary that separates and must separate God from the world, Creator from creation, the Holy One from sinners, the heavenly idea of the good from all its necessarily fragmentary and infinitely imperfect appearances. Would God be God if he met us in any other way? Would he be the Source of all being and Creator of all things, unless, in comparison to him, all being had to be disqualified as not being, and all things recognized as estranged and fallen away from the good and perfect life which belongs to him alone? And can man conceivably enter in to him except through that door of death and hell which is the perception of his remoteness from him, his condemnation by him, and his powerlessness before him? We meet our doom upon the rocks of imperishable *truth*, but that is the only way we may be *saved* from the sea of

appearance and delusion. The devastating negation under which we live has its positive, obverse
side.

The meaning of our situation is that God does not
leave us and that we cannot leave God. It is because
God himself and *God alone* lends our life its possibility that it becomes so impossible for us to live.
It is because *God* says Yes to us that the No of
existence here is so fundamental and unescapable.
It is because the answer to all our questions is *God*
and *God's* conduct toward *us,* that the only answers
that we can find in terms of our own conduct either
change immediately into questions or are otherwise too vast for us. It is because the deathless life
of *God* is our true portion that the necessity of
death reminds us so inexorably of the sinful nar-
rowness of our will to live. *Through* our doom we
see therefore what is beyond our doom, God's love;
through our awareness of sin, forgiveness; *through*
death and the end of all things, the beginning of a
new and primary life. It is when man is most remote from God that God in his mercy seeks out and
finds him. In order to let him realize his own relation
to him in its positive significance, that is, as love,
forgiveness, life, mercy, *grace,* God waits only — if
God may be said to wait — for the submissiveness
which gives to him the glory due unto his name,
for the penitence in which man makes an uncondi-
tional surrender, for the *desperatio fiducialis,* the
confident despair in which man joyfully gives himself up for lost — joyfully, because he knows what

it means to be lost in this way. The ethical question not only casts a dark shadow upon what we do in life, but lets through, at the very point where it is *darkest,* a new light. If the primary and positive relation of man to God is brought out by a last wholly negative and annihilating crisis, then evidently the whole conduct of man, since it *is* determined and disrupted by this valley-of-death crisis, participates in the justification, the promise, and the salutary meaning which are hidden there.

To be sure, this *participation* is of such a kind that the infinite separation of the righteousness of God from that of man is *not* reduced by it but is only the more clearly brought out: it is promise, not fulfillment, meaning, not fact; it pronounces guiltless, it does not make guiltless. The new creation of man, the renewal of the unrenewable old man is a *justificatio forensis,* a *justificatio impii,* a surpassing paradox; and so also is the positive relation of God's will to man's conduct. Man's will is and remains unfree: he lives and will live to the end of his days under the annihilating effect of the fall; his goals from the least to the highest will be of a different kind from the final goal, his conduct will be evil, and his achievement not only incomplete but perverted. Therefore the law is and remains in force, and is by no means abrogated by the gospel. In other words, the ethical question remains *open,* and its grave demands and obligations unslackened. There is no escaping the problem of life, no hope of covering the conscience up and lulling it to sleep.

There is no security here, not even religious security.

One of the dangers of Lutheranism, old and new,
is the teaching that there is a hierarchy of so-called
offices, or sacred functions, from that of the father
and mother through that of the pastor to that of the
God-sent king — a hierarchy which is supposed to
be part of the actual order of creation and within
which the conduct of man is justified in a special
way. Now what is this but an evasion of the question, What ought we to do? — a question which may
not really be evaded, because the justification of the
sinner is inseparably bound up with it. It is the
very grace of God which gives this question its serious aspect. It is knowing how merciful he is that
keeps us aware how holy he is, how terrible he is in
his holiness. Why should the *religious* man enjoy
special justification — he with his more than questionable "certainty" — as if it were not he of all
men who ought most to feel the need of the *justificatio impii?* And what reason has he for trusting
his life relations to save him, as if they were
somehow ultimate? The dignity of ultimateness, of
needing no other, can belong only to *One;* never to
the creation; *only* to the Creator. In this world
there is no salvation and no certainty apart from the
unique forgiveness of God, by which the sin of the
pious and the not pious, the sin discoverable in *all*
life relations, the sin underlying the *whole* system
of human ends, is *covered.*

What insures our thoughts of forgiveness from

being exchanged for a cheap quietism is the fact that forgiveness is found only in *God,* and God found only in the sense of *need* into which the problem of ethics plunges us, and the salutary sense of need only in the midst of real *struggle.* And it is this fact also that makes it superfluous, not to say wrong, to assume that special offices are let down from above into the life of man. This fact *not only* assures the continuance and proper continuance, in all its relative dignity and authority, of that system of human ends which is wholly profane, wholly set up from below by fallen man, *but also* authorizes and necessitates a struggle for relatively higher ends — with, or if possible, without revolution — in the political, social, and other spheres. In a word, the uncertain shining of the sun of forgiveness upon the shadowy realm of our ethics makes it certain that our ordinary work will go on, and that it will be broken in upon only by more of the very light that already lightens it.

Since there is such a thing as forgiveness (which is always forgiveness of *sin!*), there is such a thing as human conduct which is justified. There is an *obedience unto salvation* which begins when we come down from our high places, from our High Place — as the moralists would apparently conceive it — and declare a thorough-going religious and moral disarmament. There is an effective *brotherly love* which provides a "service" different from the Christian charity with which we are familiar; it begins with our forgiving our debtors — with empty hands! — as we also are forgiven.   And if there is forgiveness, there are *worse* and *better* goals: there is such a thing as conscious choice and the establishment of a definite habit for the better.   There is such a thing as cooperation in the tasks of industry, science, art, politics, and even religion; *civilization* possesses its own true dignity, not as the very order of creation made manifest but as a *witness,* a quite earthly *reflection,* of a lost and hidden order — and as such it is seen neither to call for nor to be capable of sustaining any special sacredness.   In brief, there is such a thing as the *possibility* — and possibility here means *necessity* — of saying Yes both to the ethical question and to its *answers* — and in a way not sicklied o'er with doubt and pessimism. This possibility arises both in spite of and *because* of the questionableness of our answers, both in spite of and *because* of our being unequal to the ultimate question.   The No under which all life is lived in the first instance, grows not out of pessimism and doubt, but out of understanding.

In these thoughts, which might certainly be better formulated and more richly unfolded in detailed dialectic but which are none the less the teaching of Paul and the Reformation, I see the only possible principles upon which the difficulty of the ethical problem *today* may be met.   If I have one hope for church and contemporary theology it is that these thoughts — by which Christianity has more than once ere now regained awareness of itself — may once more become alive and operative.   I think I make no mistake when I say that countless people of our day, Christian and non-Christian, are waiting to hear this gospel once again.

But! Is there still a But? When we have unfolded the dialectic of Paul and the Reformation, is there anything more to be said? I think not: the words that we have spoken are *final*. We may and we must develop from them much deeper and more inclusive meanings, but the main principle of our thought will always be the vast reversion — from the end to the beginning, from sin to grace, from doom to righteousness, from death to life, from man to God, from time to eternity.

But does it not give us some disquiet that our final resources for meeting the problem of ethics to-day are merely *words* — and of all words, *these* that we have used? During the past year I have had to listen to many objections to the view here set forth. Few of them have made much impression upon me, for as a whole they were based upon a failure at some point to hear correctly or to understand — and at what point should we not expect that many would fail to hear correctly or to understand? My critics certainly have in their libraries copies of the New Testament and editions of Luther; yet to most of them this type of thought seems incredibly new. I have met some of the objections by going forward guardedly, step by step. I have been unable, however, absolutely unable, to meet that objection which is the most obvious, the most hackneyed, not to say the most stupid of all, the objection that fundamen-

tally I am only playing a great intellectual game
which was played much better by Hegel and his
school long ago, and which leads not one step further toward a real solution of the problem.

What lies behind this objection? Is it due, fundamentally, to mere laziness? Have we here the type
of intellect that falls exhausted when the road takes
the second turning and, after it regains its breath,
excuses itself from going farther, with the inspired
words, "not doctrine, life . . . !" The first notes
suffice for the whole melody of anti-intellectualism.
Or is it simply a kind of godlessness, ἀγνωσία Θεοῦ,
that cries for the forbidden fruit that Kierkegaard
called "direct information," that desires those con-
solations and remembrances that one can take to
himself without thinking of God and eternity? But
even supposing that the *theologia irregenitorum*
peeps out of every fold of our critic's mantle, what
certain right have we to accuse a fellow man of this
second sin, or even of the first — unless he be a
student taken *in flagranti?* May he not possibly be
more right than *we,* for all that our dialectic is that
of Paul and the Reformation? May not *our* dialectic be at least as much a *theologia irregenitorum* as
his? And may not the shocking fact of his intellectual laziness cause us to be aware that our own thinking, and perhaps all thinking, soon reaches its limit?

We certainly cannot defend ourselves against the
reproach that our thought is a "mere play of
words" by referring to the divinity of the Logos,
for what *we* say, were it literally the word of Paul

or Luther, is not the divine Logos: what we say
breaks apart constantly into a multiplicity of logoi,
first into two, and finally into a limitless system,
producing paradoxes which are held together in
seeming unity only, as we know, by agile and arduous running to and fro on our part. How can any
one, even the most rigid disciple of Paul, escape that
to-and-fro movement? What does the Epistle to
the Romans constantly imply that it expects of us?
— and Luther, on his almost every page? — and Calvin as well (read the chapter *De Fide* in the Institutes, III, 2, which in itself alone is a veritable sea
of paradoxes)? — not to speak of the nineteenth-
century master of dialectic, Kierkegaard? The word
of God is a real two-edged sword: it does not need
to be turned around in order to cut on the other
side; but our words, even our so-called final words,
do — even our word "God," however emphatically
we may pronounce it.

In short, we must be ready to accept the criticism
that our thought *looks* like a "mere play of words."
It *looks* like a game. (It has been likened explicitly
to a foot-ball game.) It cannot possibly be gainsaid
that games have often been played with the words
we have used, wise games and foolish ones, pious
games and not pious. We shall have to reckon with
the possibility that our thought may fall short of
what we mean it to be. We have no way, of ourselves, of capturing *truth*. We are not capable of
making *reality* correspond to what we say when we
repeat the Pauline paradoxes. *God* alone can do

that. We shall not dispose the mind of God, however neatly we dispose the dialectic of the thought of God. That the question is the *answer,* that No is *Yes,* that doom is *grace,* that death is *life* — in a word, that this valley of the shadow of death is yet God's world, that there is such a thing as a *desperatio fiducialis,* and that there is therefore such a thing as a life justified in its sanctity and obedience — this may all be true, but it is not true because we think it and say it. It is logically no *truer* than Kant's postulates, God, freedom, and immortality, and the ideal of a historical goal. Its truth is derived from the same source. Let us not deceive ourselves: if we consider our thought true, we appeal to a tribunal to which we can no more than appeal, the judgment of which we can in no wise influence.

We are tempted in Fichtean insolence to grasp for ourselves what does not belong to us. But we must once again and with special urgency be reminded — so near we stand to the burning bush — that man is not in a position to solve the ethical problem by his thought — not even by his thought of the correct solution. There is no way from us to God — not even a *via negativa* — not even a *via dialectica* nor *paradoxa.* The god who stood at the end of some human way — even of this way — would not be God. Our supposedly correct solution of the problem might conceivably serve only to establish our inability to solve it of ourselves. *Our* solution might also be interpreted in the manner of Feuerbach. So far as we can govern circumstance, the hope and promise upon which we think we lay hold at the peak of the crisis *might* be even a hopeless fata morgana. So far as our abilities are concerned, the trustful moment when we give ourselves up for lost *might* be the moment of our accepting condemnation to eternal death, and we might better feel stark despair than any confident despair, our final word being our final reality, our end. The ethical problem undeniably brings us to the reality of God — that is to say, to the *judgment* of God. It is a dangerous nautical maneuver that Goethe describes in the last two verses of the Tasso: the sailor finally clings to the rocks which would have wrecked him. We count upon God's *grace*. But it is not our own! *Everything* depends upon that grace! But we do not bring it into being by any magic turn of our dialectic. He *is* and he *remains free*: else he were not God. "Therefore hath he mercy on whom he *will* have mercy, and whom he will he *hardeneth*." From the summit of the Pauline *dialectic* this is all we can really see — the landscape of an eternal *predestination* which stretches out not only toward redemption but in the opposite direction as well. From *this* lookoff we learn nothing as to whether we are cast away or *elected* — as to whether there is a *reality* waiting upon our final words or not — as to whether, holding to these words, we may live adventurously or must live despairingly.

I had thought of bringing my theme to a close at this point either abruptly or by reading to you from

the eleventh chapter of John the story of the raising
of Lazarus, which contains certain words that still
remain to be spoken. But I must not dismiss you
with a riddle. Let me assure you that if I have led
you to an *impasse*, I am at least aware of it. You
will hardly expect me now to add a "happy ending"
(positive Ergänzung). There is none for *me* to
add. The circle of our survey of the question, What
ought we to do? must be broken off at this point.
What still remains to be added is not a part of it.
I am not equivocating. This is simply the fact.
Before I close I want briefly to plot the curve of a
wholly other circle by which this one is intersected.

Up to now I have designedly omitted two central
conceptions of the dialectic of Paul and the Reformation because, though they belong theoretically
to the curve of our circle, they are part of another
also: these are the conceptions of "faith" and of
"revelation." For a definition of *faith* I go to that
place in the gospel where the words are found,
"Lord, I believe, help Thou mine unbelief"; and for
a definition of *revelation* to a sentence of Luther,
"I do not know it and do not understand it, but
sounding from above and ringing in my ears I hear
what is beyond the thought of man" (Erlangen Ed.,
20, 133). Faith and revelation expressly deny that
there is any way from man to God and to God's
grace, love, and life. Both words indicate that the
only way between God and man is that which leads
from God *to* man. Between these words — and this
is the inner kernel of the theology of Paul and the

Reformation — there are two other words: *Jesus Christ*. These two are also dialectical. They were for Paul himself. A deluge of arguments and counter-arguments has flowed over them in the past; and there is nothing to indicate any change in the future. By *words, we* shall never reach the place where problems cease — not even by these words. We can only say that by these words Paul and Luther and, finally and most positively, Calvin — whatever they thought about the moral conduct of man on *his* way — meant to point toward another world, toward that other circle which cuts the circle of our ethical problem, toward that way of God to man which is the channel by which all reality reaches us.

They meant Jesus Christ *himself* — if I may speak as a fool — when they preached the change from the No to the Yes, from doom to grace, and from death to life. They meant Jesus Christ himself when they preached the certainty of solving the ethical problem — a certanity that has *absolutely* nothing to do with so-called "religious certainty"; for it is not our certainty but *God's*. Solution is certain because salvation is certain, the salvation of man, the redemption of the body, of the creature, of the lost and imprisoned creation of God. Salvation is certain because the new man is present from above, bringing the new heaven and the new earth, the kingdom of God. His entrance into our world was not violent in character, such that no one could see without believing. There would then have been no necessity for any words, for any dialectic further. He chose rather to approach infinitely near, whence he could be seen in faith and believed. This is the reason that the witness of Paul and his successors as a word of *man* is as weak as any human word; but as a witness to the word of *God,* is the truth itself. This is the reason they preached the forgiveness of sins as the fundamental answer to the ethical question.

But note that forgiveness always takes the *way from God to man* and never otherwise. And note also that there is no other way to this way, but that the way is itself the way to this way. *I* am the way! *Our* ways lead elsewhere. Jesus Christ is *not* the crowning keystone in the arch of *our* thinking. Jesus Christ is *not* a supernatural miracle that we may or may not consider true. Jesus Christ is *not* the goal which we hope to reach after conversion, at the end of the history of our heart and conscience. Jesus Christ is not a figure of our history to which we may "relate" ourselves. And Jesus Christ is *least of all* an object of religious and mystical experience. So far as he is this to us, he is not Jesus Christ. He is God who becomes man, the creator of all things who lies as a babe in the manger. But as such he is to be understood by the other fact that he is the one who was crucified, dead, and buried, who descended into hell, but rose again from the dead. It is this, at all events, that Paul and the others meant when they spoke of Jesus Christ and him alone. *This* is the reason they dared speak of a solution to the ethical problem, for *this* is the reason they dared speak of a salvation. And if we do not learn *what* they meant, their theology will help us today no more than any other. And even if we do learn what they meant, we shall be helped only by reason of the fact that Jesus Christ is what he is whether we begin to think of him or not.

And now let me close with a word from the story of Lazarus: "Whosoever liveth and believeth in me shall never die." I beg you not to take religious rest in this, for the question asked of each one of us is "Believest thou this?"

VI.

THE WORD OF GOD AND THE TASK OF
THE MINISTRY

I.

WE whose profession it is to teach the inner meanings of religion find ourselves in perplexity. We may be hopeful but cannot be happy. We darkly suspected when we were yet students that it would be so; we have grown older and it is worse than we suspected. Whether we are ministers in parishes or ministers in professorial chairs, it is always the same perplexity: none of us can avoid it. I am surprised that there are still some of us who go to the Catholic church — and who knows where else? — for the so-called numinous influence. As if that influence were not about us, disquieting and real, when we sit at our desks, when we go to sleep the night before or after our church services, or when we rise on the morning we are to preach!

Our perplexity comes to us simply and solely because we are ministers. It cannot be accounted for in any other way. Psychology — if I may anticipate

This address was delivered at the meeting of the "Friends of the Christian World" (Freunde der Christlichen Welt) on the Elgersburg in October, 1922.

a claim from that quarter — may serve to describe it but can explain it no better than it can explain, for instance, the question which the imminence of death seems to write on the souls of men. And the strange rhythm of the spiritual life, to which we ministers are as surely subject as any man, comes and goes as it will, having no essential relation whatever to our perplexity. Even the problems of the mechanical side of our profession are quite apart from it and do not cause it. Our systematic theology, for instance, has been many times altered and sometimes improved; so also has our practical theology; and every possible variation of our personal attitude toward our profession has long since been tested and tried out. But has this meant anything more than the turning over of a sick man in his bed for sake of change? Have we not learned in the church as well as in the university that what gave us rest yesterday will certainly make us restless tomorrow? At any rate we cannot hope that modifications of method and attitude, necessary though they will always be, can give us freedom from our perplexity.

This embarrassment is not peculiar to the present day. Ministers have always believed that it was especially difficult to pursue their profession in their particular times. But as a matter of fact it is easier to be a minister today than it was ten years ago, and easier here in Germany, perhaps, than in the neutral countries, because the general scarifying of the ground by the events from which we are just emerging has provided a uniquely favorable soil for our sowing.

Neither does our embarrassment lie in the fact that our position in society is questionable, that as ministers we are not held in affection and respect by the majority of men but are surrounded by a cloud of suspicion such as Overbeck so often speaks of. Being readers of the Gospel, we should hardly be surprised at this situation; nor should we be if we were otherwise sure of ourselves. But as a matter of fact the situation is not so very bad. Even the new Germany was shocked when recently a discussion threatened as to whether we were really needed or not. On the whole we certainly have not much to complain of in the treatment we have received at the hands of either the educated or the uneducated. The real and alarming question is not whether we are needed but whether our own need can ever be supplied.

That need is not felt because of our association with the church; it is not that we chafe under the conservative spirit of our leadership, our bureaucracy, or the restraints of our creed. I come from that heavenly land where a minister, from the professor at the university to the simple pastor in the village, can do what he wishes in his own sphere; where there are no preambles, and where the mildest and most adaptable theology of the middle way prevails among the leaders; and I can only warn you against the illusion that the burden which is laid upon ministers is lightened in the slightest degree by these circumstances. On the contrary, when once the struggle against the old church in behalf of the new loses its outward as well as its inward purpose, if it ever had any, and when the zeal thus set free turns to purposes upon which zeal may more profitably be spent, the essential need of the minister only assaults him the more furiously.

Our difficulty lies in the content of our task. How far this is *felt* by this man or that is a question which we should not need to raise; for here we are discussing our common *situation*. This situation I will characterize in the three following sentences:— *As ministers we ought to speak of God. We are human, however, and so cannot speak of God. We ought therefore to recognize both our obligation and our inability and by that very recognition give God the glory.* This is our perplexity. The rest of our task fades into insignificance in comparison.

I will attempt to elucidate my sentences in order.

II.

We ought to speak of God.

What is our *aim?* Even ministers should be able to answer this question. Why did we take up this work, and why do we keep at it? What do the people who support us — or at least tolerate us — really expect us to do? And if they begin to feel they have been deceived in their expectations, what does their growing contempt for us indicate?

Of course, they will not be able to tell us what they want offhand. We shall learn nothing from their more superficial motives. If we are to understand them and their expectation of us better than they understand themselves, we must look for the motive of their motives. And from that viewpoint, can we possibly explain our existence as ministers upon any other ground than that of the existence of a basic need in other men? The people do not need us to help them with the appurtenances of their daily life. They look after those things without advice from us and with more wisdom than we usually credit them with. But they are aware that their daily life and all the questions which are factors in it are affected by a great What? Why? Whence? Whither? which stands like a minus sign before the whole parenthesis and changes to a new question all the questions inside — even those which may already have been answered. They have no answer for this question of questions, but are naïve enough to assume that others may have. So they thrust us into our anomalous profession and put us into their pulpits and professorial chairs, that we may tell them about God and give them the answer to their ultimate question. Why do they not themselves seek to master it, as they have sought to master everything else? Why do they come to us, when they must long since have made the discovery that they cannot expect the same service from us as they do from an attorney or a dentist, for instance, and that if the truth must be told we can answer their question no better than they themselves? One may well ask. Their coming gives evidence not so much of their hope for an answer from us as of their inability, shared with all mankind, to answer their question themselves.

However this may be, we *are* asked the question; and we ought to understand what the people have in mind when they ask it. It is evident that they do not need us to help them live, but seem rather to need us to help them *die;* for their whole life is lived in the shadow of death. History takes its course without assistance from us; but when the eschatological, the *ultimate,* appears upon the horizon — and what problem in history does not open upon the ultimate? — then the call does come for us, and we are supposed to be able to speak words of revelation and finality. Within the sphere of their own abilities and possibilities, the people are tolerably well adjusted; the reason that they come to us, strange as it may seem, for wisdom, is because they know the whole network of their life is hung upon a thread like gossamer. They suddenly awake to a realization that they are walking upon a ridge between *time* and *eternity* that is narrower than a knife-edge. The theological problem comes into being at the *boundary* of mortality. The philosophers know this, but theologians many times seem not to.

Obviously the people have *no* real need of *our* observations upon morality and culture, or even of our disquisitions upon religion, worship, and the possible existence of other worlds. All these things belong, indeed, to their life and are bound up, whether they know it or not, with their life's *one* need. But these things are not that need. We may

possibly be able to give pleasure or help to this man
or that, or perhaps even to hundreds, by our more or
less stimulating preaching and satisfying teaching
in regard to these troublesome questions. And I
suppose there is no reason why we should not. But
let us *not* think that by doing so we face the question
which really brings the people to us; or that we dis-
charge our duty as ministers of the Gospel by making dexterous answers, or otherwise performing useful ministries (religious ministries included) on *this*
level. And let us not plead as our excuse for doing
so that we owe the people some measure of love; for
the question must first be asked, What *is* the love
that we owe them? *We* may be *least merciful* when
we think we are most so — though a thousand should
thank us for having helped them live. When they
come to us for help they do not really want to learn
more about *living*: they want to learn more about
what is on the farther edge of living — *God*. We cut
a ridiculous figure as village sages — or city sages.
As such we are socially superfluous. We do not
understand the profession of the ministry unless we
understand it as an index, a symptom, say rather an
omen, of a perplexity which extends over the whole
range of human endeavor, present and future. It is
a perplexity felt by man simply by virtue of his
being a man, and has nothing to do with his being
moral *or* immoral, spiritual *or* worldly, godly *or*
ungodly. However conscious or unconscious of his
situation he may be, man cannot escape his humanity, and humanity means limitation, finitude,

creaturehood, separation from God. And if he is
not conscious of it, if he cannot tell us about it, and
if his fellow men who want to help him cannot
understand it, the more serious his plight.

Man as man cries for God. He cries not for *a*
truth, but for *truth;* not for *something* good but for
the good; not for answers but for the answer — the
one that is identical with its own question. *Man*
himself is the real question, and if the answer is to
be found in the *question*, he must find an answer in
himself: *he* must be the answer. He does not cry
for solutions but for salvation; not for something
human, but for God, for God as his Saviour from
humanity. He may be told a thousand times that in
order to reach infinity he has only to keep walking
along finite paths — and this he certainly does: he
keeps walking — and the splendor and horror of the
deeds that he does to make headway on these the
only paths actually open to him, are witness enough
of the driving and unendurable urgency of this
search for the impossible. But a thousand times, in
spite of all the guidance and instruction he has received, he fails for one reason or another to find
satisfaction in the path of finitude. What he finds
is related to what he seeks as $1 : \infty$; and this is an
intolerable state of affairs to him, for he cannot
believe that $1 = \infty$. And why should he, how dare
he, when the whole sea of answers which are at his
disposal seems continually to evaporate in his hands
into a single drop of a question — a question which
is himself, his own life? The answer pointed to in

his life's relationships, the subject implied by his
life's predicates, the meaning hinted at in his life's
runes, the end suggested by the abortive beginnings
which together constitute his life's endeavor — the
reality, in a word, lies beyond the sea of his experience, always beyond.

This answer, this subject, this meaning, this end,
this reality, is never quite *here*. The answer we
may give is not also its own question; by it *here* and
beyond are not merged in one. And yet when people
ask for God, they do ask for an answer which is identical with their *question,* for an infinite which is also
finite, for One who is beyond and also *here,* for a God
who is also *man.* To meet their question with an
answer commending or condemning civilization, culture, or piety, however well it may be meant, is simply to refer them, is it not, to the world they already
live in? Are we to keep this up forever? Are we
never to learn for what reason, for what amazing
reason, they endure us and think they need us? If
we believe it in secret, why not admit to them openly
that we cannot speak of God? Or if we have serious
compunctions against saying so, or saying so in just
this way, may we not at least make their *question*
about God our own? Why not make it the central
theme of our preaching?

Up to this point, for the most part, I have had in
mind the scene in the *church.* The same basic principles hold, however, for the *theological classroom
in the university* — and this quite apart from the
fact that such a classroom, as a training place for

future ministers, is an adjunct of the church. Theology is an omen, a sign that all is not well, even in the *universitas literarum*. There is an academic need which in the last analysis, as might be inferred, is the same as the general human need we have already described. Genuine science is confessedly *uncertain* of itself — uncertain not simply of this point or that, but of its *fundamental* and ultimate *presupposition*. Every science knows well that there is a minus sign in front of its parenthesis; and the hushed voice with which that sign is ordinarily spoken of betrays the secret that *it* is the nail from which the whole science hangs; *it* is the question mark that must be added to the otherwise structurally perfect logic. If this question mark is really the ultimate fact of each of the sciences, it is evident that the so-called academic cosmos is an eddy of scattered leaves whirling over a bottomless pit. And a question mark *is* actually the ultimate fact of each of the sciences.

So the university has a bad conscience, or an anxious one, and tolerates theology within its walls; and though it may be somewhat vexed at the want of reserve shown by the theologians when they deliberately ask about a matter that cannot with propriety be mentioned, yet, if I am not mistaken, it is secretly glad that some one is willing to be so unscientific as to talk aloud and distinctly about the undemonstrable central Fact upon which all other facts depend — and so to suggest that the whole academic system may have a meaning. Whatever the indi-

vidual opinion of this or that non-theological doc-
trinaire may be, there is a general expectation that
the religious teacher will give an answer to what for
the others takes the shape of a question mark in the
background of their secret thought. He is believed
to be doing his duty (let him beware of doing it too
well!) when he represents as a *possibility* what the
others have known only as an impossibility or a
concept of limitation. He is expected not to whisper
and mumble about God, but to *speak* of him: not
merely to hint of him, but to know him and *witness*
to him; not to leave him somewhere in the background, but to disregard the universal method of
science and place him in the *foreground*.

It is obvious that theology does not owe its position at the university to any arbitrary cause. It is
there in response to a need and is therefore justified
in being there. The other faculties may be there for
a similar reason, but theology is forever different
from them, in that *its* need is apparently never to be
met. This marks its similarity to the church. It is
the paradoxical but undeniable truth that as a science like other sciences theology has *no* right to its
place; for it becomes then a wholly unnecessary
duplication of disciplines belonging to the other faculties. Only when a *theological* faculty undertakes
to say, or at least points out the need for saying,
what the others *rebus sic stantibus* dare not say, or
dare not say out loud, only when it keeps reminding
them that a chaos, though wonderful, is not therefore a cosmos, only when it is a question mark and

an exclamation point on the farthest rim of scientific possibility — or rather, in contradistinction to the philosophical faculty, beyond the farthest rim — only then is there a *reason* for it.

A faculty in the science of religion has no reason for existence whatsoever; for though it is true that knowledge of religious phenomena is indispensable to the historian, the psychologist, and the philosopher, it is also true that these scholars are all capable of acquiring and applying this knowledge themselves, without theological assistance. Or is the so-called "religious insight" the property only of that rare historian or psychologist who is also a theologian? Is the secular scientist incapable of studying the documents of religion with the same love and the same wisdom? Palpably not.

If then we say that theology is the science of religion, we deprive it of its right to a place at the university. Religion may be taught as well as anything else — but then it must be called into question as well as anything else. To be sure, it is both necessary and possible to know something about religion, but when I study it as something that may be *learned*, I confess thereby to having the same need above and beyond it as I have above and beyond any science — above and beyond the study of beetles, for instance. New and remarkable and highly intriguing questions about it may keep me busy, but they are questions like all other questions, questions which point on to an ultimate and unanswered question. They are not *the* question which is also the ultimate answer. They are not *the* question by virtue of which theology, once the mother of the whole university, still stands unique and first among the faculties, though with her head perhaps a little bowed. However adroit in the eyes of other men I may be in manipulating theology as a science, I have not thereby necessarily lifted one finger to meet their deeper expectations of me.

Let me conclude this part of our discussion with a historical note. Those who accept the thoughts I have brought forward as germane to the essential facts thereby acknowledge themselves descendents of an ancestral line which runs back through *Kierkegaard* to *Luther* and *Calvin,* and so to *Paul* and *Jeremiah.* There are others, to be sure, who claim the same ancestry. Perhaps, therefore, for the sake of clearness I ought to add that our line does *not* run back through Martensen to Erasmus, and through those against whom the fifteenth chapter of First Corinthians was directed, to the prophet Hananiah, who took the yoke from the neck of the prophet Jeremiah and broke it.

And to leave nothing unsaid, I might explicitly point out that this ancestral line — which I commend to you — does *not include Schleiermacher.* With all due respect to the genius shown in his work, I can *not* consider Schleiermacher a good teacher in the realm of theology because, so far as I can see, he is disastrously dim-sighted in regard to the fact that man as man is not only in *need* but beyond all hope of saving himself; that the whole of so-called religion, and not least the Christian religion, *shares* in this need; and that one can *not* speak of God simply by speaking of man in a loud voice. There are those to whom Schleiermacher's peculiar excellence lies in his having discovered a conception of religion by which he overcame Luther's so-called dualism and connected earth and heaven by a much needed bridge, upon which we may reverently cross. Those who hold this view will finally turn their backs, if they have not done so already, upon the considerations I have presented. I ask only that they do not appeal *both* to Schleiermacher *and* the Reformers, *both* to Schleiermacher *and* the New Testament, *both* to Schleiermacher *and* the Old Testament prophets, but that from Schleiermacher back they look for another ancestral line. In such a line the next previous representative might possibly be *Melanchthon*. The very names Kierkegaard, Luther, Calvin, Paul, and Jeremiah suggest what Schleiermacher never possessed, a clear and direct apprehension of the truth that man is made to serve *God* and not God to serve man. The negation and loneliness of the life of Jeremiah in contrast to that of the kings, princes, people, *priests*, and *prophets* of Judah — the keen and unremitting opposition of Paul to *religion* as it was exemplified in Judaism — Luther's break, not with the impiety, but with the *piety* of the Middle Ages — Kierkegaard's attack on *Christianity* — all are characteristic of a certain way of speaking of *God* which Schleiermacher never arrived at.

Man is a riddle and nothing else, and his universe, be it ever so vividly seen and felt, is a question. God stands in contrast to man as the *impossible* in contrast to the possible, as *death* in contrast to life, as *eternity* in contrast to time. The solution of the riddle, the answer to the question, the satisfaction of our need is the absolutely *new* event whereby the impossible becomes *of itself* possible, *death* becomes life, *eternity* time, and *God* man. There is *no* way which leads to this event; there is *no* faculty in man for apprehending it; for the way and the faculty are themselves new, being the revelation and faith, the knowing and being known enjoyed by the new man. Jeremiah and the others — may I point out? — at least made a *serious* attempt to speak of God. Whether they succeeded or not is another story. They made at least the necessary start. At least they *understood* the need in which man finds himself simply by virtue of his being man. They *understood* the question man asks in his need. And they linked their attempt to speak of God with that need and that question and with nothing else. They tore aside every veil from that *need* and that *question*. They were in dead earnest. And this is the reason we claim descent from that historical line. We hear the imperative even from history: we ought to speak of God! It is an imperative which would give us perplexity enough even if we were in a position to obey it.

III.

I turn to my second sentence: *We are human, however, and so cannot speak of God.*

We may recall the words of the first of our authorities: "Ah, Lord God! behold, I can *not* speak." After twenty-three years of *preaching* he still allowed these words to stand — and not, certainly, as an evidence of his development but as an estimate of everything he had said: I could not really say it. And Jeremiah was a man called and consecrated by God himself.

We will not stop to ask whether it is possible to consider a church appointment in itself a call of God. Luther identified the two with arguments that are lucid enough. But even if we assumed that with our appointment we acquired also our spiritual equipment, that is, that we were thereby divinely called and endowed, we should still be men, and being such, could not speak of God. And yet our fellows in the community hold to the amazing idea that they can push us into saying the word which, as we know well enough, must be heard at any price, which they cannot say, but which, much as they desire to have us and we desire to do so, we can say no better than they. They delegate to us as ministers the same task assigned us by the university.

But we are men as well as they. We cannot speak of God. For to speak of God seriously would mean to speak in the realm of revelation and faith. To speak of God would be to speak God's word, the word which can come only from him, the word that

God becomes man. We may say these three words, but this is not to speak the word of God, the *truth* for which these words are an expression. Our ministerial task is to say that *God* becomes *man,* but to say it as *God's* word, as God *himself* says it. This would be the answer to the question put to us by frightened consciences. This would be the answer to man's question about redemption from humanity. And it is this which should be sounded as with a trumpet in our churches and our lecture halls, and out from our churches and lecture halls upon the streets, where the men of our time are waiting to have us teach them — and not as the scribes. The very reason we occupy our pulpits and our professorial chairs is to say *this* to them. And as long as we do not say it, however plausible we may be, we deceive them. The only answer that possesses genuine transcendence, and so can solve the riddle of immanence, is God's word — note, *God's* word. The true answer can hardly consist in neglecting the question, or merely underscoring and emphasizing it, or dauntlessly asserting that the question itself is the answer. Such an assertion may be true beyond dispute, but upon our lips it has a way of being now too definite, now too ambiguous. The question must *be* the answer, must *be* the fulfillment of the promise, the satisfaction of the hungry, the opening of the eyes of the blind and of the ears of the deaf. This is the answer we should *give,* and this is just the answer we can *not* give.

I see three ways we might take in the direction

of finding such an answer, and they all three end
with the insight that we cannot reach it. These are
the ways of dogmatism, of self-criticism, and of
dialectic. They are distinguishable from one
another, we may note, only in theory. No real religious teacher has ever lived who took only one of
them. We shall meet Luther, for instance, on all
three.

The first is the way of *dogmatism*. Leaning more
or less directly upon the Bible and upon dogma, a
man who takes this way comes upon the familiar
Christological, soteriological, and eschatological
ideas which grow out of the thesis that God becomes
man. So far forth his need is satisfied and his question answered. Luther suggests in his sermons, and
I agree, that it is better for us to take *this* way than
to revert to and depend upon history, even Biblical history; better than to be satisfied with the
mere forms of thought and worship, and so to forget what is essential and what *un*essential; better
than to forget that it is our task as ministers to
speak of God.

Orthodoxy doubtless has much to live down, but
it has nevertheless a powerful instinct for what is
superfluous and what is indispensable. In this it
surpasses many of the schools that oppose it. And
this, and certainly not the mere habit and mental
inertia of the people, is the primary reason why it
still continues to be so potent both in cultus and
church polity and even in state politics. In this
respect it is quite superior.

We may also remark that there are times when even the most convinced heretic desires to depart from his customary psychologisms into positive statement, when, almost against his will, he wants to talk not of religion but of God; and on these occasions he can but employ dogmatic expressions.

When the minister is given the final insight that the theme of the ministry is not man becoming God but God becoming man — even when this insight flashes only occasionally upon his mind — he acquires a taste for objectivity. And he ceases to view objectivity as a mere psychic instrument for use in analyzing the Bible and the dogmas. He finds a world which previously he had despised and hated as "supernaturalistic" slowly but surely becoming reasonable and purposeful. He understands it, so to speak, from within, from behind. He sees that what is written must be written. He gains assurance and freedom of movement in corners of that world so remote and strange that he had not allowed himself to dream he could ever be at home there. And at last he is perhaps able to find in the Apostles' Creed, with all its hardness, more truth, more depth, and even more intelligence than in any other that short-breathed modernism would put in its place.

But obviously one cannot speak of God even in the most powerfully and vividly conceived supernaturalism. He can only witness that he would like to do so. The weakness of orthodoxy is not the supernaturalistic element in the Bible and the dog-

mas. That is its strength. It is rather the fact
that orthodoxy, and we all, so far as we are in our
own way dogmaticians, have a way of regarding
some objective description of that element — such
as even the word "God" for instance — as the
element itself. We have our myths and accept
them pragmatically: a working faith! We have all
come upon those places in Luther — in his teaching
about the trinity, for instance — where we are
simply left standing with instructions to give up
thinking, lift our hat, and say Yes. We feel in
spite of ourselves that it will not do thus to slay the
harlot reason, and we remember with dismay how
often we who are not Luther have done so, in public and even more often in private. Why will it
not do? Because by this kind of answer a man's
question about God is simply quashed. He no
longer has a question. In place of the question he
has an answer. But as long as he remains a man
he cannot let the question go. He himself, as a
man, *is* the question. Any answer would have to
assume his nature, and become itself a question.
To hold the word "God" or anything else before
a man, with the demand that he believe it, is not
to speak of God. The fact is that a man can *not*
believe what is simply held *before* him. He can
believe nothing that is not both *within* him and
before him. He can *not* believe what does not *reveal* itself to him, that has not the power to pene-
trate *to him.* God by himself is not God. He might
be something else. Only the God who reveals him-

self is God. The God who becomes man is God. But the dogmatist does not speak of this God.

The second way is that of *self-criticism*. Here at any rate we have a very clear, a disturbingly clear, account of God's becoming man. On this way any man who desires to have part in God is bidden as a man to die, to surrender all his uniqueness, his selfhood, his ego-hood, and to be still, unassuming, direct, to the end that finally he may become as receptive as the Virgin Mary, when the angel came to her: Behold the handmaid of the Lord — be it unto me according to thy word! God is not this or that; he is no object, no something, no opposite, no second; he is pure being, without quality, filling everything, obstructed only by the particular individuality of man. Let this latter finally be removed and the soul will of a certainty conceive God.

This is the way of mysticism, a way that must be reckoned with! Who would turn his back upon a way along which, for a little, the best spirits of the Middle Ages inspired Luther to travel? We must reckon with the mystic's awareness that God never aids man in his growth but fundamentally aids him only in his decline. The mystic knows that man really desires One who is *not himself*. I call this the way of self-criticism — though it may also be understood as the way of idealism — because by it a man places himself under judgment and negatives himself, because it shows so clearly that what must be overcome is man as man. We have all at one time or another been found upon this way, and we shall never be able to give it up altogether. Even Luther could not do so. It will always be necessary to tell the man who is puffed up by his culture or his want of it, who in his morality and religiosity reaches toward heaven like a Titan, that he must wait, that he must go from less to less, that he must learn to become small, to become nothing, that he must die. There is something of ultimate truth in this idea of the catastrophe of man as such. Whatever objections may be raised against mysticism as a whole, one may not neglect this doctrine with impunity.

Mysticism is strongest where dogmatism is weakest. Here something happens; here we are not left standing with instructions to believe; here we are seriously attacked; here God becomes man with such vigor that there is nothing of man, so to speak, left over. Yet even this is better, infinitely better, than the pagan cultus of the intellect and the human will.

But even here we cannot speak of God. The mystics, and we all in so far as we are mystics, have been wont to *assert* that what annihilates and enters into man, the Abyss into which he falls, the Darkness to which he surrenders himself, the No before which he stands is *God;* but this we are incapable of *proving.* The only part of our assertion of which we are *certain,* the only part we can *prove,* is that man is negatived, negated. But man here on earth can never be more negative than the negativity from which he *emerged.* What then can the way of self-criticism do but somehow magnify to gigantic size the question mark set up beyond life's boundary? A disquieting conception!

Certainly it will always be well for men to understand that the question with which they turn to us is far more radical than in the random perplexities of life they have imagined it to be. Certainly it will always be well for them to look at their culture or their want of culture under the blinding light of the infinite distance between Creator and creation and to see clearly what they are really asking for when in their need they cry for God. But let us remember that no self-negation to which we may refer them (were it even suicide!) is so great and so profound as the actuality, as the self-negation to which all other negatives can only point, the self-negation which is immediately imbued with the positivity of God. The keener the criticism of man, the more keenly man's question is emphasized as a question. But this is only to indicate — although it is to indicate correctly — how God might be spoken of if man were denied. It is not however to speak of God. Not quite. Even the attack of Luther and Kierkegaard upon Christianity was not quite that. The cross is erected, but the resurrection is not preached; and therefore it cannot be really the cross of Christ. It is some other cross. The cross of Christ does not need to be erected by *us!*

The question has received no answer. *God* has not become man. *Man* has become man with a vengeance, but there is no salvation in that. Sub-

jectivity only lifts itself the higher toward heaven,
like a glorious but broken column. God may be
spoken of only (in that objectivity of which orthodoxy knows only too much) when God *himself* becomes man and enters with his *fullness* into our
emptiness, with his *Yes* into our No. But neither
the mystics nor we speak of that God.

The third way is that of *dialectic.* It is the way
of Paul and the Reformers, and intrinsically it is
by far the best. The great truths of dogmatism
and self-criticism are presupposed by it, but so also
is their fragmentariness, their merely relative
nature. This way from the outset undertakes seriously and positively to develop the idea of God on
the one hand and the criticism of man and all things
human on the other; but they are not now considered
independently but are both referred constantly to
their common presupposition, to the living truth
which, to be sure, may not be named, but which lies
between them and gives to both their meaning and
interpretation. Here there is an unwavering insight into the fact that the living truth, the deter-
mining content of any real utterance concerning
God, is that God (but really God!) becomes man
(but really man!).

But how now shall the necessary dependence of
both sides of the truth upon this living Center be
established? The genuine dialectician knows that
this Center cannot be apprehended or beheld, and
he will not if he can help it allow himself to be
drawn into giving direct information about it.

knowing that *all* such information, whether it be positive or negative, is *not* really information, but always *either* dogma *or* self-criticism. On this narrow ridge of rock one can only walk: if he attempts to stand still, he will fall either to the right or to the left, but fall he must. There remains only to keep walking — an appalling performance for those who are not free from dizziness — looking *from one side to the other,* from positive to negative and from negative to positive.

Our task is to interpret the Yes and the No and the No by the Yes without delaying more than a moment in either a fixed Yes *or* a fixed No; to speak of the glory of God in creation, for example, only to pass immediately to emphasizing God's complete concealment from us in that creation (as in Romans 8); to speak of death and the transitory quality of this life only to remember the majesty of the wholly other life which meets us at the moment of death; of the creation of man in the image of God simply and solely to give warning once and for all that man as we know him is fallen man, whose misery we know better than his glory; and, on the other hand, to speak of sin only to point out that we should not know it were it not forgiven us. According to Luther, God's justification of man is to be explained only as *justificatio impii.* When a man realizes, however, that he is an *impius* and nothing more, he awakes to the fact that as such he is a *justus.* When a man becomes really aware of the incompleteness of all human work, the only

possible response he can make to this awareness is
to go eagerly to work — but when we have done
everything we are responsible for, we shall have to
say we are unprofitable servants. The present is
worth living in only in reference to the eternal
future, to the hoped-for latter day — but we are
mere visionaries if we think that the future of the
Lord does not lie at the very door of the present.
A Christian is the master of all things and subject
to nobody — a Christian is the slave of all things
and subject to everybody. I need not continue. He
that hath ears to hear will understand my meaning.
I mean that the question is the answer because the
answer is the question. We take joy in the answer,
once we have heard it clearly, in order at the same
moment to ask our question anew and more in-
sistently, because we know we should not have the
answer if we did not continue to have the question.

An onlooker — if he be a ''Flatlander'' — will,
to be sure, stand by perplexed, and understand
nothing of all of this. Now he will bewail its supernaturalism, and now its atheism; now he will see
in it old Marcion, and now Sebastian Franck, who
is not exactly the same as Marcion, rising from the
grave; now he will call it Schelling's philosophy of
identity; now he will be frightened by its denial of
the world, which deprives him of sight and hearing,
now he will grow angry that its affirmation of the
world should be so incredibly different from his
own; now he will rebel against the positive position,
now against the negative, and now against the

"irreconcilable contradiction" between the two. How shall the dialectician — who is a "Space-lander" — meet his critic? Must he not say, in effect: "My friend, you must understand that if you ask about *God* and if I am really to tell about *him*, dialectic is all that can be expected from *me*. I have done what I could to make you see that neither my affirmation nor my denial lays claim to being God's truth. Neither one is more than a *witness* to that truth, which stands in the center, between every Yes and No. And therefore I have never affirmed without denying and never denied without affirming, for neither affirmation nor denial can be final. If my *witness* to the final answer you are seeking does not satisfy you, I am sorry. It may be that my witness to it is not yet sufficiently clear, that is, that I have not limited the Yes by the No and the No by the Yes incisively enough to set aside all misunderstanding — incisively enough to let you see that nothing is left except that upon which the Yes and the No, and the No and the Yes, depend. But it may also be that your refusal of my answer arises from your not having really asked your *question*, from your not having asked about *God* — for otherwise we should understand each other." So the dialectician might answer; and he would evidently be right.

But perhaps he would *not*. For even the dialectic method suffers from an inherent weakness. This shows itself in that when the dialectician desires to convince he is dependent upon having his ques-

tioner *ask* the real question about God. If he
actually spoke of God, if he gave the answer which
is at the same time the question, he would never
have his questioner shaking his head and thinking
he had not yet asked the right question. He might
better shake his own head over the fact that he
himself evidently has not yet found the right
answer, the answer that would also be the other's
question. His utterance is based upon a mighty
presupposition, upon the presupposition of that
living original Truth there in the center. His utterance itself, however, does not establish that presupposition. It could not, it might not, do that. It is
an affirmation and it is a denial, both of which, to be
sure, refer to that original presupposition, but only
in the form of *assertions* that it is what it is. The
positive assertion sounds unambiguous and so does
the negative, but the further assertion that both the
positive and the negative in the last analysis assert
the same thing is ambiguous in the highest degree.

*How can human utterance carry an irresistible
and compelling meaning? How can it be capable of
bearing witness?* This is the problem which arises
with special vividness in any consideration of the
dialectic method, because here everything is done
that can be done to make it carry meaning and bear
witness. But on occasions *when* dialectic utterance
has seemed to succeed in doing so — and to several
questioners of Plato, of Paul, and of the Reformers
it appears to have succeeded — it was not because
of what the dialectician did, not because of the

assertions he made, for these were in fact questionable, more questionable than his most indignant
critics might have suspected, but because, through
his ambiguous and unambiguous assertions, the
living Truth in the center, the reality of God,
asserted *itself*, created the question upon which his
assertions depended, and *gave* him the answer which
he sought, because it *was* both the right question
and the right answer.

But this possibility, the possibility that God *himself* speaks when he is spoken of, is not part of the
dialectic way as such; it arises rather at the point
where this way *comes to an end*. It is evident that
one is under no divine compulsion to listen to the
assertions of the dialectician. In this respect the
dialectician is no better than the dogmatician and
the self-critic. The real weakness of the dogmatician and the self-critic, their inability really to
speak of *God*, the necessity which is upon them
always to speak of something else, appears to be
raised even to a higher power in the dialectician.
For the very reason that he refers *everything* to the
living truth itself, the inevitable *absence* of that
living truth from his own references must be only
the more painfully evident. And even if his own
references were accompanied by that which gives
all things their truth and meaning, even if God
himself should say through him the one true word,
his own word, *by that very fact* the dialectician
himself would be proved wrong and could only confess that he could not speak of God. God may speak

for himself, but that has nothing to do with what others, the dogmaticians, the self-critics, and perhaps even the more primitive prophets may say. There is no reason why the dialectic theology should be *specially* capable of leading one up *to* a gate which can be opened only from within. If one should fancy that it possesses a special pre-eminence, at least in preparing the way for the action of God, let him remember that it and its paradoxes can do no more *to this end* than can a simple direct word of faith and humility. In relation to the kingdom of God any pedagogy may be good and any may be bad; a stool may be high enough and the longest ladder too short to take the kingdom of heaven by force.

And what man can understand all this, what man can have probed into all these possible ways (I have spoken only of those which deserve serious consideration), what man, in a word, can be a minister — for dimly or clearly all ministers have understood or probed into them — and not be submerged in perplexity?

IV.

My third sentence reads, *We ought therefore to recognize both* that we should speak of God and yet cannot, *and by that very recognition give God the glory.*

There is not much to be said about this sentence. It may serve only as a finale to emphasize the meaning of what I have already said. The word of God

is at once the necessary and the impossible task of
the minister. This is my ultimate conclusion. Further than this I have nothing to say.

And what is to be done in face of such a paradox?

Shall we go back and live in Flatland, where we
may appear to be ministers but in reality are something quite different, something that the others
might also be, if they cared to, something for which
they have *no* fundamental need? Even if we were
capable of such a *tour de force,* I fear the logic of
the situation would soon bring us back to the point
where we stand at the present moment.

Or, for the sake of change, shall we substitute
for the service of the spoken word a service of
silence? As if it were easier, as if we were any
better able, to be silent before God (before real
God) than to speak of him! What meaning can
mere silence have?

Or shall we say farewell to the ministry, give up
our positions, and become what all the others are,
or something like it? But the others are not happy,
else we should not be what we are. The perplexity
of our task is only a token of the perplexity of all
human tasks. If we were not ministers, others
would have to be — and under the same conditions.
The cobbler must stick to his last, the mother must
stick to her children — and we may be certain that
the dialectic of the nursery is no less trying than
the dialectic of our study chamber. Giving up the
ministry would be as sensible as taking one's life;
nothing could come of it, absolutely nothing. But

nothing comes of keeping on with it either. We should be *aware* of both the necessity and the impossibility of our task. And what does that mean?

It means that we ought to direct our vision fixedly and changelessly upon what is expected of us, even when we are left in the uncertain position that we now occupy. What comes of it, or whether people are satisfied with us, is not the question. Our task may be classified in the ordinary economy of human nature and human civilization as being concerned with the question as to how this economy itself may be classified in the world and creation of God. But from the human viewpoint this question must forever remain a question. And so our task must be classified as unclassifiable. There is a logic, a categorical imperative of reality, which inheres in every vocation, and for ours it has this particular content. We should keep this imperative before our eyes as fixedly as every railroad official, for example, must keep his before his eyes. More cannot be desired of us — nor *less*.

And it must be equally well remembered as we look toward our task that only God *himself* can speak of God. The task of the minister is the word of God. This spells the certain defeat of the ministry. It is the *frustration* of *every* ministry and *every* minister. But even here it is best to face the facts and not to look away to one side or to the other. There are certainly many ways, edifying and unedifying, of veiling and cloaking the actual situation; but we must be clear upon it that, even if there were Luthers or Calvins among us, there is no more hope of our finding a way to our goal than there was of Moses' finding a way into the promised land. As surely as we must take some way, and as surely as it pays to make a choice and not to take any way that may open, quite as surely we must keep it in mind that our purpose is that God himself should speak; and we need not be surprised, therefore, if at the end of our way, however well we should have done our work — nay, for the very reason that we have done it well — the Word should still remain *unspoken*.

Let me conclude with three observations.

1. I hardly dare and yet I do dare to hope that no one will come to me now and say, Well then, what shall we do about it? What do you think ought to be done in the church and at the university, if *this* is the situation? I have no proposition to lay before you for the reform either of the pastoral office or of theological education. *That* is not the primary question. *If* the situation is as I have described it, it seems to me that it is out of place to speak of what we ought to do. The question is simply whether or not we recognize this to be the situation. If we do, perhaps some practices in the church and at the university may be changed from what they are. And perhaps not. In any case it is only upon the background of our recognition of the ulterior situation that a discussion of the question of reform would be possible or profitable.

2. Our perplexity is our promise. When *I* say it,

it is a dialectic sentence like any other, and we now know what dialectics are. You may say, I thank you for a promise which I can experience only as an embarrassment! and I shall have no answer for you. But it may be that it is not only *I* who say that our embarrassment is our promise. It may be that the living Truth beyond Yes and No, the reality of God beyond my dialectic turns, has of its own might and love ordained that promise should enter into our embarrassment. It may be that the Word, the word of God, which we ourselves shall never speak, has put on our weakness and unprofitableness so that *our* word *in* its very weakness and unprofitableness has become capable at least of being the mortal frame, the earthen vessel, of the word of God. It may be so, I say; and if it were, we should have reason not so much to speak of our need as to declare and publish the hope and hidden glory of our calling.

3. I have touched a few times upon the *real* subject of my presentation, though I have never named it explicitly. All my thoughts circle about the one point which in the New Testament is called Jesus Christ. Whoever can say "Jesus Christ" need not say "It *may* be"; he can say "It *is*." But which of us is capable, of himself, of saying "Jesus Christ"? Perhaps *we* may find satisfaction in the evidence that his first witnesses did say Jesus Christ. In that case our task would be to believe in their witness to the promise, and so to be witnesses of their witness, ministers of the *Scripture*.

But my premises in this address have been the Old Testament and the tradition of the Reformed Churches. As a Reformed Churchman — and not only, I think, as such — I must keep my sure distance from the Lutheran *est* and the Lutheran type of *assurance of salvation*. Can theology, should theology, pass beyond *prolegomena* to Christology? It may be that everything is said in the prolegomena.

VII

THE DOCTRINAL TASK OF THE REFORMED CHURCHES

L ET me begin by sharing with you a few sentences from an account of a recent conference.

"It could not escape an attentive observer that *fruitless theological discussion* played a very small part. The conference was suffused with a strongly spiritual striving to comprehend *as untheologically as possible,* and to bring to life in their religious meaning for the present day, the old truths of the Reformation; and with this reversion to the sacred inheritance of the past there was at the same time a spirit of resolute determination to press *forward* and make practical test of the old truths in the new relations."

These sentences occur in a report of the last meeting of the Eastern Section of the World Union of Reformed Churches (der östlichen Sektion des Reformierten Weltbundes) in Zurich and come from the pen of one of the leading personalities of that organization. If such a suspension of theological discussion expresses — and there is no doubt

---

This address was delivered at the General Assembly of the Union of Reformed Churches (Hauptversammlung des reformierten Bundes) at Emden in September, 1923.

that it does express — the real inclination, or rather
disinclination, of the largest and at present the
most authoritative circle of our modern Reformed
churches, the task assigned to me today is no grateful one. I have been asked to speak on the subject
of the doctrine, the theology, the preaching message of the Reformed churches: I have been asked,
in a word, to speak on the subject on which in
Zurich they were as silent "as possible," and on
which elsewhere and in increasing numbers we prefer rather to be silent than to speak.

Why do we prefer silence? I think I see three
reasons.

In the *first* place, among Protestants and, curi-
ously enough, especially among Protestant
theologians, the tide of conviction is still on
the rise that "doctrine" is something else and
something less worthy and less important than
"life." The adjectives "theological" and "un-
fruitful" seem to many of us in certain respects
synonymous, and if we are not wholly indifferent
to the question as to what the content of
preaching ought to be, we are certainly ready
at any time to defer it in favor of a discussion
of ways and means of promoting good will, of co-
ordinating the various practices of the churches,
of reaching an inner and outer unity, of actualizing
our community of interest against "Rome" and
modern unbelief, of lending moral and material aid
to each other, of organizing and developing our
potential powers, and, in general, of "moving with

conviction in the direction in which the *spirit* of
Jesus Christ points us," as the report already
quoted says at its close.

In the *second* place, the question of right doctrine,
if we may judge from the experiences of the past,
would not be especially conducive to the Christian
unity so much desired today. It is obvious that no
serious attempt to understand *wherein* the members
even of the "Eastern" (not to speak of the
Western!) "Section" of the so-called "family of
Reformed churches" are in agreement, *wherein*
theirs is a common struggle, and *wherein* they owe
each other mutual aid, could possibly have results
so harmonious and edifying as those which followed,
I doubt not, from the strategic tactical compromise
effected in Zurich, and which indeed must always
follow from that mood of Christian world-brother-
hood which seems to descend upon such festivities
when the surroundings are picturesque and historical. When a man studies into the contents of Reformed doctrine, and into its points of difference
from other doctrines, how can he help calling up
the ghosts of Marburg and other surly shades? And
who would not avoid this if he could?

And in the *third* place and above all, the question
of right doctrine cannot be opened up without the
discovery and the acknowledgment of a great *perplexity* in modern Protestantism. Perhaps it is the
greatest of all perplexities. Our disparagement of
"doctrine" is the fox's disparagement of the
grapes. *Had* we something more essential and

authoritative to say, *had* we a theology convincing to, and accepted by, definite and increasing groups of people, *had* we a gospel which we *had* to preach, we should think differently. On the whole we do not have such a gospel in our churches. I think I am not mistaken in saying that this is so even where we are not so irreverent — or prudent — as to have explained away and abolished as obsolete the doctrinal norms we have inherited. The question of right doctrine introduces us to the vacuum *inside* our churches and *inside* Christianity. The discovery of that vacuum is discouraging and upsetting, not to say mortifying, enough. It may well put a question mark after our cheerful summons to turn to the "sacred inheritance of the past" and to "press forward" to the practical test of that inheritance.

From all sides there comes the cry, "O touch it, touch it, not!" And am I now to blunder into touching this sore spot? Would it not be better to follow the well-established instinct of most of our Protestant contemporaries and, like the priest and the Levite, hurry past what has fallen among the thieves? Would it not be better, as it were, to bracket the question of doctrine, and assume that "somehow" it has already been solved or been made capable of being solved? Would it not be better to turn with "resolute determination" to questions in which Christians, and the people of our Reformed churches in particular, are interested, and about which they can talk peaceably and happily? Would it not be better to do so especially in these days, when the life of the churches is already so complicated, and when it is so entirely fitting that simple ways and simple watchwords should obtain a more excellent name?

I think not. In spite of all, I feel sure we have occasion to be thankful to the executive committee of the Reformed Union for having had the courage to make the treatment of this sore spot part of the order of the day. It is a question which would have to be taken up sometime: why not by us today? The Reformed churches of the world at large, and Protestant Christians in general, will sooner or later have to face it more seriously than they do now — whatever the costs and whatever the results. The melancholy earnestness of this period we have entered will not permit the churches (of Europe at any rate!) to be satisfied with sham solutions, even though they possess the virtue of clearest simplicity.

The talk of pressing forward to practical tests of the old truths in new relations *is,* however, a *sham solution.* What is to be tested? In the long run will it escape the sharp eyes of the children of the world, to say nothing of ourselves, the children of the household, that we have here a predicate without a subject? Is it so indisputably certain that even where the creeds are still in force, or are so at least on paper, our Reformed churches do actually echo with the "old truths of the Reformation"? "In their religious meaning for the present day," we read. Even if we were familiar with the original message of the evangelical Reformed churches, are

the readjustments, reinterpretations, and other
changes which officially or unofficially have been
introduced into it really so insignificant that we
may spare ourselves the asking by what right or by
what authority this doctrine or that is preached
under the name of that message today? I do not
recall that the struggles engendered by this question in the nineteenth century came to any victorious conclusion. Is it really practicable to "press
forward," while this question remains behind us
unsolved? How can we longer close our eyes to the
fact that there is an end to the repair work, the
organizing, and the religious education upon which,
rather than upon theology, the people of our
churches today declare they prefer to busy themselves? The fatal moment is at hand when the men
of the East and West, whose attention has been
caught by so much preparation, must needs be
offered something tangible or at least told what is
really the matter, and when even the most active
and enthusiastic parish must be *still,* in order at
last to hear what words of consequence the ministers or even the professors of the Reformed
churches may have to say, to see what real light
they may be able to shed upon man's strange situation midway between heaven and earth, and to in-
quire into their claim to be in possession of redeeming truth. Is it wise to suppress or to relegate to
the end of the whole program a question upon which
everything else depends for its meaning and value?
Would it not be better for the whole program to be

held in abeyance until we are clearer, more definite, more forcibly convinced upon this question?

In Zurich a good deal was said about the coming controversy with *"Rome."* That a serious and necessary task lies before us in this connection is not to be doubted. But how can we take issue with "Rome" before we have genuinely taken issue with ourselves as to what we non-Roman Christians are, what we represent, and what we desire? Have we today any vigorous community of purpose in distinction to Catholicism? And if we have *not* or do not rightly know whether we have or not, how can we be worthy participants — to say nothing more — in the ecumenical council planned for 1925?

Those who believe that the Reformed churches should conduct themselves "as untheologically as possible" delight in appealing to the practical unionizing tendencies of the old Reformed churchmen, especially to the active, organizing, world-embracing spirit of *Calvin;* but they constantly overlook the fact that Calvin wrote his *Institutes before* he wrote his much admired letters on church polity. In a word, he first had a *theme* and *then* developed its variations; first he *knew* what he wanted and *then* he wanted what he knew. The desire "with resolute determination" to reverse this quite natural order, to begin where Calvin left off, to reap with him without having sown with him, is neither Calvinistic nor commendable. Zwingli's reformation began with *preaching;* Calvin's with *lectures.* The talk which we hear today about the "cultivation of a stronger Reformed-Church consciousness" can acquire meaning only if we are willing to go the way that Luther *and* Zwingli *and* Calvin went, the straight and rigorous way that leads from *thought* to action — and *no* other. Later, perhaps a few years later, the conscious and "strongly spiritual striving" may come to its own.

One of the few real services which the *German* Reformed churches might perhaps perform today for their confessional brethren of the West would be to recall them (after we had recalled ourselves) to the fact that in spite of all our temporal needs and seeming necessities the Reformed churches are in possession of something peculiarly *their own*.

We must now turn to a somewhat more fundamental consideration. When a man says he belongs not to the Catholic Church nor to the Lutheran nor to the Evangelical (happy generality, covering so much and yet so little!) but to the *Reformed* — the Evangelical *Reformed*, — he makes the "reversion to the sacred inheritance" of the Reformation praised, though somewhat faintly, in the Zurich report. This is quite as true of the layman as of the minister or the theological professor — and I trust all three are interested in our question. And what is the "sacred inheritance of the Reformation" — of the Reformed-Church Reformation, especially? Every Reformed churchman must obviously give

serious attention to this question and know both the
right answer and the reasons for it. And this, *in
nuce,* is the "doctrinal task of the Reformed
churches."

There are three general answers proposed.

The first is the answer of the man who is devoted
to what is *characteristic* of his own ecclesiastical
type, which in this case is the Reformed-Church
type. He loves the Reformed Church as he loves
his country, his city, his ancestral home. He loves
it *more* than others, as he loves his native heath
more than others — simply because it is his own.
This is more than piety; it is out-and-out *pietas.*
This man takes pleasure in the distinctiveness of
the Christianity he knows and trusts, and so he
keeps his eyes fixed upon the sharper profiles and
contours of its past, its points of richer ecclesiastical self-consciousness, its classical literature, its
traditional theories and practices. With an understandable feeling of defiance for the all-leveling and
uncreative spirit of the nineteenth and twentieth
centuries, he holds to what there is of vitality, or at
least of potentiality, in the old Reformed-Church
idea. We must learn again to reverence Calvin (or
in eastern Switzerland, Zwingli) because he is *ours.*
We must return to a more frequent use of the
Heidelberg catechism — because this time-honored
treasure is *ours.* Predestination, the autonomy of
the ten commandments, the necessity of church discipline — these are doctrines we must preach because they are part and parcel of a history which

is *ours*. For these reasons our friend points us to
the Reformed confessions of faith.

And perhaps he will later be good enough to tell
us to which one or to which ones of these hardly
concordant documents we ought, according to his
view, to be most obediently respectful!

But though his answer may not be finally proved
to be the correct one, its significance cannot be
questioned. It is a fact that a Reformed churchman is one who is at home within a particular historical Christian tradition, that is, within a
particular spiritual community which is defined by
its past — and more by its distant than by its more
recent past. Our open or secret rebellion against
the particular in our life situation, against those
elements which are the results of chance and history — our desire, at least in Christian relations,
to take direct flight into the general and absolute —
our impatience at being Reformed churchmen (how
petty!) when we might be simply disciples of
Jesus — indicates a mode of thought which in many
of us has become almost chronic. But it betrays
a view of things which, to say the least, is one-
sided. Even as Christians we all belong somewhere, whether or not we realize it or care to realize
it. To accept, to understand, or at least to be aware
of the particularity of one's historical relations is
an act of simple obedience to life which one may
forgo for a time but certainly not forever. The
place where the Absolute *witnesses* to itself is the
relative; and though later discoveries and advances

may be made, its immediate witness is always in
that which lies *nearest to hand*. The place where
the Holy Catholic Church is *believed in* is the *particular* church which has its own history and its own
outlook. Appreciation of the last things cannot be
won by hurriedly passing over the things that come
before. A will to unite cannot be developed by
people who have not yet taken themselves, to say
nothing of the others, seriously; the peace of Christendom cannot be served by understandings that
lack content. The fact that one *is* a Reformed
churchman is reason enough why he should be one
and why, if no obstacle arises, he should *remain*
one; and to be a Reformed churchman in earnest
means as a matter of fact to pay deference to the
Reformed-Church idea as it is expressed in its beginnings. So much the first answer makes clear.

But this answer also gives rise to serious and
crowding reflections. The Reformed churches are
the last in the world to be benefited by the interest
of the antiquarian, of the *laudator temporis acti,*
of the religious patriot, of the one who loves Reformed-Church ways because they are those of the
Reformed churches. In this as in other respects
our churches will be found to be very poor ground
for the blue flower of romance. In contrast to the
Lutheran churches, ours from the beginning have
shown a great irreverence and fundamental dis-
taste for the whole of Christian tradition, so far as
it lays claim to possessing religious meaning in
itself, so far as it cannot be justified by the Scrip-

tures witnessed to by the Spirit of truth in our spirit. To our fathers the historical past was something which called not for loving and devoted admiration but for careful and critical scrutiny. They cherished the conservative principle, it is true, but with them it was so often crossed and broken by the opposite one that their beginnings at best show only a fragmentary loyalty toward the past, and for the most part represent a clean and merciless break with it.

The one who loves the old Reformed ways will hardly desire to declare them antiquated, and yet he will do so if he creates a finality and sacredness for the Reformed tradition. There is, to be sure, a history of the Reformed churches, and there are documentary statements of their beliefs, together with classical expositions of their theory and practice, which command (and will always command) the attention, respect, and consideration of every one who calls himself a Reformed churchman; but in the truest sense there is no such thing as Reformed doctrine, except the timeless appeal to the open Bible and to the Spirit which from it speaks to our spirit. Our fathers had good reason for leaving us *no* Augsburg Confession, authentically interpreting the word of God, *no* Formula of Concord, *no* "Symbolic Books" which might later, like the Lutheran, come to possess an odor of sanctity. They left us only *creeds,* more than one of which begin or end with a proviso which leaves them open to being improved upon in the future. The Reformed churches simply do *not* know the word dogma, in its rigid hierarchial sense. In those churches Christian history has no doctrinal *authority* whatever; the authority lies rather in the *Scriptures* and in the *Spirit,* both of which (even the Scriptures!) are beyond Christian history. The part of loyalty to the fathers, then, is to hold to the past as they themselves held to it; to look to history but to note that it points beyond itself to revelation; to guard against confusing antiquity with the primal order, and the authority which the Church posses-ses with the authority by which it was founded; to reject every invariata and invariabilis but *one;* to refuse to bow to any cap set up in the market place, were it even the cap of Calvin himself; to let Scripture and Spirit, and Spirit and Scripture alike, work their way to authority through criticism; and to let them do so in face of what is best in the *Reformed* theory and practice of the present day, *as* they did in our father's time in face of what was best in the Christian tradition of the Middle Ages.

From this viewpoint, Reformed doctrine would be the ideas which took shape in *our* minds as a result of the unavoidable necessity *both* to regard Reformed Christianity *respectfully* in terms of its concrete beginnings *and* to *criticize* that Christianity in accordance with the character of those beginnings. It *may* be our doctrinal task to make a careful revision of the theology of the Geneva or the Heidelberg Catechism or of the Canons of Dort, or, if we credit ourselves with the necessary author-

ity and insight, it *may* be our task to draw up a
new creed, a *Helvetica tertia,* in the same way that
our fathers substituted a *posterior* for a *prior.*
Both are real possibilities for the Reformed
churches.

The second answer to the question, why and in
what sense we call ourselves "Reformed" churchmen, is that of the man who is interested in certain
ideas, tendencies, and institutions which have become associated eclectically with the Reformed
churches of the past and present. Perhaps he
takes pleasure — if I may put the best first — in the
Deo soli gloria! of the Reformed churches, in the
rejection and relative discrediting of all human and
personal righteousness expressed in the phrase, in
its exposure of all pietistic and methodistic illusions, and in its hint that the God who forgives sins
is one to be feared. Or perhaps it is just the opposite
element that appeals to him, the rigorous individual
and social ethos of the Reformed-Church idea, the
emphasis it places upon law and obedience — so
much more intimately and plausibly than the
Lutheran confessions do — the *vita hominis Chris-
tiani* set forth by Calvin as the central theme of his
Institutes. Perhaps it is neither of these; perhaps
he senses the humanistic element in Reformed
churchmanship and is pleased by the keen and penetrating intellectual quality of its Christianity, its
resolute refusal to deify any created thing —
vividly witnessed to in its doctrine of the sacra-
ments — its *finitum non est capax infiniti,* its affinity

with Plato and Kant and the best traditions of philosophy. Perhaps he comes from the school of Bengel or of Blumhardt and is attracted and intrigued by the great Coccygian spectacle of a coming kingdom of God. Or he prizes his Reformed churchmanship on account of its tartly wholesome *abnegatio nostri,* which seems so meaningful to the true Calvinist in his inmost heart, and in which there glows something of Tersteegen's mysticism. Or perhaps, on the other hand, he is drawn by that very open-mindedness toward the world which has made the Calvinist an active and stimulating, an even creative, factor in modern life, capable at least of allying himself in every possible way with movements spiritual, cultural, and economic. Or as a churchman he is convinced of the value and practicability of the Reformed type of church government and cultus. He is a Reformed churchman because and in so far as he approves of synodic-presbyterian polity, because his ideal envisages an actively interested laity gathered in vigorous autonomous congregations (in distinction to the pastoral congregations of Lutheranism), or because he has been won by the severe and earnest quality of the Reformed service, with its renunciation of all crypto-Catholic forms.

All these possibilities might be named — and more. They contain treasures of truth, purpose, and ideal of which any person who cannot be satisfied with being obedient and loyal to the Reformed idea without further question (and of course that

sort of satisfaction cannot last) might profitably
possess himself. Many a half-hearted Reformed
churchman not rightly certain of himself would do
well to study them more intimately, to the end that
he might in some way lend his church his thought,
leadership, gifts, and position, not only as a member born but as a member convinced: Has not
almost every one of the possibilities mentioned sufficient meaning and vitality in itself alone to give
nurture and support to a revival touching all
phases of religious, theological, and ecclesiastical
life, and even reaching out beyond? Of reasons
why a man *may* be a Reformed churchman there is
certainly no lack.

But it is just this plural and this "may" that
betray the weakness of this comprehensive way of
answering our question. A church does not live
upon truths, however many and vital and profound
those truths may be; a church lives upon *truth*,
which men do not take up *selectively*, choosing between this and that doctrine, theory, and principle,
but which they take up *of necessity* because it has
first taken *them*, and thus of itself has established
the church. It is not for many reasons but only for
one that a person may be a Reformed churchman.
This confusion of many motives, however excellent
they may be if taken singly and however clearly
they may be illustrated in Zwingli and Calvin, gives
aid and comfort *not only* to the Reformed churches
but also to their critics. The way in which one man
will give consideration only to the doctrine of sin

and grace, another will preach a part-heathen, part-Christian *lex naturae,* another will pitch his tent hard by perfectionism, another by antinomianism, and another, enthusiastically, by communism, while a sixth will expect salvation, or something close to it to result from a reestablishment of psalm-singing and the Calvinistic ordinances, and a seventh, reckoned the boldest of all, will have found his shibboleth for time and eternity in the Reformed conception of God — all this, if we are not worldly enough to confuse it with "richness," suggests disorder and must arouse serious misgiving.

At any rate the Reformed churches did not come into being in this manner. They were born not in this pantheon of ideals but in a place of prayer to *one* God. All the lights by which we variously think we see were originally fire from *one* altar. The doctrines, laws, and commandments which we now affirm as existing separately and each in its own right — as if separately and each in its own right they were not erroneous, dangerous, and un-Christian (the dominating *Deo soli gloria* not excepted, for why should even *this* idea become an idol?) — all were once a unity; and their unity was not that of a fundamental idea which bracketed them as a system of thought but was rather that of original truth, which is of an order above that of ideas. The Reformed creeds differ from the Augsburg Confession and others by the fact that in committing themselves, at a measured distance, to the *one object* of all thought, they follow a course which, though less dramatic and effective for theology, at least saves them from staking everything upon the card of *any doctrine*. They refer all doctrine away from itself to the one Object. To them *truth* is God — not their *thought* about God but God *himself* and God *alone,* as he speaks his own *word* in Scripture and in Spirit. And if we are to take our Reformed churchmanship seriously, the reasons for it, be they never so convincing in themselves, must all lead us up to this, which, as a revelation witnessed to and perceived in the Scriptures, is itself no idea, no principle, no doctrine, but the origin of all doctrine and the standard by which all doctrine is and forever must be measured.

The characteristic expressions of Reformed Christianity, which seem so clear and real and are in general so congenial to us, must command our serious attention; but this attention will presently be broken in upon, and ought to be broken in upon, by the majestic murmur of the *fountain-head* of all these rivulets which so gayly ripple past us in all directions. That fountain-head may perhaps seem to us forbidding, uncongenial, and possibly unreal; but it is in no way dependent upon our understanding or approving it. What makes us Reformed churchmen is not the pleasure we find in certain aspects of truth but the recognition of the *one* truth, the recognition of that word of God which must prevail, if the worst comes to the worst, even *against* our own ideals — a recognition which is occasioned and caused *by* the *truth* itself.

According to this second point of view, Reformed
doctrine would be that which we would express if
we could speak as bond and not free, in subjection
to overmastering truth and not in gratuitous self-
expression, under the necessity of a reality which
threatens on every side and not under the illusion
of a sovereign power of choice. This would not
necessarily bring out any particular idea which we
have upon our own hearts. It might be no more
than an acknowledgment. Essentially it would
serve not so much to produce a correct formula or
a doctrinal system as to let man know there is a
necessity upon him, a necessity for saying in human
terms, both general and particular, what is first
said to him in divine terms. Whatever language
or thoughts we used to meet the fashions of our
time, our school, or our social group, it would be
our task to work out not so much a scheme of right
"teaching" as a statement of what we have learned,
not so much a *doctrina* as a διδαχή.

The third and most modern answer is that of the
man who is interested in the inner attributes of
personality which are peculiarly the possession of
the Reformed churchman. The key word here is
"godliness" (Frömmigkeit). This man knows the
Reformed churches: he knows the fathers, the
founders, and the heroes. He is fascinated not only
by the character of these men, their life of struggle
and suffering, their austere accomplishments, but
even more by the particular tinge and temperature
of their devotion to their faith. The figure of

Luther has been so towering and overwhelming that this quality in the Reformed fathers has only recently received attention, though it has been known that popular piety did play its not always happy rôle in relation to Zwingli in the church of the sixteenth century. But modern times with their somewhat Epigonian regard for the past *have* discovered the fathers and honored them. Words like "Calvinistic" and "Calvinism," which were once scornfully left to the use of opponents, have now lost their unpleasant note, and "Reformed" seems almost to mean admiring of, commendatory of, and sometimes actually imitative of, Calvin. Delighted appreciation of the man and the men has grown into delighted acceptance of their manner. Their ways are followed, or at least recommended, by many.

And why stop here? It is a simple historical truth that the beginning of our churches is associated to an arresting degree with the strange riddle of the religious personality, the man who individually ventures with God against half the world, and whose historical portrait, therefore, in a unique fashion acquires the character of the heroic, evoking reverence and love in his posterity. It is quite time to remember, in our admiration of Protestant man, that Luther was not the only possible type to imitate. These great ones of the former time, who believed, prayed, and worked, have something to offer the small-calibred Christianity of the present day; they are a wholesome incitement to us to think of our origins, and perhaps even of the Origin.

But a fair warning must be given here. The confessions of faith of our churches, in striking contrast to the Formula of Concord, make absolutely
no appeal to the authority of Zwingli or of Calvin.
They allow even their authors to be quite submerged in substance of doctrine. The old Reformed
dogmatics knows *no* analogy to the old Lutheran
rubric *"de vocatione Lutheri."* To the grief of
Calvin's modern biographers, the story of his conversion was of so little interest to the man himself
and to his circle, that there are only two words,
subita conversione, among a multitude of guesses,
which serve to impart information — we can hardly
say edification — to his disciples. In old Geneva
they were so irreverent as to let the burial-place of
the great man pass wholly into oblivion. The
legends of the saints of the Reformed churches and
the cult of their heroes did not grow up until people
were no longer certain of the Reformed *idea.* One
may well ask what Calvin himself, if he were to
return, would say of the five-volume panegyric of
his French admirer, and whether for his own interest and delectation he would not much rather
read the work of the angry Kampschulte. And who
could persuade him that the Triumphal Parade of
the Founders of the Reformed Faith, which *new*
Geneva has built in stone to his memory and to the
memory of his grim companions, was not simply an
abomination?

According to the undeniably "unhistorical" opinion of the fathers themselves, a church should take

its rise *not* from a "religious personality," but a — *law*. The question of Reformation times in *old* Geneva was not whether one would allow himself to be religiously moved, impressed, attracted, and inspired by this man or that, but whether one would *vivre selon la parole de Dieu*. The man who was called to the preaching and execution of the law was not for a moment considered a prophet, let alone a Christian hero; he was a *minister*, a *servant* of the divine word. And his "godliness" had no value nor independent meaning of its own; it was an anonymous, colorless, virtueless, purely private act of *obedience*. The greatness of the fathers lay in their ability to see the gate definitely shut against all human greatness, and especially their own. It lay in that freedom from self-concern which made their creeds not expositions of their own inner experience, remarkable as that was, but something quite different: *testificationes conceptae intus fidei*. Does the fact that they were not always completely successful in shutting the gate, that there crept in something of the human, of the personal, of their own, give us occasion to view their lives otherwise than as they viewed them themselves?

Is there any other way for us to honor and imitate Calvin than to take our stand where Calvin stood? — to obey the law as men who are called to obey, or if we no longer know what *law, calling,* and *obedience* in the Christian sense are, then to ask what they are until we find it out again — but not under any circumstances to give time and strength to admiring Calvin or playing Calvin. The revitalized godliness of the fathers is exactly what we do not need. What has been cannot return and should not.

Those creative geniuses might make the demand upon us that we become creative *ourselves* and in our own time enter into the searching, the questioning, the perplexity, and the embarrassment — into the whole limitless difficulty and need of men who stand before their Lord. The mission which was laid upon them as men, as personalities, as heroes, would then be fulfilled in us. What we should dare to profess when, thrown back upon ourselves by these historical examples, we stood before the same shut gate as they, would be (and here we have a third aspect of it) Reformed doctrine. The historical character, the emotional coloring, the mode and tone of that doctrine would be to us necessarily a *cura posterior*. It would not be the service of man nor the service of the community but the *ministerium verbi divini* that would be laid upon us as an immediate demand, in the same inglorious but rigorous way that it was laid upon the men whose graves we else must decorate in vain.

The consideration of these different answers to the question, *Dic cur hic?* focuses our attention upon *one* point which is a primary characteristic of Reformed doctrine. It is known in church history as the *scriptural principle*. At their very beginnings the Reformed churches saw that truth is contained only in the word of God, that the word of God for them lay only in the Old and New Testaments, and that every *doctrine* must therefore be measured against an unchangeable and impassable standard discoverable in the Scriptures. What one may be moved to say concerning God, the world, and man because he *must* say it, having let the Scriptures speak to him — the Scriptures themselves, and not the Scriptures interpreted by any particular tradition; the whole Scriptures, and not a part of them chosen to suit a preconceived theory; the Scriptures, and not the utterances of pious men of the past or present which might be confused with them; the Scriptures, and not without the significant word of the Spirit which sustains them — what, after *those* Scriptures have spoken to him, one may be moved to say in fear and trembling concerning the things about which man of himself may say nothing, or only foolishness, *that,* if we may judge from our beginnings, is Reformed doctrine. *Doctrina* is the word of the Christian man at crisis with the word of God: it is penetrated by that merciless purifying and cleansing which is witnessed to in the Scriptures. It remains the word of man. It does not itself become the *verbum divinum,* but in this relation it is none the less a legitimate and pure *praedicatio verbi divini.*

This principle of *conformity* with the Scriptures has been called the formal principle of the Reformation — and not without silent regrets that for our Reformers it was, primarily at least, a matter "only" of form and not of content as well: how much profounder in this respect was Lutheranism!

Now it is highly advisable to be cautious in making this assertion. Too easily we betray the fact that we Epigoni are spectators of and not participants in the great event. *God's* witness to himself in Holy Scripture was certainly not "only" form to our fathers; "form" is precisely what it was not: it was the most immediate, most vital, fullest kind of content. It was a content immeasurable and inimitable, unalterable and inexhaustible; and as such it was too great to be identical with the content of this or that particular viewpoint or experience — even with the experience of the forgiveness of sin! No such particular viewpoint or experience could contain the concept, *God* is speaking, when the fact is that all particular viewpoints and experiences are themselves contained by *that concept*. *God* is speaking — he! — and not even the highest and most specifically religious element in the experience of grace *through* which he speaks may itself take the place of God. *God* is speaking not only in the Gospel but also in the Law; not only in the New Testament but also in the Old; not only of forgiveness of sins and of eternal life (although he mentions *these* even in "Eden") but also, and with the same earnestness, of our ordered temporal existence; not only as the open and friendly God, but also and constantly as the hidden and terrible One who demands not only faith but also obedience (and that is not quite the same, though it *also* depends upon grace).

This *"God* is speaking!" of the fathers, clear and compelling, brought to the fore the ultimate ques-

tion and demanded mighty decisions all along the
line, being concrete for the very reason that it was
absolute, and releasing a veritable flood of "teaching" for the very reason that fundamentally it com-
manded man to be silent. When the Theses of Bern
of 1528 began with the rigid words, "The holy
Christian Church, of which Christ is the only head,
is born of the word of God, abides therein, and
knows not the voice of strangers," not the second
but the first word, the causal word, of the Reformed
Reformation was spoken. That "Holy Writ"
(Gschrift) must decide concerning the truth and
falsity of all doctrine was a premise which, not
without prejudice to the Catholic participants, was
incorporated in the very rules of that disputation
from which the oldest creeds derived; it was taken
for granted, to say nothing of being recognized and
approved, even before a sentence of the creeds
themselves had been written down. It is clear that
even theoretically the fathers had no idea of
attempting to establish it in advance, for it was a
basic thing that needed no basing: spirit is recognized only by spirit, God only by God. The appeal
to this principle was meant in a sense neither
mechanical and rational nor experimental and
irrational — for what has the category of revelation to do with *these* categories? — but was meant
rather as a simple submission to God's manifestation of himself: *Summa scripturae probatio passim
a Dei loquentis persona sumitur* (Calvin).

God does not ask "why?" What he wills and

speaks and does depends both for its reality *and* its human realization *only* upon himself. "Thou reignest over *all* and in thine hand is power and might," applies also to the question of truth. God himself not only *is* the truth and the whole truth, but he is also the *revelation* and the whole revelation that he is the truth. How could the statement that the Bible is his word be proved in any other way than by an act of free grace by which he *himself* makes the proof? Would it be the word of *God* if it could be verified except by him? The astonishing statement that the Bible is his word has been called an axiom. But it is such only in its logical form. In content its certainty is wholly unlike the self-evidenced certainty of mathematical axioms. It expresses rather the self-evidenced *revelation* which God gives simultaneously to his Biblical witnesses and to those who accept their witness. It expresses obedience to the *testimonium spiritus sancti internum,* to the spirit of God in which the human spirit of the writer and the reader become one in common adoration; and the truth of the statement stands or falls with the reality of this sovereign act proceeding from God and authenticated by him.

It was just this submitting of doctrine *not* to the authority of logic but to the authority of *God* that was the secret of the fathers, of *their* Reformation, and of the churches *they* founded. The essential characteristic of their genius was not any special insight or type of godliness but their clear understanding of the basis of things: they knew that that

basis was God and God alone. In other words, they
had the courage to allow so accidental, contingent,
and human a thing as the Bible to become a serious
witness of the revelation of God, to allow a book
which was in itself profane to become *Holy* Scripture. "Abraham *believed* God and it was counted
unto him for righteousness." So, and not otherwise, the doctrine, the message, the preaching arose.

We must be clear upon it that today our eyes are
holden in just this regard. In just this critical
respect ours is an era of pygmies.

The days soon came when this clear understanding was lost, when it was forgotten that *God* was
spoken of when the Bible was called the word of
God, when people wandered off from the vital area
inclosed by the Scriptures and the Spirit and completely forgot the meaning of the statement, *God*
is speaking! Truth substantiated in itself, and therefore serving to substantiate doctrine, degenerated
into a theorem which, however ardently one might
assert it, itself needed substantiation. People began
surrounding the witness of the Holy Spirit with
other reasons for belief in order to support a proof
in which they no longer had perfect trust. An
apologetic friendly to man began to twine about the
trunk of *"God is speaking"* and to rob its roots of
nourishment. In this way the written page, coming
to be considered lifeless and no longer a witness, was
left in isolation; and its situation grew steadily
more dangerous. And when historical criticism
began objecting to the antiquity, the genuineness,

the historical reliability of Biblical literature, no one any longer knew the only possible answer, the answer of freedom and Christian reality, and we either fell back (like the authors of the Helvetic Consensus Formula of 1675) upon dogmatic assertion which was well enough meant but which had lost its vitality, or we developed a guerrilla warfare in apologetics, the blind fighting the blind, the outcome of which could be no other than what it has actually been. We had lost the wonder of *God,* and now we had to learn to eke out an increasingly difficult and miserable existence by asserting the wonder of the *world,* the miracle of history and of the inner life (all equally questionable!). The great misery of Protestantism began: doctrine, parted from its life-giving origin, hardened into *Orthodoxy;* Christian experience, confusing itself with this origin, took refuge in *Pietism;* truth, no longer understood and actually no longer understandable, shriveled into the moral and sentimental maxims of the *Enlightenment;* and finally even Christian experience was reduced in *Schleiermacher* and his followers, both of the left wing *and* the right, to the hypothesis of being the highest expression of a religious instinct common to all men.

These are the four cornerstones of the prison in which we all (I say it advisedly, we all) are living. Some of us are nearer to this corner, others to that: "Every man may choose his own hero!" Whether we are aware of it or not, the roof which is supported by these four pillars, which unites them to each other, and which shuts off from us, the inmates, the sight of heaven, is their denial of revelation. Within the walls of this prison Reformed doctrine cannot prosper, but only its substitutes which we have mentioned — which are the result of anti-quarian, theoretical, or emotional predilections. Reformed doctrine, in order to be itself at all, needs the free winds wherein the word of God is recognized in Scripture and Spirit; it needs the vastness and energy of untamed nature whereby once the Reformed churches, as by a volcanic erup-tion, were "born" — or, as Christian churches, born again. "Reformed *by God's word*" is the ancient and real meaning of the name we bear. What is the use of any "reversion to the sacred inheritance of the Reformation," if it is *not* to be conscious that *this* is the meaning of our name? That we are still vaguely conscious of this (especially perhaps where we rely most upon the fathers) but that our name in most quarters really has no meaning because it has not this rightful one — this is the source of the great perplexity of which we were speaking at the beginning, this is the *only* serious, but certainly *very* serious, reason why we today are going out of our way to avoid the question of Reformed doctrine.

———————

Of the specific content of Reformed doctrine I have spoken only in passing. For it has seemed to me that the first question before us today in this connection is concerned with the *genesis* of doc-trine: we must ask what it presupposes. With what

right and with what meaning can we speak of the
Reformed attitude toward predestination, the
atonement, and the Lord's supper, if we are not
agreed as to the reason for that attitude — and
agreed not only in hope and ideal but in fact and
practice also? Only upon the basis of such an
agreement can we speak of these or any kindred
themes with the old authority. Upon any other
basis — were we even to reaffirm the Canons of
Dort literally, were we even to preach Calvin's
original ideas regarding man and the church — we
should not be producing Reformed doctrine; we
should merely be reproducing doctrine now obsolete.
Form and content are in this case identical; and
the doctrinal task of the Reformed churches does
not go further, even in its secondary phases, than
the preaching of the Cause that occasioned it. Here
the beginning is finally identifiable with the end.
When a man has accepted in faith the doctrine born
of the word of God, the result is not one of many
possible insights or sensations or resolves; whatever may have been the particular medium of its
coming to him, whatever the particular thing he
may have heard or read, learned or felt or decided,
the result is always a renewed awareness of the
word of God as the word of *God,* a consciousness of
a Majesty to which in joy or fear he may only listen
and pray expectantly, ready to believe and ready
to obey: Speak, Lord, for thy servant heareth!

If, in our churches or, let us say more modestly,
in our study chambers, we could take it for granted

that this is the alpha and omega of Reformed doctrine, not its formal but its material, its vital principle, we should not need to be anxious about the content, the genuinely Reformed content, of our Dogmatics II. Then, as in the beginning of our history, we should have a relatively simple agreement which would not exclude but include freedom of system and formula, and above all insure greater doctrinal unanimity for the future. Perhaps, if there is as yet no desire to strike out into wholly new paths, it would be an agreement upon the interpretation of the old Reformed doctrinal standards. In that case I for my part should decidedly favor the interpretation given in the *Catechismus Genevensis* of 1545. Perhaps — though it is farthest from my thought to ask for this today — it would be an agreement upon a creed which should be Reformed but also plainly and explicitly *new*, speaking in *our own* language out of *our own* experiences to *our own* times. But first our churches must certainly be far wider awake to the question as to what is presupposed by a Christian creed. Before that is taken up there is little use in racking our brains about what follows after.

For the immediate future the one serious necessity I see for Reformed theology is to study toward a new conception of the *"scriptural principle,"* which should contain much more than that term now implies. I say study, for this new conception does not allow of sudden creation. So far as human endeavor will have any part in making this study successful, we shall need to think through the category of *revelation* again, and learn again to read the Bible, both Old and New Testaments, from that viewpoint.

By way of indicating the main divisions of this supremely important task, which for us is also supremely perplexing, let me take up briefly the matter of so-called substance of doctrine, the so-called fundamental affirmations of the Reformed creed. This I may do best, perhaps, by calling your attention to three questions asked at the beginning of the history of our churches.

If one reads the writings of Zwingli and Calvin and the oldest Reformed creeds with a view to finding out what their authors really objected to in the Medieval *Catholic Church,* he will everywhere find himself penetrating through their strictures upon its dogma and ritual to one crowning criticism: they charged that church with falsifying the theme of Christian preaching and perverting Christianity itself by the disastrous expedient of putting man — man's history and his traditions, man's intelligence and his possibilities, man's good will and his capacity for grace — in the place of God. In ecclesiasticism's whole solemn and splendid attempt to become a means of salvation, in its vast system of compromise between nature and grace, in the genius of its endeavor to make an impossibility possible — in all these devices characteristic of the last phase of medieval Christianity, they saw only an offense to the God who refuses to be possessed and from the beginning to the end remains the Possessor. They wanted to have it reëstablished unambiguously that the subject in the religious relation is God and not man.

That this objection is not wholly identical with Luther's contention that the old church led the poor frightened conscience astray into frivolity or despair, is instructively brought out by a comparison between the Augsburg Confession and the contemporaneous Confession of the Four Cities of the Oberland: the Reformed creed lays emphasis not so much upon the idea that man is justified by faith and not by works as upon the prior consideration that it is God and not man who accomplishes the justification. The Reformed leaders are interested in this primary aspect of the religious relation. They are also interested in its final aspect, the glorification of God. They are less, much less interested, at least in the older and classical times, in what comes between in the way of salvation as such. The Reformed thesis from the very start is too comprehensive to center its interest there; it goes on energetically from the antithesis of faith and works and discovers a series of them — Creator and creation, God's truth and man's invention, God's law and the church's law.

And so the Reformed Church criticized not only the more narrowly religious dialectic of sin and forgiveness but the whole existence of man as well. In its breadth it thus corresponds to the Catholicism which claims the whole man, and not his heart and conscience only. But what Catholicism claims, the Reformed Church renounces. The Reformed doctrine of God, with its blunt underscoring of God's uniqueness, sovereignty, and freedom, is only the positive expression of its renunciation of the medieval doctrine of man. In the process of controversy the gist of the Reformed doctrine was finally discovered to be a belief in divine providence and eternal election, but this belief did not at first (as it did later) so much represent interest in the conduct and destiny of *man* as it bespoke attention to the will and way of *God* with man.

The relation of this belief to the "scriptural principle" understood in terms of its positive content — *God is speaking!* — is evident. The old Reformed churchmen heard the voice of very God in the Scriptures — the voice of a God jealous in the Old Testament sense, who will not give his glory to another, the one, only, unique, almighty and all-glorious God who governs in unconditioned freedom, grants no hearings, but dispenses grace to man in perfect sovereignty; — and their passionate appeal to truth and authority and salvation as they were exclusively contained in this one book was simply a confession of *this* God. It was not by any means a "speculative" confession; it was concrete, empirical, answering to life. The question is whether we are ready to support the Reformed Reformation at this point.

It is thought — it is announced — that there is to be a controversy with "Rome." But let us not too quickly agree to it. Do we feel the renunciation of man to be a necessity? Is the pressure of our perception of God so overpowering that we cannot do otherwise than protest against Catholicism's Church of Man, and protest in behalf of God — rather, let us say, than in behalf of individualism or modern enlightenment? I dare say that more than one Reformed churchman, if called upon to justify his belief, would be likelier to present a Lutheran than a Reformed thesis — or still likelier, a thesis based upon a deteriorated form of the doctrine the Reformers all fought, Semi-Pelagianism. Is modern Protestantism of the Left *or* of the Right — with its broken relation to revelation, its fear of every either-or, its fundamental concession to the rights and dignities of man — anything more than a Catholicism tempered by negligible heresies? How fruitless, how mortifying, the expected controversy might be!

There must be some meaning in the fact that the same front which Zwingli and Calvin presented to Catholicism was defended by the fathers of Dort against the Arminians one hundred years later. But where today will not the careful observer find Arminian teachings taken for granted? I have no thought of repeating the *"Ite, ite, dimittimini!"* of the grim Bogermann of that day; but the question must be asked, if we feel ourselves honestly to be more closely related to the Arminians than to their hard-headed opponents, by what right and to what end we wish to take sides as Reformed churchmen against the Pope. Might not the controversy as well be omitted? Or, if we do not care to omit it finally, is it not fairly clear that the task of examining *ourselves* as to what we want and do not want will for a long time keep in the background any thought of a clash of wits with better-weaponed opponents?

Note that this is not a question of Zwingli's doctrine of providence, nor of Calvin's doctrine of election, nor of the Canons of Dort. It is the fundamental question whether we still own the opinion which brought the fathers to so sharp a break with the old church and at the same time to so unbelievably exclusive an insistence upon their doctrine of God; it is as to whether, for want of this opinion, it would not be better for us to admit to all that our position is untenable — as we long ago admitted it to ourselves. The question is whether we still see the same enemy that our fathers thought they saw, and whether we are armed with the same truth as they: the question is whether both that enemy and that truth are so vividly real to us that somehow, either in the words of the past or in our own, but in either case clearly and unambiguously and without shunning the necessary attack upon our *own Protestant* Church and *Protestant* Christianity, we *cannot stay from speaking*. The answer to this question will decide whether in the future there will be any first article of Reformed doctrine.

A second important part of the old Reformed literature is devoted to the controversy with *Lutheranism*. I am surprised to find so little attention given by historical research to answering the riddle why the old Lutheran and Reformed churchmen never disputed about the things which interest the two communions today: they were concerned neither with the relation between religion and morality nor with sociological ideals, but with subjects to our thinking as remote and even as abstruse as the Lord's supper and Christology. Is it not as if history wished to mock us by being silent just at the point where we should like to have information and by speaking just where we should prefer to hear nothing? For all that our fathers loved peace, for all that they were really no petty generation (and for all that the Thirty Years' War might be thought to have made them trouble enough!) they felt for two reasons that they must definitely separate themselves from the church established in the name, by the life, and upon the doctrines of Luther: first, they could not part with the belief that in the Lord's supper there is a double appropriation, a physical appropriation of the bread and wine and a spiritual appropriation of the true body and blood of the Lord, both united in the *unio sacramentalis* but *in* that union still remaining qualitively distinct; and, secondly, they could not disavow the kindred beliefs: that Christ, the man who was born, dead, buried, rose again, and ascended into heaven, is now no longer here but lives in heavenly glory in a world different from this — that without departing from his indissoluble *unio personalis* with the omnipresent Godhead, he still remains distinct in that union and is not a part of Godhead's omnipresence — and that therefore he is hidden from all thought, being approachable by faith alone and by faith only through the Spirit from above.

What does all this mean? The question of the nature of Christ's humanity and of the form of his presence in the Lord's supper leads directly to the problem of revelation understood specifically as God's communication of himself; it leads to our facing the reality of the relation between him and ourselves in the world. Is it possible, is it to any degree possible, for man to declare this reality clearly and logically in any word of his own? Yes, said Luther and his followers, it *must* be possible for man to do so, for otherwise the salvation of God which it predicates would become a question again. No, said the old Reformed churchmen, it may not and cannot be possible, else the question would arise whether the salvation here set forth were really the salvation of *God.* At least *two* human words are necessary to make known the real word of God. The founders of the Reformed churches agreed with the Lutherans that Christ was true man and true God in indissoluble unity, that God's revelation in him was really the eternal majesty become finite, temporal, and contingent, and that Christ's presence in the Lord's supper, that is, in the concentrated self-offering by which he witnessed to himself in his church, was really the presence of this God made flesh and blood. But they felt they could carry their agreement no further when the Lutherans, insisting upon the unity of God and man, arguing a *communicatio idiomatum,* and exaggerating the measure of the gift of grace in the sacrament, went so far in their own strength as to tear down that thin but real wall between God and the world which God both razes and reëstablishes in Christ. The Lutheran elimination of the quality of hiddenness from the Lord who had become man was, to the Reformed thinkers, tantamount to eliminating the miracle of grace and faith of Hebrews 11:1. The Lutherans made out of the indirect identity consummated only in God a *direct* identity between heavenly and earthly gifts, substance and symbol, witness and revelation. But this was to make revelation a kind of miracle that began and ended on earth, a piece of direct information, a religious fact; whereas, when it is genuine, revelation is always in part concealment. The idea of the notorious *Extra Calvinisticum* was that there is a divine reserve which, being maintained even in revelation, is not to be forgotten nor neglected.

On this ground at any rate the founders of the Reformed churches criticized the second article of doctrine as taught by Luther and his followers; and though their criticism may have been unfair, the Lutherans were not able to convince them that it was — any more than they themselves were able to convince the Lutherans that their own thesis was not a darkening of the reality of revelation, a hidden denial of the incarnation and of the self-offering of

the Revealer. So much by way of rough outline of
the facts.

The relation of these facts to the all-supreme
scriptural principle is evident in this case also.
What is the vast distance from us of Christ in
heaven, as the Reformed churches conceived it, but
an expression of the attribute of hiddenness and
transcendence which God maintains for our salvation, even when and just when he gives himself to
us in his word? And in the Lord's supper (precisely as in God's word, wherein also he surrenders
— and does not surrender — himself) is not the
Spirit which adds substance to the symbol and revelation to the witness of revelation, poured out
according to his own free pleasure — and yet not
poured *out?* May any man join together what God,
because he is and remains God, has put asunder?

It is evident that the church which arose out of
the idea that it is God who both gives and conceals
himself in the Scriptures could take no view of the
second article dissimilar to the one I have outlined.
But what of ourselves? Must we take this view as
well? The battle which took place about this article
has long since died away, not because it ended either
by victory or truce, but because — aside from the
stubborn protest of a few Lutheran "Outsiders" —
it wore itself out. Even in Germany, the chief
arena of the old feud, it was proclaimed ended by
command of the king of Prussia. Certainly none of
us will desire a return of the days of a Matthias Hoë
of Hoënegg. But whether or not we wholly enjoy

the denominational peace in Protestantism, as today
all proper men doubtless do, the question of our
duty will not down. What is the real cause of our
peace? Is it strength or weakness, insight or blind-
ness? Can the busy ingenuity of our historical theologians have been really insufficient for proving
what we have heard a thousand times, that these
were not mere empty disputes of the schools nor
contests in the splitting of hairs, but that they were
serious and even critical problems which, if our
churches are eventually not to mumble but to speak
the word which became flesh, must still be discussed
from both sides?

But who would say that we are prepared for
the discussion today? Doubtless the doctrines of
the fathers stand in need of supplementing, but is
it well that we should have become obtuse and indifferent to their virtues and ideals — their perseverance in the direction of a dialectic and indirect understanding of the revelation and self-
communication of God — their restraint, which in
the act of most intimate communion between God
and man still allowed God to be *God* and caused man
to remember he was dust and ashes — their protest
against the heaven-assailing aggressiveness in
which Luther tried to make news of a secret and
preached the real presence of the incarnated God in
the elements without the arresting But — their
recognition that in spite of all their faith, say rather
because of all their faith, they could not eliminate
nor deny the character in man which makes him a

stranger and a pilgrim — their ability in general to make haste, because they made it slowly, under the inspiration of their "Seek those things which are above"? If we do not revive our interest in these qualities of the fathers, how can we talk about the "cultivation of a stronger Reformed-Church consciousness?" We might as well all become Lutherans.

But that we cannot do. It is true that uncertainty prevails in the Lutheran communion also, and that they have crypto-Calvinists and even crypto-Zwinglians among them in fairly large numbers — at least in respect of the question of the Lord's supper, — but the aspect of truth which their church traditionally represents, in distinction to the Reformed, is in no way modified by those circumstances; and we must not give up the struggle (as with an opponent who is also a friend, and properly a friend) to declare truth accurately — even though today, if we may judge from what our nearest Lutheran friends are saying, there is none of the old Lutheran directness, Titanism, or over-confidence left to oppose. It is not a question of the continuation of a quarrel — we shall all heartily approve the mildness which has come over the theological manner — it is a question of the continuation of a discussion, but of a discussion not about formulas but about facts, not necessarily about Christology and the Lord's supper but about the problem of contingent revelation, which is today more urgent than ever before. What pulpit is *not* concerned with it? We may, we must, address ourselves to it, and not in a haphazard, but in our specifically Reformed fashion; and some day, if the old discernment becomes new in us, we may reëstablish for ourselves a theology of the second article, which today is sadly lacking.

At the heart of the Reformed confessions — we come now to the subject of the third and fourth books of Calvin's Institutes — there is a definite conception of what practical, personal Christianity stands for in the world. It is a conception uncontroversial but positive. Nothing could be further from the truth than the assumption that the Reformed fathers, because of their absorption in the pure *gloria Dei* and *meditatio futurae vitae*, failed to give serious attention to the situation of man in time. On the contrary, they could not escape doing so. Upon the shoulders of each of them, as they set out, was laid, like a block of stone, the self-manifestation of God; and in consequence the impact of their feet upon the ground wanted nothing of firmness. They did not too noisily and emphatically commend as God's earth this valley of the shadow in which we walk, for they knew that the world as the creation of *God* — like the true humanity of Christ — is hidden from us and is evident only to the eye of the spirit. But it is just because they possessed the humbling insight that in this valley we can be happy only by hoping, that they were prepared to move forward here with certainty.

Within the ensemble of the Reformation, Re-

formed churchmanship represents a resolute turning away from the contemplation of God (which in
this temporal realm can be only one thing and not
everything) to life, to man, and to the world of man.
Lutheranism turned away, too, but if its peculiar
genius is represented in the Augsburg Confession,
which was duly approved by Luther himself, we
cannot mistake the fact that its emphasis lies elsewhere, and that its turning back to life is always
something secondary, something merely stated and
not inevitable. To the question, *Quis humanae vitae
praecipuus est finis,* Zwingli and Calvin respond,
The knowledge of the divine majesty. This seems
a remote and surprising enough answer for these
erstwhile humanists to make. Calvin puts it in his
catechism in the simple words, To know God; but we
must see that this overpowering knowledge entails
in specie real faith, obedience, prayer, and thanksgiving. One might say that a whole program for
living is set forth there, a program almost painfully
precise in the lines of activity it exacts. It is obviously because the Reformed thinkers definitely took
this question, rather than the specifically monastic
question about grace, as their point of departure,
that they had to meet in the Scriptures that unapproachable God who is strange to this world and to
this life, being known only in the realm of truth —
that God before whom man must finally stand subor-
dinate in a creaturehood which may not be relin-
quished and may not be disregarded. But it was
the knowledge of just *that* God which prepared them

to take the genuine human earthly question, What are we to do? in earnest — Zwingli in happy earnest, Calvin in bitter earnest.

There is no great significance to be attached to this nuance of difference between Zwingli and Calvin, though Calvin's somber manner doubtless expresses more. The God they knew was such as to cause them both to face life without illusion.

So they gave to faith a no less central place than Luther gave — being unmistakably beholden to him here. But the Reformed faith differs from the Lutheran in that the essence of it is not *fiducia*, though that is part of it: the essence of it is that it is *God's gift*. Obedience to the demand of this same God therefore goes along with faith as a primary fact of no less importance. The laborious discussions in the Augsburg Confession as to whether and how far faith and good works are compatible with each other are beside the point for Reformed doctrine; here faith has not, as in Lutheranism, the character of a hypostasis mediating between God and man; here all of Christianity, including faith, is a human totality pointing to a Creator and Redeemer; here the final interest is in God and only in God, the Giver *and* Demander, and not — as the simpler and more satisfying Lutheranism would have it — in faith and only in faith.

We have here, on the one hand, a belief that the act of faith is relative, and, on the other, a belief that works of atonement, if equally relative, are a serious need — being not only steps toward faith but acts of response to the presence of God, necessary in themselves, though in no way meritorious. There is therefore abiding and positive meaning in the Old Testament with its never arriving but forever wandering patriarchs, its Moses who preaches the Gospel but preaches the Gospel as Law, its prophets who are by no means concerned only with the "inner life" of the individual but also with the politics of their nation as well, its David, in whom Calvin recognized another Elijah and saw rather a prototype of himself than of Jesus. The Reformed fathers foresaw no human conditions in which faith would have been so perfectly realized in love that the law could be suspended and all action take rise in freedom. With them ethics was grounded not upon love but upon obeying the commandments as *God's* commandments. The Law keeps its place beside the Gospel as another, a second, reality, equally true and commanding and necessary because the one God stands behind both, because the one Holy Spirit imparts both to men. The sinner's felt certainty of justification before God does not follow from his striving for salvation (for no iota of righteousness will be imputed to him for that); the certainty and the striving go together, however, for there is no such thing as justification without salvation. Operating in parallel they are the work of the spirit of the Lord, whose glory is made evident in the very fact that *both* faith *and* obedience exist, and both as a response to *his* call. And both, in the last and most accurate analysis, are *his* work.

It was an outside and apocryphal interest which won the day when in the second and third generations (with Beza first, if I am not mistaken, and later and above all with the English Presbyterians) the question of the "assurance of salvation" took the chief place and became regulative for the whole of the Reformed doctrine. The Reformed Christian of the first generation was a fighter who had no time nor interest for this sorry consideration, because he knew that he was lifted up by the hand of the Lord. "Their salvation," said Calvin of the elect who form the true church, "is supported upon a foundation so secure and solid that, even if the whole world-machine collapsed, it could not be shattered nor overturned. For it rests upon the election of God and could no more change nor fail than his eternal wisdom. However, therefore, they may tremble, as they are wrenched hither or thither or even dashed to the ground, they cannot perish, because the Lord sustains them in his hand."

Upon the rock of this divine and invisible church of the elect, the human and visible church, the church for action and enterprise, is to be built in fear and trembling. It will be constituted not only by the true preaching of the word of God and the pure power of the sacrament instituted of the Lord but also by the discipline in which it holds its members. The interpretation of the *communio sanctorum* in the Augsburg Confession, which rejects human sainthood, was too earthy for Calvin, who consciously parted from it without dreaming, on the other extreme, of the idea of any church of sinless saints, any community of perfect love. There *is* a holiness of the individual and the community *below* which is not to be mistaken for the holiness of God *above*. It is not an affair of good works, it is not a bridge into heaven, not a union with divinity, not an anticipation of the final state. It is rather a signpost which points toward the millennium — that millennium which we do not seem able to argue out of the Bible. It is a demonstration which we make to the glory of God as *peregrinantes* and which we may not abate, however infirm our desire and meager our accomplishment; for the goal, the *vita futura,* is ever before us.

The Scriptural principle understood in terms of its content is obviously the key even to this third article of doctrine, concerning the Holy Spirit and its works. The fathers conceived that principle as referring to the place and task assigned to man by the word of God; they conceived it as meaning that man should *know God*, as Calvin so plainly put it. But to these people, who from the beginning approached the Bible — and the Bible to them was the whole Bible — with a more than theoretical interest, the idea of knowing God developed a variety of inferences — inferences related to each other as parallel lines which meet only in the infinite. It was an urgent fact that man should become, be, and remain a tree planted by the rivers of water; but it was no less urgent that he should bring forth his fruit in his season. To this end they commended the Epistle to the Romans but did not despise that of James as an "epistle of straw." The heart of man, and even of believing man, can grasp faith and works as a unity only in so far as he perceives God's sovereignty in both. What appears as the duality of human action and experience is grounded and articulated in God and in God alone. But in God it *is* grounded — and consequently for human life the duality, or the variety, has a basis in ultimate value — and consequently for Calvin there must be obedience as well as faith, prayer as well as obedience, a visible community giving thanks to God as well as the invisible company of the elect. These are all one to God, but they are none the less, therefore, to be taken seriously by us men as separate necessities, each occupying its particular place in the logic of Christian life. It is sufficient that man in the contradictions of his existence, in the different relations in which *he* stands to God, should yet enjoy a unified life by virtue of the fact that as an actual creation of the Creator and as a true member of the body of Christ, he stands in his several relations — humility and exaltation, unrest and peace, assurance and apprehension, illumination and correction — before *God*. So the fathers understood the answer of the old and new covenants to the question as to the end of the *vita humana*.

And what shall *we* say? Here if anywhere we might think we were ready to join hands with the fathers understandingly and joyously. But here if anywhere we must conduct ourselves with the independence and dispassionateness demanded by Reformed doctrine.

The whole inspiration and strength of the Reformed idea depends upon the fundamental separation between the heavenly and the earthly solutions of the problem of life, between unity and variety, between fulfillment and promise; and it depends upon one's courageously looking at the second solution in the light of the first and yet (in spite — no, by virtue — of their separation!) taking the second seriously in its own right. The premises of Reformed Doctrine are that Reformed *awareness* to which the whole *vita humana* is a real and limitless and unsolved problem, and that Reformed *readiness* to accept an answer to that problem freely and without prejudice from the whole Bible — in a word, that Reformed *universalism,* that intensive universalism which consists in feeling the compulsion and having the daring to go the whole way into the world with God. But the ultimate premise even here is the majesty of God's utterance, which comes through Scripture and Spirit to the present generation, to ourselves.

Without consideration of these premises, say rather this premise, how foolish and dangerous it is to desire to repeat the words of the fathers! — even to desire it never so sincerely, passionately, and confidently. The fathers' words cannot become truth and life and therefore a *way* until and unless they rise again out of the same premise as before; and then they not only *may* but must be spoken. They were spoken not in the resplendent dawn but in the somber twilight of the Reformation, when the shadows were growing longer and it was becoming certain that not all the dreams of the dawn would be realized. Into that situation, into the grim renunciation it calls for, into that "sacred inheritance of the past," it is not so easy for us to enter as the orators at our conventions would seem to think.

We all live more or less in the narrower, more one-sidedly "religious" spirituality of Lutheranism, which though clearly less equal to the problem of actual life is therefore incontestably more emotionally, logically, and theologically satisfying. Lutheranism is indubitably sib to the "German soul" and when slightly rationalized admirably meets the so-called religious needs of the average church congregation, not only inside of Germany but outside as well. And we ministers, above all, feel ourselves continually attracted as by a magnet to its (at least apparent) centrality. It is therefore well worthwhile for us to know what it stands for; and to many a Reformed churchman there would be no better counsel to give than that he should at first become fundamentally and really Lutheran, as Zwingli and Calvin were.

The decisive step out beyond the Lutheranism of the Augsburg Confession — I am not yet clear whether or not this would really be a step back to the *younger* Luther — is a hazardous one. It leads into a wilderness where not only privations but also temptations wait. For where the answer to the question of human life is drawn so definitely from the word of God, it not only liberates knowledge but occasions the gravest misunderstandings and abuses. Everything, then, depends upon our holding fast inexorably to the consciousness that even the question of human life is a question put to man by *God*. It is not easy actually to hold fast to it. Zwingli and Calvin themselves came within a hair's breadth of letting it go in preaching and practicing their own doctrine of the spirit. And after them, the sovereignty of God fell on evil days and even in the Reformed churches became the sovereignty of man. And how can we hope to escape the curse of Pharisaism and all the horrors, great and small, connected with it, if we attempt to arm ourselves with the spirituality without the spirit of the fathers? For the sake of the pure Reformed doctrine, I repeat, let us have no experiments in the imitation of Calvin! They can bring us only evil. Μὴ παιδὶ μάχαιραν is the word, until we are again bold enough to pick up the lost clue.

Is there not need for an extension of Reformed doctrine in the direction indicated by this all-important theme? Is not the chief demand of theology coming to be a relentless renunciation of too self-centered a religiousness, too much logic, and too much unity (God having reserved the perfect theology to himself)? Is not the most timely message of salvation for the peoples of the declining West coming to be a declaration of their need for the Gospel *and* the Law? Is not the reasonable, not to say the really inevitable, theory of the church coming to be that communities are holy when they are constituted by a common apprehension of the judgment of God? The teaching of the Reformed doctrine of the Holy Spirit will become for us a commanding task when in *our* way amidst *our* surroundings we witness to God's revelation as the fathers did in *their* way amidst *their* surroundings. Until we do that we can hardly hope to attack our task with power, and the Reformed doctrine of the Spirit must remain what it now is: a corpse, say rather, a ghost.

I should be delighted now, as is the custom in such addresses as this, to close with a joyous trumpet-blast. But even in conclusion I cannot represent the situation except as we must see it today: everywhere great vision nourished upon history, but little actual and convincing insight derived from reality — excellent pathfinders but few passable paths — good hope but little present strength to bring forth — and in our own midst, a supreme weakness. Are we to call this guilt or fate? The "Doctrinal Task of the Reformed Churches" today has reached the point perhaps where we may soberly and seriously call our weakness guilt and not fate. If we are willing to do so, and if we earnestly desire and call upon the creative spirit to come and breathe upon this valley full of bones, we shall at least have begun to take possession of the inheritance of the fathers which today seems so far removed from us.

VIII

THE CHRISTIAN'S PLACE IN SOCIETY

I.

THE thought of the Christian's place in society fills one with a curious blend of hope and questioning.

The Christian's place in society! Society is not left wholly to itself. It is not left wholly without urgings and restraints. Married life and the family, civilization and the economic order, art and science, the state, the party, and international relations not only take their familiar course in accordance with the laws of their own logical inner workings but are also at least modified by another factor full of promise. That their familiar course is a wrong one is plainer to our eyes than formerly. The catastrophe from which we are emerging but are not yet free has brought this fact for many, though not for all, into devastating clearness. If we had our first wish, would we not turn away from life and society in utter scepticism and discouragement? But whither? From life and society one cannot

This address was delivered at the Conference on Religion and Social Relations (die religiös-soziale Konferenz) held at Tambach in September, 1919.

turn away. They surround us on all sides; they set
questions for us; they confront us with decisions.
We must hold our ground. The fact that today our
eyes are opened wider to life's realities is the very
reason why we long for something else. We should
like to be out of this society — and in another. But
this is only a wish; we are still painfully aware that
in spite of all the social changes and revolutions,
everything is as it was of old. If out of this situation we ask, Watchman, what of the night? the only
response which carries any promise is, *"The Christian."*

Here is a new element in the midst of the old, a
truth in the midst of error and lies, a righteousness
in the midst of a sea of unrighteousness, a spirituality within all our crass materialistic tendencies,
a formative life-energy within all our weak, totter-
ing movements of thought, a unity in a time which
is out of joint.

The Christian: we must be agreed that we do *not*
mean *the Christians,* not the multitude of the baptized, nor the chosen few who are concerned with
Religion and Social Relations, nor even the cream of
the noblest and most devoted Christians we might
think of: the Christian is *the Christ.* The Christian
is that within us which is not ourself but Christ in
us. "Christ in us" understood in its whole Pauline depth is not a psychic condition, an affection
of the mind, a mental lapse, or anything of the sort,
but is a presupposition of life. "Over us," "behind us," and "beyond us" are included in the

meaning of "in us." And "Christ in us" understood in its whole Pauline breadth is a warning that
we shall do well not to build again the fence which
separated the chosen from the rest — Jews from
Gentiles and so-called Christians from so-called
non-Christians. The community of Christ is a
building open on every side, for Christ died for all
— even for the folk outside. There is in us, over
us, behind us, and beyond us a consciousness of the
meaning of life, a memory of our own origin, a
turning to the Lord of the universe, a critical No
and a creative Yes in regard to all the content of
our thought, a facing away from the old and toward
the new age — whose sign and fulfillment is the
cross.

That is Christ in us. But *is* Christ in us? Is
Christ even in present-day society? We hesitate to
answer and we know why we hesitate. But whence
do we come by the right to say he is not? Christ
the Saviour is *here,* else the question would not
have been provoked — the question which is the hidden meaning of all the movements of our era and
which brings us together for these days as strangers
and yet as friends. There are questions we could
not ask if the answers were not already to hand,
questions which we could not even approach without the courage of the Augustinian thought, Thou
wouldst not seek Me hadst thou not already found
Me! We must acknowledge this courage as our
real possession. In doing so, we acknowledge
Christ, his present, and his future. But if Christ

is in us, then society, in spite of its being on the wrong course, is not forsaken of God. The "image of the invisible God," the "firstborn of every creature" in us (Col. 1:15), indicates a goal and a future. We think of the leaven which a woman took and hid in three measures of meal, till the whole was leavened. Paul called this "mystery among the Gentiles" "the hope of glory" (Col. 1:27). So: we bid you hope.

But our theme has, alas, another aspect, and it is doubtless this one which was chiefly in mind when it was chosen. The Christian's place — in society! How these two magnitudes fall apart! How abstract they are to each other! How foreign, how almost fantastic the great syntheses of the Epistle to the Colossians seem to us today! And why?

What does "the Christian" suggest to us? What *must* it suggest to us? It can suggest only a holy domain set apart by itself,— whether we explain it more in terms of metaphysics or psychology. Christians seem to us to be special people apart from other people, Christianity seems a special fact apart from other facts, Christ a special manifestation apart from other manifestations. The complaint of philosophy in regard to religion's arrogant aloofness is not new, and neither is the theological argument which provokes it.

Today there are many, taught by the experience of the times, who perceive behind this religious aloofness mere religious indigence. And the fact that the indigence seems unavoidable, and that even philosophy has not spoken the word to overcome it, is leading us to believe that the meaning of so-called religion is to be found in its relation to actual life, to life in society, and not in its being set apart from it. Holiness in itself is no holiness whatever. From the safe and once lauded domain of religion we are beginning to look out on the world with real longing; for we suspect, and even many theologians are beginning to suspect, that there can be no inside to that domain so long as there is no outside.

We may well look out and over; but the setting apart of the religious domain is not done away by our discovery that it really ought not to be. The relation between the "Christ in us" and the world is not merely a matter of opening the sluices and allowing the ready water to stream over the thirsty land. Immediately to hand we have all those combinations — "social-Christian," "social-evangelical," "social-religious" (christlich-sozial, evangelisch-sozial, religios-sozial) and the like — but it is highly questionable whether the hyphens we draw with such intellectual courage do not really make dangerous short circuits. Clever enough is the paradox that the service of God is or must become the service of man; but that is not the same as saying that our precipitate service of man, even when it is undertaken in the name of the purest love, becomes by that happy fact the service of God. We may well remember that according to the gospels the seed is the word and the field is the world, but just what is the word? Which of us has it? May we not well shrink from the task of becoming sowers — from the task which at first brought consternation to men like Moses, Isaiah, and Jeremiah? Is our swift readiness to plant the divine seed in life more fitting than their hesitation to do so? Jonah's flight from the presence of the Lord was something more than an expression of the aloofness of religion. He knew that what is called for in a prophet is more than a bit of experience, judgment, and good will.

The Divine is something whole, complete in itself, a kind of new and different something in contrast to the world. It does not permit of being applied, stuck on, and fitted in. It does not permit of being divided and distributed, for the very reason that it is more than religion. It does not passively permit itself to be used: it overthrows and builds up as it wills. It is complete or it is nothing. Where then has the world of God any available connection with our social life? How do we come to act as if it had?

Today for the sake of social democracy, or pacifism, or the youth movement, or something of the sort — as yesterday it would have been for the sake of liberal culture or our countries, Switzerland or Germany — we may very well succeed, if the worst comes to the worst, in *secularizing* Christ. But the thing is hateful to us, is it not? We do not wish to betray him another time.

So we find ourselves in perplexity, needing Christ and yet not knowing how to bring him into society

— to help us to *do* the things which vision and good will urge upon us and to *leave undone* those things which we ought not to do! How difficult it is, with pure heart and in awe of the Holy One, to take even the shortest step with Christ into society! How unapproachably the Divine, when it is really the Divine, veils itself from the human, to which today we would so gladly unite it!

And how dangerous, too, among the questions, cares, and excitements of society, to invite the presence of God! What would it mean if we gave up trying to treat with him merely in a special religious domain and invited his presence among us *in earnest;* and what, if we did not?

God is in truth to be had less cheaply than ever today. We shall do well to take this thought very seriously as we consider what should be done. "Which of you, intending to build a tower, sitteth 'not down first and counteth the cost, whether he have sufficient to finish it?" (Luke 14:28) This is one side.

And on the other side we have *society,* also a whole in itself, broken within, perhaps, but outwardly solid — without connections with the kingdom of heaven. Where is God in all the human? Where is the meaning in all the meaninglessness, the original purpose in the degeneration, the wheat in the midst of all the weeds? Dust thou art and unto dust thou shalt return. Is this not the right verdict concerning humanity, and is it not humanity's own creed? Here is another instance of a setting apart which, as we who endure the present days know well enough, leads only to bitter pains. All that is within us revolts against the idea of the autonomy of culture, the state, and economic life, which was exploited so exhaustively before the war.

So readily, so very readily, would we today conceive society in Christ, renew it in Christ, and, as you say in your program, "use the thought-forms of Jesus as the law for every economic, racial, national, and international order!"

If, to such an end, we had only the transfiguring optimism of a Richard Rothe! But there is no going back in that direction.

Neither, apparently, is there any going forward; for the way forward seems to lead to Friedrich Naumann, who himself once started from this very point. Our serious use of "the thought-forms of Jesus" is prevented at the very start by the brutal fact that the autonomy of social life is by no means done away by our having become thoroughly tired of it. It is with us: it is actual: even in this time of revolution it is increasing. Once we wished to have it so, and now we must. At the beginning of the century, Naumann and his disciples, with the courage of despair or a flair for esthetics, placed a religious halo over society's acting as a law unto itself. We may now remove the halo, but we do not thereby alter the state of society. If today, with all propriety, though to our grief, the Holy asserts its rights over against the profane, the profane asserts its rights over against the Holy. Society is now really ruled by its own logos; say rather by a whole pantheon of its own hypostases and powers. We may compare ourselves to the best and most spiritual thinkers of the Hellenistic or even the pre-Reformation period; we are beginning to suspect that the idols are vain, but their demonic influence upon our lives is not thereby allayed. For it is one thing to entertain critical doubts regarding the god of this world, and another thing to perceive the δύναμις, the meaning and might of the living God who is building a new world. And yet without that perception the idea of "social Christianity" is sheer nonsense.

There is always the possibility of patching the old garment with pieces torn from a new one; we may always, to change the figure, attempt to furnish worldly society with an ecclesiastical cupola or wing and so render unto Caesar the things which are Caesar's and unto God the things that are God's according to the old misunderstanding of Jesus' words. The attempt of the Christian Middle Ages to *clericalize* society may perhaps be undertaken once more and once more meet with the success it deserves. Already there are signs in Protestant circles of a disposition to make the experiment. Let us establish a new church with democratic manners and socialistic motives! Let us build community houses, push our young people's program, organize discussion groups, plan special services of music! Let us step down from the high buskin of the clergyman and invite the laity into the pulpit. Let us go the old way with fresh inspiration — the way that begins with a fervor for social work and with deadly certainty ends in the liberalism of Naumann. For all our new patches, the old garment still remains the old garment.

Surely we shall resist this temptation to betray society; it is no easier to bring it to Christ than Christ to it. For it is God's help that we still have really in mind; and we shall deceive society about it if we set to work building churches and chapels and do not learn to wait upon him in a wholly new way. Let us not be lulled to sleep by the siren tones of modern ecclesiasticism; but let us not be surprised to find that our proposed *omnia instaurare in Christo* in face of the naturally developed and immutably continuing solidarity of society is for us an act of biting upon granite! Let us withstand the new temptation of ecclesiasticism! But the more bravely we do so, the more mightily the giant evils of the day against which we have come up to do battle will stand and defy us.

God alone can save the world. When we approach the execution of our program we shall not be able, as the familiar warning goes, to reckon too soberly with "reality"; and there is good reason why we should not, *rebus sic stantibus* — our ideals being impossible and our goals unattainable. This is the other side.

————

So this is what I find in our theme: on the one hand a great promise, a light from above which is shed upon our situation, but on the other hand an unhappy separation, a thorough-going opposition between two dissimilar magnitudes. We must keep both clearly in sight. This is our hope and our need both as Christians and as members of society. But do not expect me to provide a solution! None of us may boast a solution. There is only one solution, and that is in God himself. Our task is only the candid, absolutely thorough, and — I should like to venture the expression — *priestly agitation* of this hope and this need, by means of which the way to the solution, which is in God, may be made clearer to us. It is obvious that all I can offer you today is a statement as to the *points of departure* from which this agitation, as the one thing needful, must proceed. My description of them will be inadequate, but I am at least sure that those of which I should like to speak are the necessary ones. As a matter of fact there are no others.

II.

Before taking up the main question of the hope and the need indicated in our theme, let us note what our general standpoint must be — remembering that it is not a new standpoint on our part, for we assumed it when the situation first became a problem for us.

"Standpoint," however, is hardly the right word. For our position is really an instant in a *movement*, and any view of it is comparable to the momentary view of a bird in flight. Aside from the movement it is absolutely meaningless, incomprehensible, and impossible. By "movement," to be sure, I do not mean either the socialistic movement, the social movement in religion, or the general, somewhat problematical, movement of so-called Christianity. I mean a movement from above, a movement from a third dimension, so to speak, which transcends and yet penetrates all these movements and gives them their inner meaning and motive; a movement which has neither its origin nor its aim in space, in time, or in the contingency of things, and yet is not a movement apart from others: I mean the movement of God in history or, otherwise expressed, the movement of God in consciousness, the movement whose power and import are revealed in the resurrection of Jesus Christ from the dead. This must be the gist of all our thinking about the Christian's place in society, whether that thinking arises from hope, from need, or from both alike.

Be assured that you will have the weakest part of my exposition at just this all-important point! Theoretical discussion always involves something uncertain, impracticable, and dangerous. Almost unavoidably it ends in the ridiculous attempt to draw the bird flying. Almost unavoidably it ends in making the movement a theme *in itself,* a fact *in itself,* entirely apart from the motion. Kant had good reason for guarding so anxiously lest his critique of reason should be taken as a new philosophy rather than as a prolegomenon. And the very way in which

his warning has been neglected is evidence of the
danger we ourselves face. A critique of reason is
complete only when it issues in applied science; God
comes in history only through deeds and evidences;
he manifests himself in consciousness only through
compelling, revealing, immediately self-confirming
insights and communications — else what is the
meaning of all the words about the Word? Life can
be lived only by being lived. The philosopher has
his difficulty when he attempts to explain the idea
of a First Cause in which consciousness and action,
future and present, are one. We have the same difficulty when we attempt to testify to the reality of
the living God. Any one who heard our testimony
might well cry, if he dared, "Put me then in the
power of the First Cause! Place me within the
reality of God!" And there, at the very outset, we
should realize our vast inadequacy. What we are
now trying to speak of must be produced, brought
out, made actual — else it is not what we are trying
to speak of. "The word of God is quick, and powerful, and sharper than any two-edged sword, piercing . . . " (Heb. 4:12). But what man can avail
of himself either to pronounce or understand this
quick, powerful, sharp, piercing word of God? I
could no more succeed in speaking it to you than you
could succeed in hearing it. To be sure, we have
always the full right and ability to declare our longing for it with appropriate religious assurance. But
that is a pleasure we shall forgo in the interest of
something larger; for it is better for us to be con-

scious of our primary inadequacy than to surrender
ourselves to a religious mood which, despite all our
sincerity, might again veil from us the real situation.

What I must give you here I therefore cannot
give except a miracle should happen. I cannot convince you by assertion that we are concerned with
something very great. There is nothing to do but
to paraphrase actuality in dead words. Do you,
however, remember that what I am attempting to
speak of is the real, the flying, bird and not the
painted picture-puzzle which I actually lay before
you. Come with me as I also seek to go with you,
as far as it is given us both to take our way.

Our concern is *God*, the movement originating in
God, the motion which *he* lends us — and it is not
religion. Hallowed be *thy* name. *Thy* kingdom
come. *Thy* will be done. The so-called "religious
experience" is a wholly derived, secondary, fragmentary form of the divine. Even in its highest and
purest examples, it is form and not content. Our
interpretation of the Bible and of the history of
the church has too long maintained the formal point
of view. The church has too long directed its
efforts to the consideration of types of godliness.
We shall turn away today entirely from form. The
Immediate, the Original, is never experienced as
form. "Experience" is only a *reference* to the
Original, to God. The new life revealed in Jesus is
not a new form of godliness. That is the reason
why Paul and John are interested not in the per-

sonal life of the so-called historical Jesus but only
in his resurrection. And that is the reason why the
synoptic accounts of Jesus can be really understood
only with Bengel's insight: *spirant resurrectionem.*
The Catholic Middle Ages and the Reformation
understood this in some measure. It remained for
pietism, Schleiermacher, and modern Christianity
consciously to read the New Testament Gospel backwards. We must win again the mighty sense of
reality in which Paul is one with Plato and the
prophets. Christ is the absolutely *new from above;*
the way, the truth, and the life of *God* among men;
the Son of Man, in whom humanity becomes aware
of its *immediacy* to God.

But keep your distance! No mental apprehension
of the *form* of this truth, however subtle that apprehension may be, can replace or obscure the true
transcendence of its *content.* The step from the
experience of the Lord to the experience of *Baal* is
a short one. The religious and the sexual are close
akin. As evidence of the purity and superiority
of the new life in which we find ourselves and as an
aid to the deepest understanding of ourselves, let me
lay stress upon the fact that this new life is not our
best understanding and experience of God, not our
best godliness, not an experience apart from others.
Let me speak as abstractly and theoretically as possible, that all emotional misunderstandings may be
eliminated: this new life is that from the third
dimension which penetrates and even passes through
all our forms of worship and our experiences; it is

the world of God breaking through from its self-contained holiness and appearing in secular life; it is the bodily resurrection of Christ from the dead. To participate in its meaning and power is to discover a new motivation.

We must return to that reserve maintained by the divine over against the human — though it must now have become clear to all that the separation of the two cannot be ultimate, for then God would not be God. There *must still* be a way from there to here. And with this "must" and this "still" we confess to the miracle of the *revelation* of God. However much the holy may frighten us back from its unattainable elevation, no less are we impelled to venture our lives upon it immediately and completely. We listen to the voice which says, Draw not nigh hither: put off thy shoes from off thy feet, for the place whereon thou standest is holy ground. And with Moses, we are afraid to look upon God. But we hear the voice continue, "I have surely seen the affliction of my people which are in Egypt, and have heard their cry, and am come down to deliver them out of the hand of the Egyptians"; and we perceive that the first forbiddance must have been only to complete and clarify the final message. Isaiah, also, and Jonah finally had to prove their devotion to the holy by daring to relate it directly to the secular life of man. The *mysterium tremendum* phase, which comes first, finally ceases, and with it that dread of the divine which is dread and dread alone. The kernel breaks through its hard shell.

The message itself, the thought of what God's "coming down" means for us, the decision to venture with him, is suffused with a dread which conquers *mere* dread. This is not the act of man but the act of God in man. And for this reason God in *consciousness* is actually God in *history* — and no mere figment of thought. God causes something to happen, a miracle in our eyes.

A *new* possibility and reality, as it were, open up to man. Once we are conscious of the life in life, we continue no longer in the land of the dead, in a life whose forms unhappily allow us to miss the very meaning of life — that is, its connection with its creative origin. We perceive the Wholly Other, the eternity of the divine life; and we cannot escape the thought that for us also eternal life can alone be called and really be "life." The Wholly Other in God — itself resisting all secularization, all mere being put to use and hyphenated — drives us with compelling power to look for a basic, ultimate, original correlation between our life and that wholly other life. We would not die but live. It is the living *God* who, when he meets us, makes it inevitable for us to believe in our own life.

Will the creation of this new life, in which God makes us believe, consist in the last end simply in the annulment of the creaturehood in which, in contrast to the life of God, we live our life on earth? Fundamentally, this is exactly what we mean. "We wait for the redemption of our body" (Rom. 8: 23). And however remote the annulment may be, it yet

influences our life on earth in every part, and the
light which rises in our soul with our growing perception of God will less and less allow us at any
point to come to an agreement with the ultimately
mortal character of our existence here.

With the insight that the divine breaks through
into the human it becomes clear on the other hand
that our human independence of the divine is not
ultimate. The unrest which God gives us must
bring us into critical contact with "life" — critical
being understood in its largest sense. To the miracle
of revelation corresponds the miracle of *faith*. God
in *consciousness,* in this aspect also, is God in *history* — no mere imaginative idea but a new compulsion from above. However clearly we may see
that the brutal prerequisites of social life — the
state and the economic system, art and science, and
even the more primitive necessities of eating, drink-
ing, sleeping, and growing old — all have their own
laws of mass and movement; however definitely we
may reckon upon the necessity of enduring these
laws still; however certainly we may be convinced
of the absolute folly of biting upon granite — one
thing is still more certain, more serious, and clearer: we can no longer submit ourselves to these laws
as *ultimate* independent authorities. And the reason is *not only* because we have been shamed into
becoming wise by the outward events of our times;
it is *not only* because we have become spiritually
tired, tired to the point of exhaustion, of our pantheon of independent divinities; it is *not only* be-

cause after our drunkenness we find ourselves
in skepticism and disillusion regarding the
κοσμοκράτορες τοῦ σκότους τούτου (Eph. 6:12) —
for there is nothing here of the meaning and power
of the resurrection. It is *rather* because our souls
have awakened to the consciousness of their immediacy to God.

And this means an immediacy of all things, relations, orders, and forms to God, an immediacy lost,
gone, and needing to be won again. When the *soul*
remembers that its origin is in God, it places the
origin of *society* there as well. When it comes to
itself, it finds a sense of *life* everywhere; and this
with the consciousness of its own participation in
the world's guilt and the world's responsibility. It
accepts for itself the judgment under which the
world stands, and takes the world as a burden upon
itself. There can be no awakening of the soul which
is anything but a "sympathetic shouldering of the
cares of the whole generation." This awakening of
the soul is the vivifying movement of God into history or into consciousness, the movement of Life
into life. When we are under its power, we can
but issue a categorical challenge to all the authorities in life; we cannot but test them by that which
alone can be authoritative. All life must be measured by Life. An independent life aside from Life
is not life but death. Dead are all things which
claim to be more than material, which claim a kind
of reality in themselves. Dead is our personal life
— were it even the noblest, finest, and most pious —

when it does not have its beginning in the fear of God. Dead are all mere parts however ecstatically we may hold them together in our hands; if the spiritual bond is wanting, all is wanting. Dead is everything which has only an inner side as well as everything which has only an outer side. Dead are all "things in themselves" (Dinge an sich), all the heres and theres, all the onces and nows, all the thises and thats which are not united to each other. Dead are all mere facts. Dead is all metaphysics. Dead were God himself if he moved his world only from the outside, if he were a "thing in himself" and not the One in all, the Creator of all things visible and invisible, the beginning and the ending. We are engaged in life's revolt against the powers of death that inclose it. We cannot longer allow ourselves to be *wholly* deceived by the theories with which those powers have surrounded themselves and by the facts which seem to point to their authority. There is something fundamental in us that denies these powers.

This then is our situation. Does it not cast upon the problems of the day a light unusually clear and significant if not new? Life has risen up against life in death. Our task is not to read something into the strangely confused and ambiguous movements of our time but rather to understand them sympathetically, hopefully, and in their deepest meaning. Let us not be deceived by the fact that the present dissolution of so many "things in themselves," so many "things for their own sake," threatens *here*

to be halted by the interdict of the old and *there* to
be formed into new and godless materialisms in
place of the old.　Let us see what the real situation
is: that what is being called in question today at
more than one point and very seriously is the
deadly isolation of the human from the divine.
However we may be justified in wagging our heads
over modern youth's fantastic drive for freedom,
it is certain that our final attitude cannot be surprise and opposition; the youth movement of the
present time in all its phases is directed against
authority for its own sake, and whoever desires to
be an educator today must, in spite of Foerster,
stand in principle upon the side of our young
people.　However dangerous to the things we hold
most sacred the present plainly observable dissolution of the family may be, we cannot, for all our
astonishment and opposition, ignore the point that
in the last analysis this is an attack upon the *family
for its own sake;* and the family has been in truth
not a holy thing but the voracious idol of the erstwhile middle classes.　However strong our aver-
sion may be to the work of the modern expression-
istic artists, it is more than clear that for these men
the chief concern is the essence, the content, the
referring of the beautiful to life's unity, in contrast to that *art for its own sake* which prevailed
during the last generation, but which, after all, can
cite precedent with certainty in neither Raphael nor
Dürer.　For this tendency as well we must spare
more than a shake of the head.　And if today in all

seriousness, for our existence depends upon it, we join in the cry, "Work! It is work that Europe needs!" we need not be surprised and indignant, at least not to the depth of our souls, if the Spartacists and communists make answer that they would rather perish and see all perish with them than return again to the yoke of *work for its own sake.*

If we try to understand the movements of our time completely, we shall come finally to the place where the church is called in question. Did it not seem to you one of the most surprising features of the German revolution, and for the immediate future the most discouraging, that the new powers so quickly made halt before the gates of *religion for its own sake?* So easily could this abstraction, this power of death in its Catholic and Protestant forms, insist upon its authority without having to meet any trace of a protest worthy the name! If this protest is not on its way, we must start it; and if it is, we must be the first to understand it — the first to understand what today's poor church-baiters themselves mánifestly do not understand, that the divine can by no possible means be managed and administered in the form of a thing for its own sake.

To *understand!* Let me compress into one word the meaning of our part in this unbroken movement of life into death and out of death into life: to understand! We must understand the mighty God-given restlessness of man and by it the mighty shaking of the foundations of the world. We must understand the raw primordial elements of motives

and motions. We must understand our contemporaries, from Naumann to Blumhardt, from Wilson to
Lenin, in all the different stages of the one movement in which we see them. We must understand
our times and their signs, and also understand ourselves in our own strange unrest and agitation. To
understand means to have the insight of God that
all of this must be just as it is and not otherwise.
To understand means to take the whole situation
upon us in the fear of God, and in the fear of God
to enter into the movement of the era. To understand means to be given in order to give. The essential thing is understanding.

For we must know that it is in this God-given unrest which brings us into critical opposition to life
that the most constructive and fruitful work conceivable is done. God judges the world by setting
over against it his own righteousness. To go back
to origins is not to go back to annihilation, if we go
back to the Origin of origins — to God. On the
contrary, it is only in God that we can come to a
positive position. The negation which issues from
God, and means God, is positive, and all positives
which are not built upon God are negative. To
understand the meaning of our times in God, to
enter into God-given restlessness and into critical
opposition to life, is to *give* meaning to our times
in God. For giving contrasts with all the theories
which attempt to palliate and explain a reality; it
is the power of God upon earth; it makes new.
When, in fear, reluctance, skepticism, and angry

disillusion we go back to the origin of things in God, we go toward the point where the living word and the creative deed must again appear.

When we seek God, let us not be bewildered by the negative appearances of disintegration in ourselves and in the world. According to Grünewald's and Rembrandt's keen intuition, the watch at the sepulchre who, at the moment of resurrection, are staggering down from their seat on the closed tomb, are certainly a negative, an "unhappy and far from exemplary sight"—but is our concern with them? We know that *they* are not the resurrection. And why direct our eyes to the by-play? What prevents us from looking at the resurrection itself, from acquiring God in consciousness, from experiencing him in history? And who could see the resurrection without himself *participating* in it, himself becoming a *living* being, and entering into the *victory* of life?

What now have we achieved by describing our situation thus as an instant in a movement? Have we only given a new title to an old and unending confusion? Perhaps. We have sought to *recollect* what we had forgotten and continually forget— God's revelation and our own faith; but perhaps we have failed to do so. We have sought to direct our vision to the *life* that conquers death in Christ; but perhaps we have seen simply one thing apart from others, and therefore a dead thing. We have sought to locate the *Archimedean point* from which the soul, and with the soul, society, is moved; but perhaps we have spoken again of a reality only metaphysical, a false transcendence. In this evil possibility lies the weakness and the danger of our position.

But ought we in honesty to take this evil possibility too seriously? If God exists, then the *pou sto* exists — and in God we live and move and have our being. Without him there could be no thinking and no object of thought. If then we appeal to this Highest Court, how can we help coming eventually to an understanding of ourselves in spite of all possibilities to the contrary; how can we help understanding that we *live* by the power of the resurrection, in spite of the inadequacy of our perception of it and our response to it; how can we help understanding that the resurrection of Christ from the dead is not a question but the answer which has been given us and which we all have somehow given? ὃ καὶ παρελάβετε, ἐν ᾧ καὶ ἑστήκατε, δι' οὗ καὶ σώζεσθε (I Cor. 15:1-2)! As a matter of fact we *do* share in the resurrection movement: with or without the accompaniment of religious feeling we *are* actuated by it. The facts of our inner life being what they are, it would be dishonest for us to deny it. There is at least something within us that shares in it; and if anything at all, then our description of our inner state is certainly more than description. We are not unofficial observers. We *are* moved by God. We are conscious of God. God in history lives in us and about us.

And so it is the light of victory into which our hope and our need have entered. The hope rather than the need is the decisive, the supreme moment. Godly and worldly interests, tendencies, and powers are not balanced. God applies the lever to lift the world. And the world is being lifted by the lever which he has applied. God in history is *a priori* victory in history. This is the banner under which we march. This is the presupposition of our being here. The real seriousness of our situation is not to be minimized; the tragic incompleteness in which we find ourselves is not to be glossed over. But it is certain that the last word upon the subject has been spoken. The last word is the *kingdom of God* — creation, redemption, the perfection of the world through God and in God. The last word concerning God is not Draw not nigh hither! but, God so loved the world that he gave his only begotten son! The last word concerning the world of men is not Dust thou art and unto dust shalt thou return! but, Because I live, ye shall live also. With this last word in our minds we feel our hope and our need stirring within us. The advancing glory of God is already vouchsafed us. The unholy equilibrium of a constant relation between God and man is overcome. Our life wins depth and perspective. We live in the midst of a tragically incomplete but purposeful series of divine deeds and evidences. We live amidst transition — a transition from death to life, from the unrighteousness of men to the righteousness of God, from the old to the new creation. We live in society as those who understand, as those who undergo, and as those who undertake.

We are surrounded by the holy, but not completely surrounded; pressed back by the profane, but not completely pressed back. The great syntheses of the Epistle to the Colossians are not *wholly* strange to us. They are manifest to us. We believe them. They are fulfilled. We fulfill them. *Jesus* lives. "By him were all things created that are in heaven, and that are in earth, visible and invisible, whether they be thrones, or principalities, or powers: all things were created by him, and for him" (Col. 1 : 16).

III.

"*Created* by him and for him." Our next prospect is surprising enough. It may not quite suit our immediate mood, but there is no escaping it. We must now follow the meaning and power of the kingdom of God into the particular.

We shall have to remember that the relation between God and the world is so thoroughly affected by the resurrection, and the place we have taken in Christ over against life is so unique and preëminent, that we cannot limit our conception of the kingdom to reform movements and social revolutions in the usual narrower sense. A protest against a particular social order, to be sure, is an integral moment in the kingdom of God, and there have been dark, blundering, godless times when this moment of protest was suppressed and hidden. But it is also a blundering and godless time when Christ is thought of as a Saviour, or rather Judge, who up to that hour for some incomprehensible reason has kept himself concealed, and is now emerging into this sin-stricken world for the first time. The kingdom of God does not begin with our movements of protest. It is the revolution which is before all revolutions, as it is before the whole prevailing order of things. The great negative precedes the small one, as it precedes the small positive. The original is the synthesis. It is out of this that both thesis and antithesis arise. Insight into the true transcendence of the divine origin of all things permits, or rather commands, us to understand particular social orders as being caused by God, by their connection with God. Naturally, we shall be led first not to a denial but to an *affirmation* of the world as it is. For when we find ourselves in God, we find ourselves committed to the task of affirming him in the world as it is and not in a false transcendent world of dream. Only out of such an affirmation can come that genuine, radical denial which is manifestly the meaning of our movements of protest. The genuine antithesis must follow the thesis: it is through the thesis that it derives from the synthesis.

We shall first then quite naïvely have to accept the world as it is — as it is given us and not as we dream it to be — and ask ourselves about its relation to God. God could not redeem the world if he were not its Creator. Only because it *is* his possession can it *become* his possession. Genuine eschatology casts a light backwards as well as forwards.

Jesus Christ *yesterday* — and not for the first time today! God desires to be known and honored as Creator even in the simple acts and facts of human life. And "simple," here, is to be understood not only as *plain* but also according to its Biblical meaning: God desires to be known even in the *foolish* acts and facts of human life. He desires to be known even in the profligate, degenerate, and confused ways of men.

Even the *regnum naturae* is the kingdom of God with the addition of — and, we might add, in spite of — the veil which now covers its glory. In this sense we must accept the well-known and often-condemned Hegelian dictum regarding the rationality of all being.

In all the social relations in which we may find ourselves, we must perceive something ultimate in the mere fact of their being and having come to be; we must affirm an original grace as such; we must accept orders of creation there as we accept the orders of creation in the natural world. We thereby commit ourselves not to what is mortal and godless in the world but to the living and divine element which is always there; and this very committing of ourselves to God in the world is our power of not committing ourselves to the world without God. "Created *by him* and *for him.*" In this "by him" and "for him," by Christ and for Christ, lies our victory over a false *denial* of the world and also our absolute surety against a *false* affirmation of the world.

In this sense we understand the practical philosophy of *Ecclesiastes,* which is Epicurean in appearance only: "Go thy way, eat thy bread with joy, and
drink thy wine with a merry heart; for God now ac-
cepteth thy works. Let thy garments be always
white; and let thy head lack no ointment. Live joyfully with the wife whom thou lovest all the days of
the life of thy vanity, which he hath given thee under
the sun, all the days of thy vanity; for that is thy
portion in this life, and in thy labor which thou
takest under the sun. Whatsoever thy hand findeth
to do, do it with thy might; for there is no work, nor
device, nor knowledge, nor wisdom, in the grave,
whither thou goest." (Eccl. 9:7-10) He that hath
ears to hear, let him hear. I pass by all explanations. One surely fails to know the Gospels if he
thinks Jesus could not also have said this. It is
quite in his character. Whoever has gone through
the strait gate of critical negation — vanity of
vanity, saith the Preacher, vanity of vanities — may
and must use such language. To perceive the
absolute vanity of life under the sun in the light of
the heavenly life of God is also to perceive its *relative potentiality*: it is to perceive that it possesses
no insignificant nor inglorious *authorization.*

In this sense we understand the strange fact that
Socrates did not work out his theory of ideas in a
retreat separated from the world, presently to
bring it forth as a new thing to unknowing men. On
the contrary, the new from above is at the same
time the oldest thing in existence, forgotten and

buried. To invent means to find, and in the streets
and market places of the Athens of the Pelopon-
nesian War, which was no *civitas Dei* — in the
physician's, the architect's, and the helmsman's
knowledge of the meaning and aim of their profes-
sions, however isolated and fragmentary their
knowledge was — Socrates *found* a direct indica-
tion of a general original knowledge of the meaning
and aim of life. His findings astonished him. And
his astonishment was genuine worship of God the
Creator.

In this sense we might understand — or misunderstand — even *Naumann's* unfortunate change from
an earlier desire for social Christianity to an interest in mere politics and economics. His "esthetic"
admiration and affirmation of simple nature, of
simple technical science, of simple humanity, — is
it essentially less than astonishment at their origin,
in the light of which we see light even in darkness?
And if today we wish to begin again where Naumann stopped, his work will have improved our
vision of the light which shineth in darkness and
the darkness comprehendeth not. Naumann
will also remind us how great is the danger that
such world-affirming perception of its Creator
within it should develop into a mere regard for the
creation. Alcibiades, as well as Plato, walked
familiarly through the market place of Athens at
the side of Socrates. But the fact alone that it was
possible to interpret the work of Socrates in the
Platonic way ought to warn us against thinking we

must come to a stop in asceticism or in protest against the orders of our age. In the opposition to life which we assume in Christ, we must not forget the very mind of Christ in regard to the events, the necessary and in their way the right and proper events, of the daily round. In our very opposition we can and must remember the much misused warning, Destroy it not, for a blessing is in it. We shall maintain toward the world, toward men and ourselves, a grateful, happy, understanding patience — better indeed than do the others who know nothing of the opposition. We can permit ourselves to be more romantic than the romanticists and more humanistic than the humanists.

But we must be more precise. Let us consider the view of life which is expressed in the *parables* of the synoptic Gospels. What is the one remarkable characteristic which sets them off in bold relief from Aesop's and Gellert's fables, Grimm's and Anderson's fairy tales, Christoph Schmid's stories, and the religious mythology of India? Is it not the simple way in which the kingdom of heaven is compared to the world? ὁμοία ἐστὶν ἡ βασιλεία τῶν οὐρανῶν it goes — and then follows regularly a picture of social life which in itself discloses nothing heavenly whatever. Not the moral world, nor the Christian, nor any theoretical and postulated world is described, but simply the world as one finds it. It is all done in the most naïve manner, without concern for the sometimes rather massive fragments of earth that cling to the events and relations described. A perfect rogue is graciously received by his father, simply because his father is his father — a reason beyond the comprehension of the onlookers. A scolding woman proves mightier than a judge who has feared neither God nor man. A king plunges into an ill-considered war and presently has retreat sounded in the nick of time. A speculator invests his whole fortune in a costly pearl. A shrewd old codger, a veritable war-profiteer, knows how to get hold of happily discovered treasure. A rascal handles unrighteous mammon as if there were no mine and thine. A group of children quarrel in the street. A farmer sleeps and rises in comfort while his land works for him. A man is mauled and half killed by robbers and, although the world is full of pious people, he must wait a long time before he finds a sympathetic soul — from Samaria. A whimsical host wishes by hook or crook to see his house full. A lone woman having lost a penny acts as if she had lost everything. A righteous and an unrighteous man stand near each other in church, each strictly in his own character.

It is all so commonplace, so lacking in illusion, and so wholly without eschatological reference — just like the actual life of men, and for that very reason brimful of eschatology! For this is not story-teller's technique nor literary form, but content itself, full of meaning, with a form which issues from an inner necessity. This view of life conceives the happenings of the day to be in their way

fully justified, inevitable, and complete. Here we
have the same free survey and understanding and
representation of the actual life of society that dis-
tinguishes the novels of Dostoevski, for example,
from the kind in which, as in most of Tolstoy's, we
feel ourselves directly preached to. Only out of
the keenest consciousness of redemption can one
represent life as it is — as Jesus did. Only from the
standpoint of an antithesis which has its roots in
the synthesis can one accept the thesis so calmly.
Only that man can speak as Jesus speaks who stands
over against life in a rôle *absolutely* critical and
who therefore, unlike Tolstoy, can suspend *relative*
criticism — who in perfect peace can recognize in
the *worldly* the *analogy* of the *heavenly* and take
pleasure in it. And this is not a matter of losing
oneself in the object of one's regard but of penetrating through the object to its creative origin —
to that kingdom of heaven whose laws cast their
shadow upon the events and relations of the present
age. "For the invisible things of God from the
creation of the world are clearly seen, being understood by the things that are made, even his eternal
power and Godhead" (Rom. 1:20).

Even more clearly brought out in Jesus than in
Socrates is that farseeing happy patience in which
all things transitory, even in their abnormal forms,
are seen in the light of the eternal. For the Lord
praised not only the good physician and the skillful
helmsman but also the unjust steward. And even
more clearly brought out in Jesus is the fact that

the transitory is *only* a parable. His very uncon-
cern for the things and events he relates makes it
quite clear that he sought their original and creative
element not in the mere things and events themselves, but in their idea, their heavenly analogue.
And even more clearly brought out, also, is the
purely miraculous element which inheres in seeing the invisible things of God and understanding
them by the things that are made. This is not
a rational, obvious, self-evident procedure, but it is
of the nature of revelation: as Paul wrote, "That
which may be known of God is manifest in them, for
God hath shown it unto them" (Rom. 1 : 19). For
it is given to some to know the secrets of the kingdom of heaven, to see the eternal in the likeness of
the transitory, and to others it is not given. To
the latter, if it is to be conceived at all rightly, the
divine must be veiled rather than revealed by its
likeness. Without eyes there cannot be sight, and
without God there cannot be eyes. But unto every
one that hath shall be given, and he shall have
abundance. The so-called Marcan theory of the
meaning of the parables (Mark 4: 10-12, Mt.
13: 10-17), though often deplored and ridiculed, is
really their most congenial interpretation, and
doubtless the one to be attributed to Jesus himself.

The parables are pictures from life as it *is*, pictures that mean something. For life as it *is* means
something. And the one who does not understand
life as it is cannot understand its meaning. He who
so clearly and broadly saw the mutual relation of

the world and the kingdom of heaven, of the present and the original-and-future, evidently had a penchant for *objectivity*. One thing does not occur in the parables: dilettantism, halfwayness, jerry-building. Even the useless fellow who buried his pound is in speech and action a complete man of his own sort. The children of this world are wise; judged by their own standards they do their work well — better than the children of light judged by theirs — and the Lord praises them for it. These are hopeful facts. When one does his work well, there comes into evidence not the kingdom of heaven itself but the possibility of it; it is then, as it were, penetrating its world-foreground and entering into consciousness, into fact. So far as we know, when Jesus called his disciples to *his* service he found them at work and not idle; *fishermen* could be made into fishers of men; from the simple duty of render-ing unto Caesar the things which are *Caesar's* it could be seen that rendering unto God the things that are *God's* was a duty much loftier and more difficult. The classical example of this parabolic character of the present world and of this penetra-tion of it by its heavenly archetype is that of the centurion of Capernaum who, whether we like it or not, becomes in his capacity as military officer a parable for the order of the messianic kingdom, and whose simple insight is presently extolled by Jesus as faith such as he had not found in Israel — in that too spiritual Israel which was forever en-gaged in protest against existing things.

What follows from all of this? Evidently the hint that the simple *objectivity* of our thought, speech, and action, even in our particular relations, even in our consciousness of imprisonment here, contains a *promise*. No more but no less follows from this. It is not ours to be onlookers; it is ours to take our appointed place in the world's march. We are forced to it by the consciousness of solid responsibility laid upon our souls for the degenerate world; we are forced to it by the thought of the Creator who is and remains the Creator even of our fallen world. However true it may be that everything we do within the limits of mere particular things and events is only *play* in relation to what really should be done, it is none the less *significant* play if it is rightly engaged in. Poor players will certainly not make good workers; camp-followers, correspondents, and spectators on the battlefield of the everyday can hardly be made into shock troops to storm the kingdom of heaven. Though we are keenly alive to the limitations of purely objective thinking and doing, we shall be prepared to respect them whenever they are honest: for, being purely objective, they *might* come to be filled with the purity of the Original — as indeed they always are for those who have eyes to see. Though we are alive to the limitation of our own work there will arise in us a will to do good, sound, finished work; for the spark *might* come from above, and the eternal be brought to light in the transitory.

The divine *commands* — "Replenish the earth,

and subdue it!" "If any would not work, neither should he eat!" "He which made them at the beginning made them male and female!" "Honor thy father and thy mother: that thy days may be long!" — these still stand in their ancient strength. With Oetinger, we shall not allow *Wisdom,* the delightful deity of the *sensus communis* of the Proverbs and Ecclesiastes, to utter her voice in the streets in vain — however late-Hebrew the writing concerning her may be. And we shall not be too proud to submit to the divine *blessing* which Isaac and Job received even on this earth, after they had gone through the strait gate. A humble but purposeful and really happy freedom of movement will always, to some degree, be allowed us even in this age — the freedom, that is, of living in the land of the Philistines: the freedom of going in quiet strength in and out of the house of publicans and sinners; in and out of the house of the mammon of unrighteousness; in and out of the house of the state, which, call it what you will, is the beast of the bottomless pit; in and out of the house of secular social democracy; in and out of the house of falsely heralded science and the liberal arts; and finally even in and out of the house of worship.

And why should we not accept such freedom? *Introite nam et hic dii sunt!* We shall go in and out in the fear of God without becoming servants of the idols: we shall go in and out in perfect liberty. The fear of God is our freedom in the midst of freedom. "There is nothing better for a

man than that he should eat and drink, and that
he should make his soul enjoy good in his labor.
This also I saw, that it was from the hand of God"
(Eccl. 2:24). We affirm the thesis of romanticism
that the kingdom of God has not yet begun, as well
as the thesis of humanism that even fallen man is
the bearer of the divine spark. We affirm life.
Even the *regnum naturae,* the vast time-being,
within the frame of which all thought, speech, and
action now take shape, may always become the
regnum Dei; and such it will be when *we* are in the
kingdom of God and the kingdom of God is in us.
This is not worldly wisdom. This is truth in Christ.
This is the solid and fundamental Biblical perception of life.

IV.

We shall do better to keep quietly to this Biblical
perception of life than to call, or at any rate to call
too loudly, for Platonic philosophy or German
idealism. This will save us from allowing the
denial of life to become a theme in its own right —
an error made by some Russian and many Oriental
thinkers. The destruction of Sodom and Gomorrah
is not a thing to be looked toward; the one who
looks toward it becomes a pillar of salt. We shall
be saved also from allowing the *affirmation* of life
to become a theme in itself. We shall not again go
back of the fundamental dualism of Dostoevski
either to the Greeks or to Goethe.

But we do not desire a harmonious balancing of

affirmation and denial. How to relate the sense of human tragedy which hovers even over the cultural consciousness of the Greeks, to the sense of human majesty with which the Greeks knew how to surround themselves, is a nice question and a serious. It is certainly not an abstract and intellectual one; it may be answered only in connection with God in history. And in that case, tragedy and majesty are not equally significant; they are not, as it were, symmetrical moments of truth. Goethe on his Jupiter-throne at Weimar and Dionysius-Nietzsche may in all sincerity have thought they were — Kutter may inform us that it suits the divine humor to manifest itself in the riddles of world history smiling through its tears — but we at least cannot afford in any way to equalize the motion and tension between these two moments and bring them to rest, not even for the sake of the integrity of the philosophical conception of man.

The fact of growth will not allow us to overlook the truth that the antithesis is more than mere reaction to the thesis; it issues from the synthesis in its own original strength; it apprehends the thesis and puts an end to it, and in every conceivable moment surpasses it in worth and meaning. Rest is in God alone. We must honestly confess, even when we seek to comprehend our situation from the viewpoint of God, that we know the element of tragedy in it better than that element of sovereignty which might reconcile us to it. Tears are closer to *us* than laughter. *We* live more deeply in the

No than in the Yes, more deeply in criticism and protest than in naïveté, more deeply in longing for the future than in participation in the present. *We* can honor the Creator of the original world only by crying out to the Redeemer of this present one. Our Yes toward life from the very beginning carries within it the divine No, which breaks forth as the antithesis and points away from what but now was the thesis to the original and final synthesis. That No is not the last and highest truth but is the call from home which comes in answer to our asking for God in the world. We shall not continue our song of work and efficiency, of culture and of evangelical freedom, in the choir of heaven without significant modulation. The unrest which God in his grace and his judgment has given us as a promise of unfolding life and as a warning, is upon us, and we cannot dream of escaping it. Too conscious are we, when we make and must make our affirmations of Life, that our work in this age, though analogous to, is also disjunct from, the work of God. Too real to us is the very presupposition of those affirmations — the thought that it is all vanity of vanities, all vanity. Too solemn is the insight that it doth not yet appear what we shall be.

There is no place in this age for Olympian ecstasy. The sovereignty which Alcibiades admires in Socrates in the *Symposium* arises from the very dualism of the Socratic perception of life; it arises from the critical power accompanying the idea — and the strength of Michelangelo, Bach, Schiller, and others like them is obviously traceable to the same source. This the Athenian blueblood did not see. But we should see it and not lose touch with facts. True perception of life is hostile to all abstractions. It may say Yes, but only in order out of the Yes still more loudly and urgently to say No. For it fixes its attention not upon any scheme of perfection but upon its own position in history, upon the order of the hour. It moves forward. And the motion in it comes from neither one of our two earthly dimensions.

So the free outlook upon the order of creation is the very thing that presently leads us on to the region where light is locked in arduous but victorious *struggle* with darkness — leads us from the *regnum naturae* over into the *regnum gloriae,* where, in Christ, the problem of life becomes at once serious and full of promise. It is the same God that "saw every thing that he had made, and, behold, it was very good" (Gen. 1:31), "who hath delivered us from the power of darkness, and hath translated us into the kingdom of his dear Son" (Col. 1:13). The same moving force that bids us take life as it comes presently prohibits us from doing so. The correctly learned answer becomes a new question; the Yes becomes No; and with the same necessity with which we perceive that God is the eternal beginning and the eternal end, we must now discover that the present, the medium in which we live, is transitional in character. At the point where society becomes a mirror of the original thoughts of God, it becomes a mirror of our need and of our hope.

So the kingdom of God advances to its *attack* upon society.

Why is God hidden from us as he is? Why is it so difficult, so almost impossible, with Socrates and the author of the synoptic parables, to feel a suggestion of Origin in what we do and see others do every day? Which is it — something the matter with our feelings or something the matter with every day? How is it that it is not given to some to see, and though given to others, is given even to these so seldom and so meagerly? Why does the conduct even of the most distinguished Christians in society leave us in doubt whether it is according to the will of God?

But given that God is hidden, why is there laid upon us so imperiously the demand — terrible in its simplicity — that we do his will? Why does the Bible speak of that will with such emphasis? And why, whenever we think of it, do our eyes turn almost of necessity to the future? *Quod vixi tege, quod vivam rege!* Shall we do better tomorrow? Why are we always making preparations for a life that never begins? Why can we not enter into the kingdom of God triumphantly, in the sunshine of humanism, proud of mind and whole of body, instead of entering, at best, lame, halt, and blind, abased, humbled, and crushed? Why is it that only the Philistines can actually be satisfied and self-satisfied? Why must we, at the crucial point, in spite of all our resistance, *give in* to the protest which *Kierkegaard* makes against marriage and the family, *Tolstoy* against the state, civilization, and art, *Ibsen* against the approved bourgeois morality, *Kutter* against the church, *Nietzsche* against Christianity as such, and *socialism,* with concentrated weight, against the whole structure of society, intellectual and material? Why can we work up no indignation against *Dostoevski's* daring to make Christ pass as an idiot in society and the real understanding of him begin with the murderer and the harlot? Why does something in us affirm the radical protest which the original *Reformation* and *Anabaptism,* as well as the *mysticism* of the Middle Ages, directed against that religion which is the only one conceivable and possible within society? Why, with a *sacrificium* of our intellects and more than our intellects, do we bow before the message of the *Sermon on the Mount,* which acclaims men blessed who do not exist; which opposes what was said to them of old time and what we must continue to say to each other, with a "But *I* say unto you" that can be applied neither to modern nor to any conceivable society; which preaches a morality that presupposes that morality is no longer necessary? Why do we find ourselves perplexed but tacitly assenting when we read the accusation which the *social philosopher of the Old Testament* brings against life — not only against this or that present situation, but against life itself? — "So I returned,

and considered all the oppressions that are done under the sun: and behold the tears of such as were
oppressed, and they had no comforter; and on the
side of their oppressors there was power; but they
had no comforter. Wherefore I praised the dead
which are already dead more than the living which
are yet alive. Yea, better is he than both they,
which hath not yet been, who hath not seen the evil
work that is done under the sun.'' (Eccl. 4:1-3)

How does it happen that we understand all this
without understanding it, affirm it without affirming
it, and that we must take part, without wishing to,
in the attack which is directed against the deepest
foundations of society?

It is quite clear that we are drawn into taking
sides with the Attacker as irresistibly as we were
into taking sides with the Defender, that the Attacker and the Defender must be one and the same,
and that the attack is the development of the defense. And it is also clear that this irresistibleness
does not have its source outside of us but rises
within our own freedom. For God the Creator, of
whom we have been thinking, is also God the Redeemer, in whose footsteps we must follow of ourselves; and the onward march of God in history,
in which we are voluntarily taking part, necessitates
our advancing from the defense to the attack, from
the Yes to the No, from a naïve acceptance to a
criticism of society. We may deny ourselves the
universal No no less than the universal Yes, for
both are one; or rather, *rebus sic stantibus,* we may

deny ourselves the No even less than the Yes, for
it follows after it.

Christ's truth contains both a warning to us to
keep to simple objectivity and an urging which
prompts us rigorously to look in our personal and
social life for a far greater objectivity. We *cannot*
rest content with seeing in things transitory *only*
a likeness of Something Else. There is an element
in analogy that demands continuity. We feel it in
the case of the centurion of Capernaum. Likeness
is promise, and promise demands fulfillment. The
child, having been conceived, must be born. There
is an expectation of the creature waiting for the
manifestation of the sons of God, and in its ὠδίνειν
and στενάζειν, its groanings and travailings, we
ourselves participate (Rom. 8: 19-23). To all our
thought, speech, and action, there is an inner *meaning* that presses for expression; we cannot satisfy
ourselves with pictures and parables. Not in vain
does the transitory show us the likeness of the eternal, for now we cannot forget the eternal — now
we can no longer find rest apart from the kingdom
of God. No relegating of our hopes to a Beyond
can give us rest, for it is the Beyond itself standing
outside and knocking on the closed doors of the
here-and-now that is the chief cause of our unrest.
Nor will any pessimistic discrediting of the here-
and-now give help for this unrest; for it is by the
very fact of our living here and now that we are
conscious alike of our fall and, in the likeness of
the eternal, of the promise to us. τὸ φθαρτὸν τοῦτο,

this corruptible, must put on incorruption and
τὸ θνητὸν τοῦτο, *this* mortal, must put on immortality (I Cor. 15:53). We must enter fully into
the subversion and conversion of this present and
of every conceivable world, into the judgment and
the grace which the presence of God entails, unless,
remaining behind, we wish to fall away from
Christ's truth, which is the power of the resurrection. We cannot look on at this subversion and
conversion as pious or clever observers nor escape
it by walking down the broad, light, well-filled
streets of the romanticists and humanists; for that
would be consciously taking a stand with those of
whom it is said: ἀγνωσίαν θεοῦ τινες ἔχουσιν
(I Cor. 15:34). When God is present we cannot
longer maintain the balance of our certain creaturehood; we can no longer appeal to "reality" when
reality is bursting forth from "reality." We *must*
take our situation seriously and become aware of
the momentum of the attack directed at once against
us and by us.

How terrible if the *church,* of all institutions,
should not see this, but put her effort into maintaining for men a balance which they must finally lose!

Yet why do we worry about the church? The question whether we ourselves are alive to the situation
is of such stubborn seriousness that there is little
need to look beyond it. *Have* we heard the call that
we have heard? *Have* we understood what we have
understood? — that the demand of the day is for a
new approach in God to the *whole* of life, and not

for mere opposition to particulars, whether few or many; and that we must guard and make good that approach by frank criticism of particulars, by courageous decision and action, by forward-looking proclamation of truth and patient work of reform. *Today* there is a call for large-hearted, far-sighted, characterful conduct toward *democracy* — no, not *toward* it, as irresponsible onlookers and critics, but *within* it, as hope-sharing and guilt-sharing comrades; — and it is largely in this field that we must work out the problem of opposition to the old order, discover the likeness of the kingdom of God, and prove whether we have understood the problem in its absolute and in its relative bearings. Who among us would boast of possessing enough of this dual perception of life? *Domine ad Te nos creasti* — that is its Yes. *Et cor nostrum inquietum est donec requiescat in Te* — this is its towering, flaming No. We are all just beginning.

But be this as it may — a new day has dawned. Jesus Christ *today* — today the *same!* "Today as you hear him speaking, let but your heart hear, too." "From the days of John the Baptist until now the kingdom of heaven suffereth violence (βιάζεται), and the violent (βιασταί) take it by force" (Mt. 11:12). And "I am come to send fire on the earth; and what will I, if it be already kindled?" (Luke 12:29). This is the *regnum gratiae*. "The kingdom of heaven is *at hand*."

V.

Let us stop for a last time to make certain we understand our position. Simple cooperation within the framework of existing society is followed by radical and absolute opposition to that society. But as we had to guard ourselves against thinking that we could set up our overturned idols again by confining ourselves objectively to the world as it is, we must now fortify ourselves against expecting that our criticizing, protesting, reforming, organizing, democratizing, socializing, and revolutionizing — *however fundamental and thoroughgoing these may be* — will satisfy the ideal of the kingdom of God. That is really beyond us. There is no such thing as perfect naïveté in this age — and no such thing as perfect criticism. The unsolved situation in which God has placed us can no more be taken as an abstraction than the order of creation in which he has given us to live. The one must be understood by the other, and both understood as God-given. If we try to understand them otherwise we pass from one piece of worldly wisdom to another. Our Yes like our No carries its limitation in itself. While it is God who gives us that rest and this greater unrest, it is clear that neither our rest nor our unrest in the world, necessary though both of them be, can be final.

The *other*, which we try to represent by parable in our thought, speech and action, the *other*, for whose actual appearing we yearn, being tired of mere parables, is not simply some other thing, but is the wholly other kingdom which is *God's*. It is the original and spontaneously productive energy of the synthesis from which the energy of the thesis and the energy of the antithesis both derive. The corruptible is not, as it were, the first step to the incorruptible; and when we read that this corruptible must put on incorruption, we must remember, in our earnest desire for it, that incorruption is "a building of God, an house not made with hands, eternal in the heavens" (II Cor. 5:1). If I understand what the German theologian meant who during the war made the discovery that instead of saying The Life Beyond it would be better to say The Life Within, I can only trust that his dictum, more serpent-wise than dove-harmless, will not establish a school. No, no — we answer — begone from us, you psychics, with your Within! *Apage Satanas!* Beyond, *trans: that* is the crux of the situation; *that* is the source of our life. Our little *within* belongs to the realm of analogies, and it is from *beyond* that realm that we draw our life. There is no continuity leading from analogy over into divine reality. There is no objective relation between that which is *meant* and that which *is*, and therefore no objective transition, to be thought of in terms of development, from the one to the other. The kingdom of heaven is peculiar to itself in its promise as well as in its revelation, though quite as surely it does not and cannot remain peculiar to itself. The goal of history, the τελος of which

Paul speaks (I Cor. 15:23-28) — which means goal
rather than end — is not one historical occurrence
among others but the summation of the history of
God in history, its glory being veiled to us but manifest to him and to those eyes which he has opened.
The kingdom of the goal, however, is confessedly
an order of things which is not to be comprehended
in the category of time and contingency.

The synthesis we seek is in *God* alone, and in God
alone can we find it.   If we do not find it in God,
we do not find it at all.   "If in *this* life only we have
hope in Christ, we are of all men most miserable"
(I Cor. 15:19).   For creation and redemption are
possible only because God is *God,* because *his* immanence means at the same time his *transcendence.*
"Flesh and blood cannot inherit the kingdom of
God" (I Cor. 15:50).   The creaturehood of the sons
of God and the manifestation of the sons of God
are mutually exclusive.

It is only in *God* that the synthesis can be found;
but in God it *can* be found — the synthesis which is
meant in the thesis and *sought* in the antithesis.
Troeltsch has the striking sentence in his *Social
Doctrines* (Soziallehren), "The energy of the life
here is the energy of the life beyond," and we add:
this is the energy of affirmation and the greater
energy of denial.   The naïve acceptance and the
criticism with which in Christ we meet the lower
order of things, both alike take their rise in the
higher order which in God, but in God alone, is one
with the lower.   Naïve acceptance and criticism

have their possibility, their authorization, and their necessity in the power of the resurrection.

The *resurrection* of Jesus Christ from the dead is the power which moves both the world and us, *because* it is the appearance in our corporeality of a *totaliter aliter* constituted corporeality. More we cannot say. Think once more of the Isenheim altarpiece, and think, if you will, of the comments of the historians of art who are wont to gather about it, shaking their heads. What more can they do? The *Holy Spirit* of Pentecost was the Holy Spirit *for the reason* that it was not the human spirit, not even in the best and purest sense, but came to the apostles, *horrible dictu,* in tongues like as of fire, with a sound from heaven which filled all the house where they were sitting — came "perpendicularly from heaven" as Zündel's pointed commentary has it. We believe there is an inherent meaning in relations already existent, and we believe also in evolution and revolution, in the reform and renewal of relations, and in the possibility of comradeship and brotherhood on our earth and under our heaven, *for the reason* that we are expecting wholly other things; namely, a new heaven and a new earth. We throw our energies into the most humdrum tasks, into the business nearest to hand, and also into the making of a new Switzerland and a new Germany, *for the reason* that we look forward to the new Jerusalem coming down from God out of heaven. We have the courage in this age both to endure limitations, chains, and imperfections and also to do

away with them, *for the reason* that, enduring or
not enduring, we are thinking of the new age in
which the last enemy, death, the limitation *par excellence,* shall be destroyed. We enjoy the liberty
of living naïvely with God or critically with God
for the reason that in either case our eyes are open
to the day of Jesus Christ, when God shall be all in
all. If we understand ourselves rightly, we shall
see that power to grow comes always from above
and never from below. For the last thing, the ἔσχατον,
the synthesis, is *not* the continuation, the result, the
consequence, the next step after the next to the last,
so to speak, *but,* on the contrary, is forever a radical break with everything next to the last; and this
is just the secret of its connotation of Origin and
its moving power.

We need not therefore be apprehensive of any
pessimistic discrediting of our life here and of
activity in our life here. *if* we conclude with Calvin
to fix the place of the Christian in society within the
spes futurae vitae. Thence the power of the consciousness of predestination! Thence the power of
the decision to live to the glory of God! As a matter of fact we are restricted to this viewpoint as
much in our naïve acceptance as in our criticism of
society. But restriction confessedly means not *loss*
but *accumulation* of strength, the salutary damming
of running water to prevent foolish waste and
dangerous excess. And it is quite clear *why* we are
so restricted. When we look from creation and redemption toward perfection, when we look toward

the "wholly other" *regnum gloriae,* both our naïve and our critical attitude to society, both our Yes and our No, fall into *right practical relation to each other in God.* The one as well as the other is freed from that danger of abstraction in which death lurks; and the one relates itself to the other not systematically but historically, in the manner of God in history, in the manner of inner necessity. And this is evidently what we need and what we are seeking here.

The more our life has really to do with God and with God alone, the less will the life-movement from God leave us high and dry either on the right bank or on the left. We shall run off neither on a wild goose chase with Naumann into the Yes until it becomes madness, nor with Tolstoy into the No until it is likewise reduced *ad absurdum.* Let us listen then to Ecclesiastes: "Be not righteous over much; neither make thyself over wise: why shouldest thou destroy thyself? Be not over much wicked, neither be thou foolish: why shouldest thou die before thy time? It is good that thou shouldest take hold of this; yea, also from this withdraw not thine hand: for he that feareth God shall come forth of them all" (Eccl. 7 : 16-18). We shall make our decisions from the viewpoint of the *regnum gloriae;* and though this will take us far away from things, it will for that very reason give us perspective upon them — and our short circuits to the right and to the left will gradually become fewer. Without being disturbed by the inconsistent appearance of it we shall then enjoy the freedom of saying now Yes and now No, and of saying both not as a result of outward chance or of inward caprice but because we are so moved by the will of God, which has been abundantly proved "good, and acceptable, and perfect" (Rom. 12:2). For "to everything there is a season, and a time to every purpose under the heaven: a time to be born, and a time to die; a time to plant, and a time to pluck up that which is planted; a time to kill, and a time to heal; a time to break down, and a time to build up; . . . . . . a time to cast away stones, and a time to gather stones together; . . . . . . a time to keep, and a time to cast away; a time to rend, and a time to sew; a time to keep silence, and a time to speak; a time to love, and a time to hate; a time of war, and a time of peace." And the passage, which was *Oetinger's* favorite, continues — if the Septuagint rightly translates the original: "God hath made every thing beautiful in his time: also he hath set *eternity in the heart of men,* without which no man can find out the work that God maketh from the beginning to the end" (Eccl. 3: 1-11). That man *can* find eternity in his heart is the synthesis. Jesus Christ, the same yesterday, and today — and forever.

Our theme contains a question which must now be upon the lips of us all: What ought we then to do? It is true that many other questions, great and small, burning questions for which we are badly in need of an answer, are contained in this fundamental question and have not apparently been met by the fundamental Biblical answer we have given. But they merely *seem* not to be answered. We are moved by the truth of Christ: why should we not then be grounded in God? We are grounded in God: why should eternity not then be set in our heart? And *sub specie aeternitatis*, why should we not know what is to be done? We can indeed do only one thing — not many. But it is just that one thing which *we* do not do. What can the Christian in society do but follow attentively what is done by *God?*